Contents

KU-201-158

Tables

Acknowledgements

The author and publishers gratefully acknowledge the following for granting permission to reproduce copyright material in this book: table 1.1 reprinted from Peter Dahlgren and Colin Sparks *Communication and Citizenship: Journalism and the Public Sphere*, 1991, by permission of Routledge; table 1.2 reprinted from Denis McQuail, *Mass Communication Theory*, 1983, by permission of Sage Publications Ltd.; table 3.1 by permission of the *Guardian* newspaper; table 4.1 reprinted from Richard Collins, Nicholas Garnham and Gareth Locksley *The Economics of Television: The UK Case*, 1988, by permission of Sage Publications Ltd.; table 6.2 by permission of *Broadcast* magazine; table 8.1 reprinted from the *Financial Times*, 12 May 1995.

The publishers apologize for any errors or omissions in the above list and would be grateful to be notified of any corrections that should be incorporated in the next edition or reprint of this book.

1
The Traditional Paradigms:
Political Theories of the Mass Media

Introduction

(The mass media have) become overwhelmingly the dominant medium
of the late twentieth century: the paramount place where elections are
conducted and where fictions are disseminated. How (they are) run, by
whom and in what interests, is arguably a more important issue for any
modern society than control over major industries, the law or finance.
Geoff Mulgan *Politics in an Antipolitical Age*

The mass media provide powerful channels of information between
the political elite and the electorate. Traditionally, the press and broadcasting act as proactive devices for encouraging the citizen to participate in the democratic process. The mass media, by disseminating
the full range of political opinions, enable the public to make political
choices and enter the national life. Therefore, they are understood as
important mechanisms in ensuring the principles of modern democratic societies.

Their political role covers several features including being a public watchdog, agenda setting and message production. Consequently,
the organization of the print and electronic media plays a vital role
in furnishing individuals with their rights. The concepts of the fourth
estate and freedom of information have underpinned the development
of British and other Western democratic media systems. The press
and broadcasting (in a more complicated variant) are meant to act as
impartial, objective and independent brokers of information. To safeguard this freedom, governments have remained vigilant in evolving
policy to regulate the ownership of media institutions and guarantee
the flow of information.

In this way, the press and broadcasters are meant to act as neutral observers of the political process. However, as Judith Lichtenberg has commented, an ambiguity exists as the media not only act as onlookers, but are political actors themselves. Whilst media organizations claim to be critical outsiders, they are simultaneously political participants who shape the public's world view:

> The press today – the mass media in particular – is one of the primary actors on the political scene, capable of making or breaking political careers and issues.[1]

Formally, the press and broadcasting both perform a negative political liberty by protecting freedom of speech, and enjoy a positive function by brokering information across society and setting the agenda. However, throughout the years the democratic role of the mass media has been challenged. The concept of a free press has been replaced by a more critical analysis. Principally, the media have been seen to perpetuate the values of the political, social and economic elites. Effectively, the mass media reinforce the dominant ideology over the mass of citizens.

A number of schools have emerged questioning the traditional orthodoxy of state–media–audience relations. These have been drawn from several sources: anti-statist liberalism; market-liberalism and the many variants of Marxism. This has led to different analyses of the media and the call for reform and this chapter will provide the context to this study of the political role of media systems. It will compare and con-

Table 1.1 Alternative perspectives of the media

	Liberal	*Marxist*	*Communist*
Public sphere	Public space	Class domination	
Political role of media	Check on government	Agency of class control	Further societal objectives
Media system	Free market	Capitalist	Public ownership
Journalistic norm	Disinterested	Subaltern	Didactic
Entertainment	Distraction/ gratification	Opiate	Enlightenment
Reform	Self-regulation	Unreformable	Liberalization

Source: Peter Dahlgren and Colin Sparks (eds) *Communication and Citizenship: Journalism and the Public Sphere*, 1991

trast the disparate theories of mass communication and citizenship which have been deemed vital in democratic societies.

The alternative concerns for the media within different state organizations

Whilst this chapter will focus on the media in liberal democratic regimes, it may be useful to consider how media systems have operated in alternative state structures. An explicit comparison between the media in feudal and totalitarian states can aid our understanding of what is attempted in a liberal democratic system.

The print media which existed during the feudal, pre-capitalist era was subject to extensive state intervention. The authoritarian rule of societies, governed by absolutist monarchs, meant that the press advanced the elite's interests. The press was subjected to pre-publication censorship and supported state despotism. To maintain this arrangement, the government determined media rights by granting royal patents. The media was effectively controlled by the guilds, licensing and overt censorship. Although the press was privately owned, it propagated governmental policy. Criticism of the political machinery was forbidden. Whilst this has been defined as a historical phase for Western nations, in absolutist states such as Saudi Arabia this remains the media's role.

Similarly, in totalitarian states such as Stalin's Soviet Union (and in many respects in Nazi Germany and Fascist Italy), a subservient media existed. This emerged out of the amalgam of Leninism and Stalinism practised there. The media was subordinate to the aims of the revolution. These included the continuation of the Soviet socialist system and the dictatorship of the Communist party. Stalin's expansion of the corporate state, governed by an inner and outer circle of party bureaucrats, meant it controlled all areas of civil life including the media institutions. Consequently, loyal party members had the right to make use of the media. Further, the media was forbidden to express criticisms of party objectives and was subject to censorship through surveillance; the state-owned media system could be controlled by the government's economic or political actions. Within totalitarian societies the media was an arm of the state and served the ends of the dominant elite.

This model was spread by the Soviet Union's control of Eastern Europe for over forty years. The subsequent collapse of Stalinist state capitalism brought to attention the democratic functions of the media. After many years of state and party control, underpinned by the secret surveillance forces, the individual's right to freedom of speech was deemed vital. The media's influence in the successive liberation drives of Poland, Hungary, Bulgaria, East Germany, Czechoslovakia and most especially Romania (where rebel and state forces engaged in running gun battles to control the television stations) has been crucial. However, throughout the post-Stalinist period the respective rewards of a capitalist, liberal democratic political system have been double-edged. The media proved to be no exception as the issues of ownership, financial control and regulation which have affected advanced Western nations have emerged. The following table signifies that there are competing views of the media in democratic societies:

Table 1.2 Dominance and pluralism models compared

	Dominance	*Pluralism*
Societal source	Ruling class or dominant elite	Competing political, social, cultural interests of groups
Media	Under concentrated ownership and uniform type	Many and independent of each other
Production	Standardized, routinized, controlled	Creative, free, original
Content and world view	Selective and coherent; decided from above	Diverse and competing views; responsive to audience demand
Audience	Dependent, passive, organized on large scale	Fragmented, selective, reactive and active
Effects	Strong and confirmative of established social order	Numerous, without consistency or predictability of direction, but often 'no effect'

Source: Denis McQuail *Mass Communication Theory*, 1987

To ascertain why these two models have been advanced, it will be necessary to consider the press and broadcast media in a liberal democratic state structure and the arguments which called for the press liberty.

Communications and Citizenship

It has been commonly suggested that there are civil, political and social dimensions to the exercising of citizenship within a democracy. Civil rights and liberties are guaranteed by laws to curtail state power. They comprise freedom of speech, movement, association and consciousness. A democracy should safeguard open debate and competition for power. The rights to own and dispose of personal property are an essential curb to state power. They establish countervailing power centres and ensure that individuals are not dependent on government subsidies.

Political rights allow individuals to participate in the diffusion of political power through exercising their franchise, occupying public office and sitting on juries. Representational assemblies enable citizens to engage in determining and administering the laws under which they are governed and distinguish them from being subjects.

Social rights ensure the basic living standards through the welfare state and universal access to communications and information facilities. Freedom of speech is the citizen's fundamental right in a modern democratic society. These conditions allow people to become full members of the society.

In this way, the mass media should secure the citizen's civil, political and social rights. The print and the electronic media's ability to disseminate critical information quickly and widely throughout society is crucial. The concept of freedom of information has underpinned the development of advanced media systems; further, within traditional liberal thought, the media should act as a public watchdog or fourth estate to reveal state abuses.

The mass media should facilitate citizenship through the provision of free and accurate information in three important ways. First, individuals must have access to knowledge and information that will allow them to pursue their rights. Second, they should be provided with the broadest range of information, interpretation and debate over public political choices. Thus, citizens can employ communications facilities to register criticism and propose alternative courses of action. Finally, they should recognize themselves in the range of representations on offer within the central communications sectors and be able to develop and extend their representations.

These rights indicate that the communications and information systems have two key features. At the production level, they should afford the maximum possible diversity of provision and the mechanisms for user feedback and participation. At the level of consumption, they should ensure universal access to services that can guarantee the exercise of citizenship regardless of income or area of residence. To this end, the citizen's access to the market-place of ideas has been understood to be an obligation of national governments. Such rights have been established through a variety of laws, policies and regulations. The right to be informed has been sustained through:

1 the population's universal education to advance knowledge and to discriminate changes in the world;
2 widespread public libraries which are repositories of historical and current information, thereby giving the public access to information about
   governmental policies and dominant societal institutional practices;
3 independent and widespread reporting of fluctuating local, national and
   international events through the press and broadcast media.[2]

The role of the press in a liberal democratic state

Freedom of speech is the citizen's fundamental right in a modern
democratic society. In traditional liberal thought the press has been
advanced as a 'public watchdog' over the state. It occupies a fourth
estate which is separate from the Crown, Parliament and the Judiciary. Therefore, it may reveal the authorities' abuses and maintain a
mature democracy. This underlying principle has dictated the press's
organizational structure. It should be lightly regulated, subject only
to libel and obscenity laws and the tenets of taste and decency. Lib-
erals maintain that if the press were regulated it would become a ser-
vant of the state. Moreover, its political liberty is guaranteed as it has
been independently funded through advertising revenues. Thus, only a
privately-owned press competing in a free market can ensure complete
independence from the government. This argument has been justified
for several different reasons, the first being *consumer representation*. The
fourth estate is ensured by the market relationship between the press
and its audience. The market enables the readers to register their preference as consumers of a product. As the buying public determines
the newspaper's success, the owners must respond to popular demand
to make profits. Consequently, it follows that to sell papers proprietors must ensure that a wide variety of opinions are expressed. Therefore, through their buying power consumers act as the controllers of
press output.

Following from this exchange between producers and consumers is
the informational role of the press. The media market is responsive to
consumer need, as it is profit-driven. This aids competition, as papers, in
order to be sold, must provide a wide variety of interpretations of the
news. Consequently, the consumer's choice of information will facilitate his or her own self-expression and will encourage political participation. In turn, this may promote public rationality and focus collective
self-determination. The press promotes the culture of a free-thinking
democracy in which no one should be subjugated to another's will but
may freely express an opinion. Individual self-realization is guaranteed
by the free market.

The liberation of the press is driven by the desire to make profits.

It has been argued that the free market allows a free trade of ideas. This is because a diverse number of owners have the freedom to publish. As this aids competition, popular representation is exercised, as the market allows the citizen to comprehend salient issues. Therefore, the free market creates a media system which reacts to and articulates the people's opinions.[3]

This free market model has been challenged by a combination of advertising pressures, monopolization and concentration of ownership. However, if the market fails another safeguard can be applied – professional responsibility. Journalistic professionalism has squared the market's flaws with the traditional conception of a democratic media. This is a conscious and an unconscious process. First, proponents argue that the journalists' first duty is to serve the public. This is reinforced through the journalistic codes on truth, accuracy and factual authenticity. Second, as journalists have to verify information by drawing on alternative sources and presenting rival interpretations they will necessarily provide a plurality of opinions. Thus, journalistic professionalism balances against the forces undermining the media's integrity. Whilst free market competition has been qualified, an 'internal pluralism' within the media monopolies counters market pressures to sensationalize and trivialize political information. Further, this professionalism allows the public to analyse important issues. Once again, the stress is on citizen empowerment as professional self-interests coincide with the public interest.

The role of broadcast media in liberal democratic societies

There are several similarities and differences between the role of the press and broadcasting in liberal democracies. The broadcasters' political independence is closely tied to the freedom of the press. They remain neutral observers committed to the principles of accuracy, impartiality and objectivity. Yet society's response toward broadcasting has been different than that of the print media. Whilst broadcasting organizations have been constitutionally independent, they have been regulated by public bodies. The electronic media has not enjoyed the press's immunity. For example, in the United States a constitutional asymmetry between print and electronic media exists. American broadcasters have been regulated by the Federal Communications Commission (FCC). The FCC, until its partial deregulation by the Reagan government,[4] was responsible for ensuring that equal-time rules for political parties and a fairness doctrine were applied. If these controls had been directed at the press they would have violated the First Amendment of the US Constitution. Several reasons have justified this state of affairs. One refers to broadcasting's power to shape opinions over newspapers. Pictures have greater influence over the public than the printed word. Television is more intrusive and less escapable as it dominates the private space. However, the justification for broadcasting regulation has been the limited spectrum of airwaves. Until the last decade, radio and television broadcasts were limited to a narrow band of nationally available frequencies. This 'limited spectrum' qualified the number of channels and affected broadcasting's organization. The early experience of the American radio system, in which competing radio stations interfered with each other, demonstrated the practical need for a regulated system. However, the mass dissemination of communications raised political as well as technical questions. For policy makers this meant that a central dilemma had to be addressed:

> How (is it possible) to reconcile within a limited number of outlets the need of the state to make judgements of national priority as to how these outlets should be used, the need of each individual citizen for maximum freedom of choice in his search for personal satisfaction and the need for the broadcaster to express the truth about the world as he sees it.[5]

In responding to this conundrum, with the exception of the United States, most advanced Western broadcasting systems have followed a variant of the British public service model. This comprises a public broadcaster, the BBC, funded through a licence fee and private channels (ITV and Channel Four) funded through advertising. Traditionally, these organizations have competed for audiences rather than revenues. They are responsible for providing a mixed schedule built on the programming trinity of educating, informing and entertaining.

In Britain, the broadcasting institutions proclaim their political independence from state control, as an arm's-length relationship is seen to exist. This liberal-pluralistic position contends that through legal, institutional, funding and ideological devices broadcasters have resisted the external pressures of government intervention. They are free to broadcast within the confines of the law. The BBC is governed by a Royal Charter which enables it to be resistant to overt state pressures. Whilst the licence fee has provided assured funds for programming requirements, it has preserved the corporation's political independence from the state. It means that the BBC is not dependent upon state funding for its revenue.[6] The corporation has been guided by the notion of impartiality in its representation of political affairs. However, in Britain and several Western states the media's 'public watchdog function' has been formally exercised in the press rather than the broadcasting system. Constitutionally, the BBC was described by its first Director-General, John Reith, as an 'institution within the constitution',[7] as it was subject to the Crown but simultaneously followed the plural- ism of parliamentary democracy. Whilst the BBC rejects any political control of content, its public accountability, in contrast to the press, is mediated through the governors and by '(its acceptance of) Parlia- ment as a natural pole and . . . (its interpretation) . . . (of its) task as one of reproducing "a picture of political discourse dominated by Par- liament. [Broadcasting] . . . operates (an) impartial brokerage within a prevailing political system'."[8]

The ITV system's political independence has been ensured through a mixture of advertising revenue and regulatory control. ITV's fin- ances were indirectly drawn from the public rather than the state. Until the 1990 Broadcasting Act, the Independent Broadcasting Author- ity's (IBA, now reformed as the ITC) position as a broadcaster meant that state intervention could be offset, as the regulator was a buffer between the government and the programme-makers. Thus, the IBA was the legally responsible party instead of the regional contractor. As with the BBC, the IBA has seen parliament as its natural pole and has understood that it should provide impartial information within the dominant political system.

Moreover, minimalist broadcasting legislation (meaning that the BBC Board of Governors and the IBA had a relatively free hand in how they interpreted directives) has been developed to stem state inter- vention and enhance broadcasting freedoms. Further, pluralists would argue that as the Home Secretary has never employed his veto power over broadcasting democracy has been served. Whilst broadcasting has not enjoyed the same liberties as the press, it has remained independ- ent within the mainstream political consensus, determined by Parlia- ment as a sovereign representative body, and has adhered to the goals of impartiality, objectivity and accuracy.

The philosophical origins of a free press

Having established the press and broadcasting's political position in a liberal democracy, the origins of a free press may be considered. The concept of press freedom emerged as a distinctive principle during the wave of democracy which affected modern European and North American states during the late seventeenth and eighteenth centuries. The call was strongest in Western Europe where it coincided with the collapse of the *ancien régime*. This campaign was led by an educated bourgeoisie who fought against the power vested in the monarchy and aristocracy. They intended to transform society by providing altern- ative political institutions rather than merely tampering with the exist- ing state apparatus. From the English revolution onwards, there was a

LIVERPOOL JOHN MOORES UNIVERSITY
LEARNING SERVICES

search for new, more secular and democratic methods to organize the state. The disintegration of absolutist monarchical power went hand-in-hand with the arguments articulating greater press freedom.

The seed of press freedom was sown in Britain and transported through the American and French revolutions to the Continent. These arguments were sustained by several imperatives: cheap presses; the English Revolution (1641–60); the Levellers; the 1694 expiry of the Regulation of Printing Act; the writings of Cato and John Wilkes; the popular discontent engendered by the Corn Laws; middle class enfranchisement; the radical press; and the parliamentary debates repealing the advertising and stamp duties known as the 'Taxes upon Knowledge'.

John Keane has identified four concepts underpinning the call for press freedom:

Theological: John Milton argued in *Areopagitica* that press freedom equated with a love of God and a free and knowing spirit. As God had allowed man to deduce between good and evil, the press must provide information. Good can only be appreciated when compared to evil. This argument criticized state censorship, as the individual had a God-given faculty for reason. From this perspective, control of the press was repugnant, inefficient and unworkable. Further, censors could not decide how others live as they were fallible and corrupt themselves.[9]

Individual rights: The natural rights theory of the press was articulated by John Locke, Cato, John Asgill, Tom Paine, Mary Wollstonecraft and most especially Matthew Tindal. Tindal rejected any religious justification of press censorship, arguing that theocratic rule should be replaced by man's ability to decide the truth. As it was man's right to judge information in religion and politics, there was a natural tendency to publish by stealth against court rulings. Press freedom guaranteed liberty from the political elite. It allowed for good government, based on the natural rights of rational citizens who were able to live, with their elected representatives, under the rule of law.[10]

Utilitarianism: From this position, press censorship was a licence for dictatorship and undermined the public's maximum happiness. William Godwin, James Mill and Jeremy Bentham argued that the best government and laws would produce the greatest happiness for the majority of the people. Bentham, however, believed that most governments were motivated by the politician's self-interest. Therefore, to check state despotism a separation of powers, a broadening of the franchise, secret ballots and frequent elections were required. Further, press freedom meant that politicians had to use newspapers during elections and there would be a free and effective expression of opinions. It would add to the general happiness by reducing the power held by the minority of governors:

> A free press is the ally of happiness. It helps control the habitual 'self-preference' of those who govern. It exposes their secretiveness and makes them more inclined to respect and to serve the governed.[11]

Attaining truth: This tradition countered Utilitarianism, arguing that it said too much on utility and too little about the truth. Utility may allow people to feel secure in their opinions but these need not be necessarily true. In John Stuart Mill's *On Liberty* truth is fundamental to utility. Three reasons were given to guarantee truth. First, those who censor potentially true opinions have naturally denied the truth itself and assume the infallibility of their opinions. Therefore, such an assumption suppresses potential truth and stems the digestion of counter-arguments. Second, prevailing sentiments often contain falsehoods; only by countering them with alternative convictions can the truth be attained. Finally, even if an opinion is entirely true it will degenerate into dogma if it is unchallenged. Truth needed to be protected as it could not protect itself. A free press would supply an abundant amount of facts and thereby a general questioning of views by voicing truth over falsehoods.[12]

These rationales led to the rise of a free press which would dismantle prejudice and foster reflectiveness. The print media constituted a public sphere in which political sentiments could be elaborated. In such a manner, popular opinion could be directed against secretive and arbitrary state action. It was contended that state despotism fed on the blind obedience of subjects and attempts to outlaw open discussion. The press could stem the concentration of secular power by criticizing the government when it overstepped its legitimate power. Collective popular representation stood against secrecy, it demanded governmental checks, was for civic humanism and for self-restraint. Thus, it would give arcane and bossy government a bad name. A free press was the stabilizing force in the precarious balance between the state rulers and the public.[13]

In Chapter 2 we shall consider how these ideas tied in with the British press debates in the eighteenth and nineteenth centuries. As we shall discover, the following issues all shaped the structure of the press: the incorporation of advertising encouraged by the repeal of the Stamp duties; the plurality of private ownership; lower cover prices and the greater commercialization of the system.

Criticisms of the pluralistic model

The pluralistic model of the relationship between media and the state has been subject to extensive criticism. From a liberal-pluralistic position a number of revisionist histories have emerged alongside those advocating anti-statism and market-liberalism. In particular, the liberal tradition has been criticized by Marxist interpretations of the media. These have ranged from political economic approaches focusing on issues of production and concentration of ownership to accounts analysing ideology, class and control.

Revisionist Histories of the Freedom of the Press

Some revisionist histories have suggested that a free press remained a utopian ideal.[14] For instance, universal public access to freely circulating books, newspapers and pamphlets was never realized. A number of qualifications existed including advertising controls, the low circulation of papers, limited distribution and working class illiteracy. However, the principal problem in Britain referred to the introduction of stamp duties (taxation on pamphlets, newspapers and advertisements) in 1712. There were many constraints on a free press as the political elites and the establishment wished to retain social control.

Yet, as John Keane has commented, there was not only a significant chasm between the free press utopianism and the reality of a poorly circulated, harassed and deeply corrupt print media, but this early European and American vision included several blindspots.[15] A series of internal pressures existed. One issue was media self censorship which contradicted the assumption that the state's political power was the main threat confronting the individual's liberty. Throughout this period pre-publication censorship occurred through the inspection of content, the provision of rewards to publishing monopolies and the various apparatus of surveillance.

The advocates of press freedom pursued an information-flow paradigm which failed to address how the media could pre-structure or bias the audience's reception of opinions. They did not recognize that information could be structured through symbolic codes determined by the citizen's ability to interpret and select material. These referred to the manufacturing of the news in which information was processed through institutional routines and technical tricks. The dissemination of data was shaped by media practices which set agendas, constrained the contours of possible meanings and determined how individuals thought about political issues. The early proponents did not understand that readers were situated interpreters.

Finally, this understanding did not appreciate that censorship has been subject to different meanings and motivations. As readers were situated interpreters, they could voluntarily restrict their comprehension of information through internal censorship. The internal censor often determined that certain information must be rejected as it undermined the individual's reputation, family, career, or could result in legal action being taken. The early modern view therefore suffered from a hidden classical bias. The face-to-face model of communications supposed that everyone could enter into public life on an equal basis:

> The early modern assumption that communications media recreate the intimacy and directness of the *polis* neglected the problem of how freedom of communication among citizens could be institutionalized peacefully in a dispersed, complex civil society.[16]

Another set of historical revisions have suggested that the fourth estate was a myth. George Boyce has shown how different motivations shaped the organization of the British press in the late nineteenth century and early 1900s.[17] Throughout this period, newspaper circulation increased and was aimed at the prosperous, literate lower middle-classes. Alongside the improvements in printing and distribution, news was parcelled into short and easily digestible packages. Underpinning these developments was advertising finance. Economic controls existed, as the paper's respective advertising, news and deliberative heads had different priorities. Boyce has gone as far as to comment:

> The paradox of the Fourth Estate, with its head in politics and its feet in commerce, can, however, only be understood if it is appreciated that the whole idea of the Fourth Estate was a myth. A myth can combine fact and fiction without any uneasiness existing between the two: nowhere is this dualism – this ability to mix mythology with reality – more apparent than in the examination of the British press at the height of its power and prestige, between 1880 and 1918.[18]

Throughout this era, newspaper editors *apparently* wielded greater power than the politicians. The press appeared to initiate policy, criticize its application, control the executive and act as an organ of public opinion. For example, the press forced the partisan truce during the First World War so that political in-fighting could be avoided and the coalition wartime government would receive all-party support. However, this understanding may be seen as an illusion when the source of this apparent power is discussed. Instead of the press being free, professional and in touch with public opinion, it was part of the political machinery and enjoyed a close affiliation with the contemporaneous partisan groups.[19] Ultimately, the press was an extension of the political system. Rather than acting as a check or balance, it was inextricably linked to the parliament and political executive. In reality government by journalism masked government by politicians, with the journalists and editors performing as advisers, brokers and, sometimes, opponents for the political elite. Moreover, many journalists aspired to enter the political mainstream. Therefore, the press and politicians worked closely for common ends. For example, the *Morning Post* editor H. A. Gwynne appeared to control the content of the paper rather than his proprietors. He was apparently free from any one party's financial commands. However, Stephen Koss has shown that a 'Byzantine network of relationships' existed between editors and politicians.[20] Gwynne, for instance, had developed a number of relationships within the political and military elites and 'was certainly not independent of the political system, nor . . . (wished) to be: the influence he possessed derived, not from any aloof, distinct posture, but from his contacts and friendships with the people at the very centre of power.'[21]

Boyce's arguments have been complemented by James Curran's analysis of the parliamentary debates surrounding the repeal of the Taxes Upon Knowledge during the 1830s and 1850s.[22] As we shall see later, the economic reform of the press precipitated by the introduction of mass advertising may equally be seen as a method of social control, incorporating the press into the dominant political sphere rather than liberating it.

Anti-statist and market-libertarian critiques of British broadcasting

The critique of the pluralistic tradition has been particularly directed at the British broadcasting institutions. In many respects, they have been unfavourably compared to the press. Whilst public service broadcasting has been governed by the imperatives of impartiality, objectivity and accuracy, a number of criticisms have emerged which have cast doubt on the traditional wisdoms.

As we have seen, broadcasting institutions have been contained within the state as they conform to parliamentary sovereignty. Supporters of the pluralist position argue that broadcasters have remained independent actors in mainstream politics. Further, it has been propagated that, as the Home Secretary has never employed his veto power over broadcasting, democracy has been served. Against this, it may be contended that the Home Secretary has never had to effect such powers due to the inbuilt self-restraint and ideological adherence of the broadcasting institutions to the dominant political culture.

Although minimalist broadcasting legislation has allowed the BBC Board of Governors and the IBA to enjoy a relatively free hand in their interpretation of policy, this position disguises as much as it reveals. Governments have been engaged in political patronage in the appointment process. Broadcasting regulators have been drawn from a list of the great and good from the political and cultural establishment. Most notably this occurred when Harold Wilson chose Charles Hill in the 1960s and Margaret Thatcher selected Marmaduke Hussey in the 1980s to chair the BBC.[23] Moreover, the setting and collection of the licence fee has provided governments with a political lever to influence the BBC. Finally, it has been suggested that the monopoly of funding and resources, and the vertically-integrated structure of a system founded on broadcast producers has stemmed creativity, access and ultimately a plurality of independent voices on the airwaves.

Kenneth Dyson has shown how two alternative models have criticized the system's norms and reformed it.[24] The first referred to what could broadly be called an anti-statist, culturalist set of arguments. The second was more directly drawn from the traditions of Adam Smith's market-liberalism. The importance of these positions was reflected in the two most recent cycles of British broadcasting policy-making centred around the 1977 Annan and 1986 Peacock Reports respectively. In Chapter 4 we shall see that these ideas were to fall on fertile soil during the seventies and eighties as the political discourse changed.

Culturalist, anti-statist traditions

The literary critic Raymond Williams has argued that the central concern of mass communications or the long revolution was the extension of social communications to enhance the learning process and restrict elitism. To achieve this, a suitable broadcasting system was required. Williams rejected the market, as it qualified human experiences and as broadcasting represented social rather than fiscal capital. He argued for a cooperative trust which would encourage communal broadcasting and democracy. Thus, the public service broadcasting system was perceived as anachronistic in solving the dilemma between the state and the democratic flow of information. First, it was accused of insularity due to the closed entry for independent producers. Second, it was unaccountable to its audience. The system was seen as unrepresentative, monopolistic and unable to respond to the public. The state's need to control a scarce national resource outweighed the citizens' rights to freedom of choice and the broadcasters' need to express their perception of the truth.

By focusing on the fourth channel, this 1970s debate raised issues pertaining to editorial control, finance, organization and the relationship between broadcasting and the state.[25] As a result, a number of different broadcasting models were proposed to encourage pluralism,

diversity and viewer choice. Public lobbies called for a central funding scheme, increased worker participation within managerial policies,
and a school for research. In particular, Anthony Smith advocated an
open access policy in which freelance broadcasting groups would produce their programmes under contract. They would be offered the
technical back-up to make alternative programmes.

To realize this aim Smith advocated an electronic publishing model
for broadcasting. At the centre of this commissioning system stood the
National Television Foundation (NTF). This would operate like a
publisher, broadcasting programmes made by independent companies rather than producing them. In contrast to the vertically integrated
system, the fourth channel's schedule could consist of independent productions which would encourage community access and democracy.
Smith contended that institutional controls should be wedded 'to a
doctrine of openness rather than balance, to expression rather than
neutralisation'.[26] As we shall consider, the Annan Report replaced
the foundation with an authority – the Open Broadcasting Authority
(OBA). The OBA would be limited in liabilities, intervening if programmes were libellous, incited riot or were obscene. The authority
was to be light in its touch, enjoying as much freedom as parliament
deemed possible.

In many respects, these ideas would be echoed, within a different
theoretical framework, in the 1986 Peacock Report's market-liberal
model. A substantive difference between Annan and Peacock was the
funding method that was recommended. Annan proposed the OBA
should be financed through a mixture of sponsorship, interest groups
and block advertising in competition with ITV. This multiplicity of
funding was conceived to ensure political independence. Moreover,
in contrast to the later report, Annan's reforms were pitched upon
the social rather than economic purpose of broadcasting to provide a
plurality of voices.

Market-liberal developments

The libertarian interpretation of broadcasting originated from Adam
Smith's market-liberal/utilitarian conception of society as a competitive market. In this construct no 'fixed' societal order exists. Instead,
society was composed of interactive and independent individuals. Thus
'the individual is the axiom, the society the derivative.'[27] Following
upon this, the individual is the principal source of economic activity
through his or her enterprise. Individual economic liberalization equated
with societal benefit. Social welfare was maximized by the individual's
preferences which were supported by pro-competitive policies and minimal public regulation.[28]

By extension, state powers have to be limited so that individual enterprise may be fully realized. For example, government policies can only be justified if their sum benefit outweighs their costs to the individual. The notion that political or societal elites can act in their own interests for the greater good is rejected, as it qualifies the individual's freedom. This contrasts with other philosophies which perceive society as embodying 'some other or higher force or purpose than simply the welfare, however, broadly interpreted, of the individuals who comprise (it)'.[29] Within this conception, social communication should satisfy individual preferences, rather than attempt to act as an unprovable public service good. As long as the public service tenets do not impinge upon the individual's right to choose, they remain acceptable. However, for libertarians, this had rarely been the case in British broadcasting.

It should be noted that whilst this conception underpinned the market-liberal analysis, this model was often developed by individual actors working within a market-liberal tradition. This was a broad approach rather than constituting a particular 'school' of thought. However, market-liberals have been unified in their unfavourable comparison between broadcasting and the press. Where the press operated as a free market, broadcasting had been duopolistic and subject to political pressure. This critique provided the basis of the two main market-liberal approaches to broadcasting. First, they have determined that a form of regulatory capture has characterized relations in broadcasting. Gordon Hughes and David Vines maintain that in the ITV sector the normative objective of regulation has been to enforce franchise agreements located around the concept of quality upon which there can be no defined agreement.[30] Invariably, the IBA reacted to interests of the ITV companies rather than to the public. Second, a significant contribution to the market-liberal approach was made by the libertarian economist Peter Jay.[31] Throughout the 1970s, Jay constructed an integrated thesis on the financial reform of broadcasting.[32] He argued that two imperatives heightened the need for reform: the incremental growth of the broadcasting organizations made them susceptible to state interference and technological developments had placed history on the side of the market. Jay contended that it was no longer acceptable to judge British broadcasting as being good through the normal criterion of its ends (programmes), instead it was necessary to assess the quality of the system by the level of access it afforded to the individual to determine what s/he wanted to view or listen to. The process, rather than the product, was what mattered. Therefore, he argued that the new technologies (cable, satellite), by removing the limited spectrum, provided the means through which the viewer might fully participate in a form of electronic publishing. He envisaged that a nationally integrated cable system could be developed through a mixture of public and private funds. This network would be generally available to the public who would then subscribe to view individual programmes. As a consequence, a true market-place could exist, as the consumer would call up the programme by dialling the correct code and paying an appropriate charge in relation to the programme's popularity or desirability.[33]

Just as 'electronic publishing' would revolutionize the individual's access to programmes, it meant that the production and regulation of broadcasting would be transformed. The broadcasting system would no longer be vertically integrated, comprised of broadcasting organizations who produced and transmitted programmes. Instead, the new broadcasting market would enable the entrance of a greater number of independent production companies. These programme-makers could produce whatever they liked in exchange for the payment of a transmission fee. Like any product, the programme's success would ultimately be decided by its ability to attract subscribers. The regulators would therefore become an irrelevance as the technological and industrial imperatives which had contributed to their existence had been overcome. This would be beneficial, as regulators had previously censored the individual's economic and societal rights. Jay contrasted the state's control over broadcasting against the freedom and liberty of an independent, printed press. The basic right to publish was contradicted by:

> our belief that broadcasting must be closely and minutely controlled . . . by accountable public bodies operating under the laws and charters which specify their duties in exacting terms. Is there any good reason why we should be appalled by the idea of making the market-place the arbiter of what should be broadcast as we would be outraged by the thought of one or two National Publishing Authorities determining what books, magazines and newspapers should be offered to the public?[34]

In Jay's construct the interventionist regulation of the public service system had no place in the future of broadcasting. Within two decades, there would be no technical pretext for a government-appointed policeman to regulate the air-waves. Consequently, government or legislative intervention could not be justified, except in applying the general print laws of blasphemy and libel.[35] In order to create a free broadcasting market-place in which the individual might exercise not only his or her economic but political freedoms, it would not be acceptable to merely tamper with the BBC's funding structure. From this perception, the ITV network also suffered from the ills that had dogged the public broadcaster – monopolization, inefficiency, the stemming of independent producers, a lack of choice in programming, and finally an overbearing regulatory authority. Essentially, both the public and commercial sectors were perceived as a 'comfortable duopoly'.[36] In a number of respects Jay's vision concurred with the arguments made by Anthony Smith during the Annan debate. However, Jay's ideas were drawn upon the market as the provider of economic pluralism and political liberty: 'The thought may have been influenced by my bias against paternalism and corporatism . . . and the general disposition to replace the sovereignty of the consumer in many walks of life by the fatherly dispositions of the benevolent.'[37]

As we shall see, these ideas were potent in the development of policy toward the British broadcasting institutions during the 1980s. Most especially, the Peacock Report was to provide a challenge to broadcasting's traditions and set the framework for the following policy cycle.

Critiques from the Marxist tradition

Beneath this market-liberal critique sits a view of individualism shaped by eighteenth-century political theories and practicalities. However, it may be asked whether this concept remains consistent with the modern political process and is an appropriate unit to judge the system. By focusing on the individual as the basic unit of analysis, it harks back to the pre-industrial conception of the polity. This dismisses the role of modern political parties, pressure groups and associations; it ignores the power blocks of an era of mass politics. Consequently, this perspective makes an artificial distinction between information and representation by detaching information from its social context. This analysis does not show how ideas and systems of representation are ideological weapons which allow societal elites to advance their interests. Whilst libertarians contend that the media should facilitate social agreement through the dissemination of accurate information and contrary opinion, they fail to understand that one class or social coalition may manipulate the media's content. An elite can naturalize and universalize its interests because it controls the cultural production. The media may give the impression of distributing accurate information and promoting a conflictual debate. However, by confining the political discourse to ' "legitimate" areas of controversy, and by grounding it on assumptions that do not challenge the structure of social power, it may be engineering a contrived form of social consent'.[38]

These points are made by Marxists, who stress that the mass media have been forged out of the capitalist relations of production underpinning society. Essentially, Marx argued that the economic base has defined the ideological superstructure. In Marx's analysis of capitalism, the bourgeoisie's control over the proletariat has been defined by its ability to shape the ideology. The neo-Marxist critique has descended from the theory of false consciousness and the basic belief that capitalism not only owns the means of production, but the cultural means of production. In *The German Ideology* Marx commented: 'The class which has the means for material production at its disposal has control at the same time over the production and distribution of the ideas of their age.'[39] Thus, traditional Marxists have argued that capitalism no longer simply owns the means of production, but also controls the superstructure through ownership of the media. The public sphere has become an arena for class domination in which elites disorganize their opposition through ideological indoctrination. Therefore, the media was straightforwardly seen to have been structured, controlled and located within the dominant framework of class interests. As Jean Seaton and Ben Pimlott state:

> The . . . (Marxist) . . . school . . . sees the media primarily not as a restraint on rules but in effect, as their servant. Thus in modern Britain, the media should be regarded as an agent of consensus; directed towards producing agreement, acceptance or the acquiescence of the masses towards policies or attitudes which are not of their making nor necessarily in their interest.[40]

Media ownership is a key element in the mental domination of the capitalist class over the working classes. The mass media's politics are determined by a concentration of capital and the tightening grip of multinationals. However, there is no single Marxist approach to the media. Several paradigms have emerged from the many revisions of Marx's work. Throughout the 1970s the political analysis of the media was underpinned by a number of approaches concerning this base-superstructure relationship; political economy; critical theory and an analysis of the workings and mass dissemination of ideology.[41] Although these approaches differed in their methodology and analysis, each remained committed to the Marxist view of the media as an agent of the dominant ideology. As Richard Collins comments: 'The role of media studies was to strip the legitimizing mask from the media and by revealing them as agents of oppression hasten the day justice would triumph.'[42]

The political economist tradition

This materialist approach asserts the dependence of ideology on the economic base, and centres on the media's financial structures rather than its content. It investigates the inter-relationships between media economies, the processes through which communications are manufactured and their ideological impact within the public sphere. A crude

Marxist would state that the direct intervention of a press baron like Lord Beaverbrook produced a particular editorial outlook. However, Marx commented that journalistic freedom (of which he had first hand experience as a reporter for the *New York Daily Tribune*) was constrained due to the economic pressure produced under capitalism, regardless of direct ownership. This manifested itself through the expansion of stock companies and corporations. The owners invariably left the running of the companies to business managers. Therefore ownership was not directly comparable to control.

Ownership has also received criticism from arguments concerning managerial revolution and professionalism. James Burnham argued in *The Managerial Revolution* that the development of capitalism on the lines of the Stalinist corporate state had produced an elite of *apparatchiks*. Through their administrative status they exercised control. Power was essentially more diffuse and organized at an allocative level. For example, the BBC is a publicly owned institution run by a managerial elite, dominated by peer professionalism where power operates at a commissioning or producer level and is funded for non-profitmaking purposes.[43] In response, modern media political economists, such as Peter Golding and Graham Murdock, are critical of this interpretation. First, they argue Marx predicted that monopolization would occur. Second, to focus on the relationship between owners and managers significantly underestimates the interconnections between shareholders of different companies and ignores this potential power base. Finally, managerial freedom is still constrained by profit-making.[44] Even public service broadcasting cannot operate outside the context of capitalism as it has to compete for audiences and is placed under political pressure to utilize the licence fee.

Golding and Murdock demonstrate that greater concentrations of ownership, media diversification, conglomeration and imperialism have emerged. In effect, a new form of empire-building has evolved.[45] For instance, Rupert Murdoch's News International has a variety of multimedia interests and involves itself in newspapers, satellite broadcasting, films and book publishing. Most recently, Murdoch has moved to tap the potentially lucrative markets in China and the Asian subcontinent through his purchase of Star Television.

The history of the modern communications media, therefore, is not only an economic history of their growing incorporation into a capitalist system, but also a political history of their increasing centrality to the exercise of citizenship. In relation to this argument, the mass media have been employed as agents of control over the full democratic process of citizenship. The media are part of the information-cultural complex with close ties to the government. Therefore, they are integrated into the political elite and remain generally supportive, although sometimes critically so, of the capitalist discourse: 'the conglomerate media are not a source of *popular* control over government but merely one means by which dominant economic forces exercise informal influence over the state.'[46]

These arguments occur in Edward Herman and Noam Chomsky's analysis of the American media.[47] Whilst the system appears to compete, attack and periodically expose corporate or political corruption, its watchdog function is qualified by the limited nature of these critiques, the huge inequality of resources held between elites and the populace, and the public's access to the media:

> What it amounts to is a technique of control. . . . this was useful and necessary (for the elite) because 'the common interests' – the general concerns of all people – 'elude' the public. The public just isn't up to dealing with them. And they have to be the domain of what (was) called a 'specialized class'.[48]

To operationalize this analysis, Herman and Chomsky have developed a propaganda model which identifies a number of filters shaping the media output. The first is the concentration of ownership. The second is advertising which is the prime source of media income. The third considers the use of legitimate sources in news production which spawns an unhealthy reliance on primary definers such as the government, business and 'experts' funded or approved by these agencies. The fourth concerns flak directed at the media as a means of discipline. Finally, they refer to anti-communism as a national religion and control mechanism. In such a manner freedom of speech is nullified and refers to the interests of the capitalist classes.[49]

The critical theorist tradition

This view is reflected in the work of critical theorists drawn from the Frankfurt School. They shared, with many others, the fears of the mass society.[50] This was a conception of modern society as a mass of alienated, atomized individuals whose social ties were undermined through industrialization and urbanization. Therefore, the isolated individual was more receptive to media messages because s/he has fewer social ties. The power and influence of the media over the 'mass' audience is highly pervasive and problematic. Essentially, it could sway audiences and set the agenda. The Frankfurt School integrated the mass society argument into the Marxist view, commenting that it impeded the proletariat's ability to create socialist political consciousness. Imminent radical social change had been denied because political awareness had been eliminated. To this end, the media expressed the dominant ideology by industrializing the cultural practices, defining the debate and manipulating the audience.[51]

In his influential work, *The Structural Transformation of the Public Sphere*, the critical theorist Jürgen Habermas provided a concrete demonstration of this abstract. He argued that the public sphere (the space between the state and the public in which mass communications operated) had increasingly been organized in the interests of the bourgeoisie.[52] Habermas demonstrated that the media's democratic function eroded from the eighteenth century, in which the press was dominated by individual rationality, into the period of mass political power. In the 1700s, the press acted as a medium through which private opinions could be transformed into public opinions. The public benefitted by having access to free discussion and participation from equal parties, thereby enabling a collective, rational arena for debate to emerge to influence public policy and criticize governments. Thus, the media expedited the political process by reorganizing the private citizen into a collective public body through different opinions:

> The economic independence provided by private property, the critical reflection fostered by letters and novels, the flowering of discussion in coffee houses and salons and, above all, the emergence of an independent, market-based press, created a new public engaged in critical political discussion. From this was forged a reason-based consensus which shaped the direction of the state.[53]

However, as monopoly capitalism emerged the press became dominated by corporatism, advertising and ownership. Rational public discourse was overridden by power politics in which major organizations negotiated with one another and the state, thereby excluding the public. In turn, the media's political discourse was state-controlled, sensationalist and market-led. Politics was defined as a predigested spectacle. For Habermas public opinion was no longer a process of rational discourse but resulted from the media's manipulation of publicity and social engineering.

Althusserian and Gramscian criticisms of the media

Habermas's view of the public sphere's decline in the light of encroaching monopoly capitalism reflects a methodology, common in critical political economy, which defined ideology as a reflection of the production process. Essentially, the ideological superstructure was a passive expression of capitalism's economic base. Stuart Hall has argued that this notion of class dominance by overt force or ideological compulsion hid the real complexities of the media's role:

One had also to see that dominance was accomplished at the unconscious as well as the conscious level: to see it as a property of the system
of relations involved, rather than as the overt and intentional biases of
individuals in the very activity of regulation and exclusion which functioned through language and discourse.[54]

Two influential sources directed this approach; Louis Althusser's analysis of ideology which focused on how the superstructure was necessary
to the base's existence and Antonio Gramsci's concept of hegemony.[55]
These ideas challenged the materialist perspective.

First, traditional Marxist analysis failed to explain how social agents,
such as the media, operated as ideological actors to create false consciousness. Althusser rejected the base/superstructure model by employing the concept of the social formation. This comprised three practices
– the economic, the political and the ideological. Although economic
determination occurred in the last instance, capitalism's contradictions never took a pure form. Althusser's idea of structure in dominance meant that whilst the economic remained a key organizing societal
principle, it was not necessarily the dominant one during a particular
historical period. In feudalism the political sphere was predominant.
However, the dominant practice in a social formation was dependent
on the economic production's specific form: 'The economic is the de-
terminant in the last instance, not because the other instances are epi-
phenomena, but because it determines which practice is dominant.'[56]
This economic determination in the last instance suggested that other
social practices were relatively autonomous and had a specific effect.
Therefore, ideology which is 'a system (with its own logic and rigour)
of representations (images, myths, ideas or concepts)' was not an expression of the economic base,[57] but a practice in itself. As economic
practices transformed raw materials into a product through channelling human labour by determinate means (production), ideological
practices could transform the individual's lived relations to the social
formation. Ideology existed to dispel the contradictions of lived experience by presenting false, but seemingly true, information. It represented
capitalism as a totally coherent system lacking any internal conflict.

Althusser contended it was at the ideological level that the repro-
duction of the entire capitalist system was secured. Ideology was a
concrete social process embodied in material institutions entitled 'ideological state apparatus'. These included the family, school, church and
the media. They reproduced ideology in a manner which stressed capitalism as being natural and inevitable. Thus, Althusser produced a
theory to demonstrate how the media presented an ideological meaning of the world by providing an imaginary picture of real conditions,

thereby concealing exploitation. The media offered citizens a position in which they misrecognized themselves as free and discriminating:

> Put simply, if capitalism is to survive as an ongoing system, then concrete social individuals must be reconciled both to the class structure and to the class positions within it which they occupy. They must be induced to 'live' their exploitation and oppression in such a way that they do not experience or represent to themselves their position as one in which they are exploited and oppressed.[58]

Second, this critique of base-superstructure relations was reinforced by the Italian Marxist Antonio Gramsci's theory of hegemony. This argued that the elite classes ruled by consent rather than force. The media had a central role in developing public compliance. For instance, it defined apparently common sense values which were a form of ideological indoctrination. Further, the ruling class constantly struggled to retain its hegemony over the proletariat. Therefore, although the media formally allowed for a contestation of ideas between political and social groups, through linguistic codes, concepts, chains of association and common sense values, the ruling classes' interests were perpetuated: 'Put another way, the media's informational role is never purely informational; it is also a way of arbitrating between the rhetorical claims of rival interests – in a form that has an indirect outcome in terms of the allocation of resources and life opportunities between different social groups.'[59]

Finally, the political economist perspective defined ideology which is concrete, identifiable and materialist by referring it to consciousness which cannot be identified. Critics have suggested that ideology did not emerge from an ephemeral consciousness but from the material world. Therefore, ideology was not a product of consciousness, as ideological forms are the producers of consciousness: 'Rather than being regarded as the product of forms of consciousness whose contours are determined elsewhere, in the economic sphere, the signifying systems which constitute the sphere of ideology are themselves viewed as the vehicles which the consciousness of social agents is produced.'[60]

The hegemonic theory of the media differed from the classic Marxist and political-economist arguments through its appreciation of ideology's greater independence from the economic base.[61] Therefore, it focused less on economic or structural determinants of class-based ideology, but more on the media's content. It stressed how ideology created its own forms of expression and signification, and was a mechanism which invaded and shaped the consciousness of its compliant victims (mainly the proletariat):

Ideology, in the form of distorted definition of reality and a picture of class relationships or, in the words of Althusser (1971), 'the imaginary relationships of individuals to their real conditions of existence', is not dominant in the sense of being imposed by force by ruling classes, but is a pervasive and deliberate cultural influence which serves to interpret experience of reality in a covert and consistent manner.

Conclusion: The Political Position of the Mass Media

This chapter has outlined some of the theories concerning the media's political position in liberal-democratic states. These have included: arguments for a free press and broadcasting system; critiques from re-visionist press historians, anti-statist and market-liberal advocates for greater independence in broadcasting; and various Marxist perspect-ives focusing on the media as agents for social control. From these viewpoints we may ascertain that the political position of the media is contested and debatable. Underpinning all these critiques is an assump-tion that the media can not occupy an autonomous position so long as the press and broadcasters simultaneously attempt to remain public watchdogs whilst being political actors.

It should be noted that these theories have been challenged by more recent developments in the academic debate and the changing media environment. To some extent, the post-modernist ideas have reformul-ated our view of the media's political position. They have argued that the concept of dominant ideology has been undermined as people are faced with a proliferation of images from which no objective truth can be drawn. In particular, Jean Baudrillard has contended that there has been an implosion between the virtual and reality, so that hyper-reality defines people's thinking, discourse and view of the world. This has coincided with new developments in transmission technology, the greater globalization of the media economy and a changing role for media owners within national and international political affairs. There-fore new forms of statecraft have emerged to challenge the traditional understandings between the mass media and the state. This brings into question the press and the broadcaster's position as public watch-dogs, as widening technological diffusion and greater concentration of media ownership have started to force a rethink over the media's role.

Throughout the following chapters we shall assess, analyse and explain how media institutions have been developed, principally in Britain, and test the applicability of some of the above media theories. It is our aim to explore the political and philosophical implications of the changing communications landscape as reformed policy agendas develop, new technologies become domestically available and there is a greater globalization of the media economy. Therefore, the structure underpinning this approach will be conditional on several major questions:

- What type of media system has existed in Britain throughout the years and how and why did it evolve in such a manner?
- In what ways has it been understood to operate and what criticisms have been levelled at it?
- To what extent have the criticisms been justified and how has the system responded?
- Have certain ideological, philosophical and political positions dominated the discourse?
- What has been the role of political actors, legislators and policy-makers?
- What shifts are beginning to occur and what will they mean to our understanding of the mass media in Britain and the world?
- What appropriate new paradigms can be employed in order to understand the mass media in the future?
- To what extent has the concept of the citizen been replaced by the consumer?

Further Reading

George Boyce, James Curran and Pauline Wingate (eds), *Newspaper History: from the 17th Century to the Present Day*, Constable, 1976.

Richard Collins, *Television: Policy and Culture*, Routledge, 1990.

Richard Collins, James Curran, Nicholas Garnham, Paddy Scannell, Philip Schlesinger and Colin Sparks (eds), *Media, Culture and Society: A Critical Reader*, Sage Publications, 1986.

James Curran and Michael Gurevitch (eds), *Mass Media and Society*, Edward Arnold, 1992.

James Curran, Michael Gurevitch and Janet Woollacott (eds), *Mass Communication and Society*, Edward Arnold, 1977.

James Curran and Jean Seaton, *Power without Responsibility: The Press and Broadcasting in Britain*, Routledge, 1991 (4th edn).

Peter Dahlgren and Colin Sparks (eds), *Communication and Citizenship: Journalism and the Public Sphere*, Routledge, 1991.

Nicholas Garnham, *Capitalism and Communication: Global Culture and the Economics of Information*, Sage Publications, 1990.

Edward Herman and Noam Chomsky, *Manufacturing Consent: The Political Economy of the Mass Media*, Pantheon Books, 1988.

John Keane, *The Media and Democracy*, Polity Press, 1991.

Stephen Lambert, *Channel Four: Television with a Difference?*, British Film Institute Publishing, 1982.

Judith Lichtenberg (ed.), *Democracy and the Mass Media*, Cambridge University Press, 1990.

Denis McQuail, *Mass Communication Theory: An Introduction*, Sage Publications, 1987.

John Storey, *An Introductory Guide to Cultural Theory and Popular Culture*, Harvester Wheatsheaf, 1993.

John B. Thompson, *Ideology and Modern Culture*, Polity Press, 1990.

Cento Veljanovski (ed.), *Freedom in Broadcasting*, Institute of Economic Affairs, 1989.

Notes

1 Judith Lichtenberg, Introduction to Judith Lichtenberg (ed.), *Democracy and the Mass Media*, Cambridge Studies in Philosophy and Public Policy, Cambridge University Press, 1990, p. 1.

2 See William H. Melody, 'Communication Policy in the Global Information Economy: Whither the Public Interest?', in Marjorie Ferguson (ed.), *Public Communication: The New Imperatives: Future Directions for Media Research*, Sage Publications, 1990, pp. 18–19.

3 James Curran, 'Mass Media and Democracy: A Reappraisal', in James Curran, Michael Gurevitch and Janet Woollacott (eds), *Mass Media and Society*, Edward Arnold, 1991, p. 92.

4 When Ronald Reagan took office in 1981, communications deregulation accelerated as it fitted in with the administration's general monetarist policies. Reagan appointed Mark Fowler as head of the FCC, and deregulatory activity peaked during Reagan's first term (1981–5). This began with Congress's extension of radio and television licences to seven and five years respectively, and culminated in the showpiece 1984 Cable Telecommunications Act which massively deregulated cable services. In between, two other decisions shaped the pace of change, both occurring in January 1982. The old AT&T/Bell monopoly was relieved of its local services control and IBM's dominance of the computer market was reinforced by its release from an anti-trust case. All these reforms were significant of an increasingly competitive set of market arrangements. For further details see Jeremy Tunstall, *Communications Deregulation: The Unleashing of America's Communications Industry*, Basil Blackwell, 1986.

5 Nicholas Garnham, *Structures of Broadcasting*, BFI, 1980, p. 15.

6 Raymond Kuhn (ed.), *The Politics of Broadcasting*, Croom Helm, 1985, p. 6.

7 See for instance Philip Schlesinger, *Putting 'Reality' Together*, Routledge, 1987.

8 Ralph Negrine, *Politics and the Mass Media*, Routledge, 1989 (1st edn), pp. 120–1.

9 John Keane, *The Media and Democracy*, Polity, 1991, pp. 13–14.

10 Ibid., pp. 14–15.

11 Ibid, p. 16.

12 Ibid., pp. 16–17.

13 Ibid., p. 27.

14 Ibid., pp. 35–42.

15 Ibid., pp. 35–6.

16 Ibid., pp. 40–1.

17 George Boyce, 'The Fourth Estate: The Reappraisal of A Concept', in George Boyce, James Curran and Pauline Wingate (eds), *Newspaper History: from the 17th Century to the Present Day*, Constable, 1976, pp. 19–40.

18 Ibid., p. 27.

19 Ibid., p. 29.

20 Stephen Koss, *Fleet Street Radical*, Penguin, 1973, p. 8.

21 George Boyce, 'The Fourth Estate', p. 31.

22 Ibid., pp. 51–78. For further details see James Curran and Jean Seaton, *Power Without Responsibility*, Routledge, 1991 (4th edn).

23 For further details on Hill's appointment see Michael Tracey, *The Production of Political Television*, Routledge, Kegan Paul, 1977. Hussey's role has been extensively discussed in Steven Barnett and Andrew Curry, *The Battle for the BBC*, Aurum Press, 1994.

24 Kenneth Dyson and Peter Humphreys, *Broadcasting and New Media Policies in Western Europe*, Routledge, 1989, p. 68.

25 Stuart Hood, *On Television*, Pluto Press, 1987, p. 79.

26 Anthony Smith quoted from Simon Blanchard and David Morley (eds), *What's this Channel Four?*, Comedia, 1982, p. 11.

27 Kenneth Dyson and Peter Humphreys, *Broadcasting and New Media Policies*, p. 68.

28 Ibid.

29 Peter Jay, *The Crisis for Western Political Economy*, André Deutsch, 1984 (9th edn), p. 226.

30 Gordon Hughes and David Vines (eds), *Deregulation and the Future of Commercial Television*, The David Hume Institute, Aberdeen University Press, 1989, pp. 38–88.

31 In various guises Peter Jay has been a journalist, television interviewer, an incomes policy adviser to James Callaghan (his then father-in-law), a British Ambassador to Washington and former Chairman of TV-AM. He is now the BBC's Economics Editor.

32 Peter Jay, 'The Future of Broadcasting: A memo to Lord Annan', *Television*, 1977, p. 68.

33 Peter Jay, *The Crisis for Western Political Economy*, p. 227.

34 Peter Jay, 'Broadcasting laissez-faire', *The Times*, 24 November 1970.

35 Peter Jay, *The Crisis for Western Political Economy*, p. 225.

36 See E. G. Wedell, *Broadcasting and Public Policy*, Michael Joseph Books, 1968 and *The Peacock Report*, HMSO, July 1986.

37 Peter Jay, *Television*, 1977, p. 68.

38 James Curran, 'Mass Media and Democracy', in James Curran and Michael Gurevitch (eds), *Mass Media and Society*, Edward Arnold, 1991, p. 101.

39 Karl Marx and Friedrich Engels, *The German Ideology: Part One*, (Students edition, edited and introduced by C. J. Arthur) Lawrence and Wishart, 1977, p. 64.

40 Jean Seaton and Ben Pimlott (eds), *The Media in British Politics*, Avebury, Aldershot, 1987, p. ix.

41 Richard Collins et al., *Media Culture and Society*, Sage Publications, 1986.

42 Richard Collins, *Television: Policy and Culture*, Routledge, 1990, p. 4.

43 See Tom Burns, *The BBC: Public Institution and Private World*, Macmillan, 1977 and Jeremy Tunstall, *Television Producers*, Routledge, 1993.

44 See Graham Murdock and Peter Golding, 'Capitalism, Communication and Class Relations', in James Curran, Michael Gurevitch and Janet Woollacott, *Mass Communication and Society*, Edward Arnold, 1977, pp. 12–43.

45 Ibid., pp. 28–33.

46 James Curran, in James Curran and Michael Gurevitch (eds), *Mass Media and Society*, pp. 87–8.

47 Edward S. Herman and Noam Chomsky, *Manufacturing Consent: The Political Economy of the Mass Media*, Pantheon Books, 1988.

48 Noam Chomsky quoted from Mark Achbar (ed.), *Manufacturing Consent: Noam Chomsky and the Media*, Black Rose Books, 1994, p. 40.

49 Edward S. Herman and Noam Chomsky, *Manufacturing Consent*, pp. 3–35.

50   For further details on Frankfurt and Mass Society theories see Tony Bennett, 'Theories of the media, theories of society', in Michael Gurevitch, Tony Bennett, James Curran and Janet Woollacott, *Culture, Society and the Media*, Routledge, 1982, pp. 30–57.

51   Ibid., pp. 42–3.

52   Jürgen Habermas, *The Structural Transformation of the Public Sphere*, Polity, 1989. Habermas's theories have influenced many scholars such as Nicholas Garnham, see *Capitalism and Communication*, Sage, 1990 and Peter Dahlgren and Colin Sparks (eds), *Communication and Citizenship*, Routledge, 1991.

53   James Curran, in James Curran and Michael Gurevitch (eds), *Mass Media and Society*, p. 83. For further details, see Nicholas Garnham, *Capitalism and Communication: Global Culture and Economics of Information*, Sage Publications, 1990.

54   Stuart Hall, 'The rediscovery of "ideology": return of the repressed in media studies', in James Curran, Michael Gurevitch and Janet Woollacott, *Mass Media and Society*, p. 95.

55   It should be noted that this amalgamation of Althusser and Gramsci has been employed for the purpose of discussing competing theories governing the media's political role in society. This narrow focus hides many issues drawn from a significant debate between Althusserians and Gramscians in their interpretation of Marx. For further details see David Harris, *From Class Conflict to the Politics of Pleasure*, Routledge, 1992.

56   John Storey, *An Introductory Guide to Cultural Theory and Popular Culture*, Harvester Wheatsheaf, 1993, p. 111.

57   Althusser quoted from ibid., p. 111.

58   Tony Bennett, 'Theories of the media, theories of society', p. 51.

59   James Curran, in James Curran and Michael Gurevitch, *Mass Media and Society*, p. 101.

60   Tony Bennett, 'Theories of the media, theories of society', p. 51.

61   Denis McQuail, *Mass Communication Theory: An Introduction*, Sage Publications, 1987, p. 66.

2
The Development of the British Press

Introduction

The concept of press freedom was developed in the eighteenth century. The press should occupy the fourth estate (separated from the Crown, Parliament and the Judiciary), be liberated from state censorship and check the political establishment. Therefore, the individual's access to unfettered information could be guaranteed. Press freedom was a method for sustaining democracy.

This philosophy underpinned the British press's development. The press was organized on market principles to be independent from state repression. It has been funded through advertising and was privately owned. British governments have avoided the establishment of a statutory body to regulate the print media. A free press market flourished so that the full range of political opinions could be expressed.

Whig historians suggest that press freedom was secured after a long struggle. They stress that the press was emancipated from state control through a series of political and economic reforms:

> Thus, in perhaps the most influential schema so far presented . . . The historical development of the British press is sub-divided in three phases; in its first phase the press was subject to pre-publication censorship and functioned to support the state; in its second phase, dating from 1668, the press became increasingly independent of state control and accountable to the public through the market mechanism; and in the third phase, dating from the twentieth century, the press became less partisan and more socially responsible due to growing commitment amongst publishers and journalists to the professional goals of objectivity, balance and accuracy.[1]

However, the press's development is contested. Several arguments have challenged the traditional scheme. They maintain that the press's history is one of capitalist incorporation. The benefits associated with the introduction of advertising have been questioned. Many Marxists assert that hidden economic controls replaced overt methods of political repression. Further, critics contend that the press's ownership, finance and partisanship continued to shape its output. Instead of being a free press, it became an agent for social control.

The development of the British press has been argued either to be explicitly pluralistic, a method for greater bourgeois domination, or a means through which different elite groups may interrelate to manipulate the press's output. Thus, we shall assess, analyse and explain the British press by addressing the political, social and economic imperatives which have underpinned its evolution. This chapter will survey the press from the start of the nineteenth century to the late 1960s. To study such a long period it has been necessary to be judicious with the material (I will not, for instance, be directly discussing the historical development of the local press)[2] and to select a number of key phases in order to discuss how academic opinions have varied over their meaning. Clearly, the 1861 Repeal of the Taxes Upon Knowledge, allowing for the introduction of advertising, provides an entry point into these arguments. Moreover, the period of the press barons, with particular reference to the 1931 United Empire Party Campaign, may be seen to be illustrative of how press power was used as political power. In regard to these case studies the pluralistic and Marxist theories, alongside Habermas's conception of the public sphere, are of key relevance, focusing on issues of political independence, ownership and finance in shaping output.

The Whig History of the Press

From this perspective, political and economic reforms emancipated the press from an overbearing state. Popular control was manufactured through an independent press.[3] This academic tradition has had a pervasive effect upon the press's consciousness.

The pre-Victorian press was subservient to the state due to censorship and licensing. Throughout the Middle Ages, the Roman Catholic church censored books. Simultaneously, in the secular institutions, absolutist sovereigns banned heretical and seditious pamphlets. Through its licensing powers, the state employed repressive measures including pre-publication censorship and the outlawing of presses. However, these restrictions were overturned by the Star Chamber in 1694. Subsequently, the print media flourished with twenty papers of two to four pages appearing on a weekly, twice-weekly and thrice-weekly basis.[4] Macaulay commented that this reform provided a greater contribution to liberty and civilization than either the Magna Carta or the Bill of Rights.[5] Yet throughout the eighteenth and nineteenth centuries, the state continued to harass and persecute the press. The general laws of sedition, decency, blasphemy and obscenity remained potent weapons. However, the main constraint on the press's freedom was financial. Throughout the early eighteenth century Parliament had unsuccessfully sought to bring back licensing controls. Instead, in 1712 Lord Bolingbroke introduced the first of a series of Stamp Acts. The state's power was sustained through these stamp taxes and advertising duties known as the Taxes upon Knowledge. Consequently, the press's expensive costs resulted in high cover prices and increased charges on advertisements.[6] Further, unstamped papers could be prosecuted due to their non-payment of duties. Circulations and readership remained confined to the well-off.

These financial qualifications led to calls for reform. The respectable campaign for press freedom was mobilized by Whig opposition to the Gagging Bills in 1819–20. The government extended the stamp duty by taxing newspaper sales, increasing the seditious libel laws and introducing a security system requiring proprietors to provide bonds of £200–300 before publication.[7] Between the 1830s and the 1850s several parliamentary debates discussed the press's financial reform. Whigs commented that freedom of expression should not be taxed as the truth exposed falsehoods and the people should be heard. To facilitate a free trade of ideas, a free press market was required.[8]

Subsequently, in the 1830s, the tax on pamphlets was removed and the stamp duty was reduced by 75 per cent.[9] The latter was abolished in 1855 and paper duty was repealed in 1861.[10] In such a manner, advertising could fully fund the press. A number of benefits accompanied this transition. In 1855, daily papers were priced at 5d; by 1870 this had been reduced to between $\frac{1}{2}$d and to 3d.[11] As cover prices were reduced, a greater number of papers entered the market and mass circulations were achieved.

This liberation enabled the press to remain independent from state influence. In turn, it could supply disinterested information to an expanded electorate to participate in the democratic process. Essentially, the press's economic reform led to the citizen's political emancipation by providing a greater plurality of views from different newspapers:

> Since sales were inadequate to cover the costs of producing a paper it was the growing income from advertising which provided the material base for the change of attitude from subservience to independence . . . It is perhaps no exaggeration to say that the growth of advertising revenue

was the most important single factor in enabling the press to emerge as the fourth estate of the realm.[12]

A cheap press became an integral ingredient for an educated democracy. The traditional wisdom saw state despotism being replaced by enlightenment. At the end of the 1860s, it appeared that through a free press a wider and more accountable representative democracy would be established.

Critiques of the Whig history

This interpretation has been criticized by Jürgen Habermas, as well as liberal revisionist and radical historians. Instead of papers being 'great organs of the public mind',[13] the press's history was reflective of elite power and public manipulation. However, whilst this conclusion unifies these critiques, their arguments over the press's development have differed.

The structural transformation of the public sphere

Jürgen Habermas reversed the progressive Whig view by contending that an independent press was made subservient. He argued that as the public sphere had eroded from the eighteenth century, the press had been transformed from an agent for the rationality of elite, private individuals, into an instrument for public manipulation during the nineteenth and twentieth centuries. Previously, the press was a forum in which private opinions could be transformed into public views and the government might be criticized. However, as the mass political processes emerged, underpinned by monopoly capitalism, the press became dominated by advertising and ownership. In turn, its political discourse was state controlled, sensationalist and market-led. Thus rational public opinion was overridden by power politics in which large organizations bargained with each other and the state, thereby excluding the public. For Habermas, public opinion no longer reflected rational discourse but was led by the press's orchestration of publicity: 'The media were an accessory to (the) "refeudalization" of society. They functioned as manipulative agencies controlling mass opinion, in contrast to the early press which had facilitated the formation and expression of organic public opinion.'[14]

Criticisms of Habermas and Whig histories

Habermas and the Whig histories were questioned by liberal revisionist historians and Marxist analyses.[15] The former argued that the eighteenth-century press was dominated by political controls and circles of influence. This contrasted with Habermas's idealistic, pre-mass politics vision. Therefore, a close affiliation between the press and the political elite had dominated the press's organization throughout its history.[16] Marxist academics have discussed the legitimacy of these positive or negative analyses of the press's history. Rather than accepting Habermas's view of gradual decline from a golden age or the dominant belief that newspaper industry was liberalized, they contend that overt political controls were replaced by covert, economic constrictions. To sustain their arguments they concentrate on the radical press which existed during the early to mid-nineteenth century.

The radical press

From the Napoleonic Wars to the middle of the nineteenth century momentous changes occurred in British society. There was a shift from an agricultural to an industrial economy. This resulted in the expansion of urban centres and a decline in rural populations. The Industrial Revolution was accompanied by extreme class antagonism. Further, the bourgeois revolutions of the eighteenth century had invested Britain with a tide of radicalism: for example, the Battle of St. Peter's Fields, Manchester (or Peterloo), the Luddite Plug riots, the Tolpuddle Martyrs, the rural Swing riots, and the People's Charter.[17]

From the late eighteenth century, attacks on the established order were disseminated through newspapers located around popular, working class movements. In 1836, London's unstamped press's aggregate readership stood at approximately 2 million.[18] With varying degrees of success, it developed an oppositional, plebian sub-culture which criticized the dominant order:

> They helped their readers to make sense of the world in a new way, most notably by popularising the labour theory of value. The assertion that the wealth of the community was created by labour that became a recurrent theme of the new radical press was of crucial importance in developing a corporate class pride and establishing an ideological base from which to resist middle-class propaganda.[19]

In the 1830s, *The Poor Man's Guardian*, *The Northern Star* and *Reynolds News* provided a class critique of Britain by arguing that economic exploitation was perpetuated under capitalism. The radical press increased class consciousness and sought out methods to transform society.[20] In particular, they attacked state institutions such as the royal family, the electoral system, the law courts, the army, the police and parliament. The House of Commons was presented as a group of landowners who operated in their own interests.[21] Naturally, the state perceived the radical press as a danger. Governments imposed controls to outlaw these newspapers. However, direct prosecutions for blasphemy or sedition proved inoperable. Juries were unwilling to convict and the publicity helped to generate public support for the defendants. Successive Attorneys-General realized that prosecutions for seditious libel were counter-productive. The heavy stamp duty of 4d per paper proved to be unenforceable, as radical papers were printed on clandestine presses.[22]

The state's ineffectiveness was apparent in the Whigs' attempt to confiscate the radical press in 1836. Ironically, a reform – the reduction of the stamp duty by 75 per cent – led this crack-down. Other measures comprised greater appropriation powers and increased penalties for being in possession of an unstamped paper. To comply with these rules, radical papers inflated their prices from 1d to 4d or 5d – well beyond the purchasing power of their readers. Yet, the strategy was frustrated by a campaign of resistance as unions, clubs and political associations funded the collective purchases of newspapers. Paradoxically, the new radical papers achieved larger circulations than those of their best-selling predecessors.[23]

After 1861, the radical press significantly declined. James Curran argues that the repeal of the stamp taxes produced repressive structural changes. He contends that their removal transformed the methods of subjugation as market forces replaced legal mechanisms to contain the radical press. The lifting of controls in the 1850s was inspired by the same beliefs which had previously prompted state restrictions. The proponents and opponents of press freedom wanted a print media which supported the status quo. The change in emphasis was influenced by a resolution to indoctrinate the proletariat through cheap papers, and a realization that free trade controls were preferable to direct state repression. This reflected the power of the Victorian middle classes who hoped to utilize the expanding press to advance their interests with Parliament's landed gentry and against the threat posed by a militant working class:

> When the organizers of the campaign against state economic controls of the press argued that the market was a more efficient control system, they showed themselves to be people of remarkable insight. Just how shrewd and perceptive they were can only be fully grasped . . . (by comparing their success with) . . . the inability of successive governments to suppress through direct methods.[24]

The middle classes' values were legitimized in the parliamentary debates which accompanied the press's reforms. In the 1850s, the discourse was underpinned by the concern for social control. As one reformer, J. F. Stephen, commented: 'a perfectly free press is one of the greatest safeguards of peace and order . . . (as journalists would come) . . . from the comfortable part of society, and will err rather on the side of making too much of their interests than on that of neglecting them.'[25]

For W. Hickson, a member of the Stamp Abolition Committee, the labouring classes would be addressed by individuals who were 'two or three degrees' their superior. Gladstone argued that a free press would enable men of quality to educate the masses. Further, it was appreciated that by employing market strategies starting costs would be increased, thereby allowing the appropriate classes to become owners.[26] These expenses were enlarged through the press's industrialization, as fixed expenditures in machinery, publishing and distribution escalated. Consequently, newspapers could only enjoy profitability if they were established as 'legitimate' business ventures and accorded to the wishes of a selective set of advertisers.

Free trade would promote newspapers to shape the public demand. This freedom enabled capitalism to indoctrinate labour as it fed the proletariat with an ideological diet which stressed conformity. Instead of class conflict, societal conflicts would be conceptualized as occurring between ignorance and enlightenment and the individual and the state. Consequently, the press's fourth estate function was contained within a dominant ideological universe.[27]

This analysis has ramifications for the progressive Whig histories of the Victorian press. The use of economic reforms established covert forms of elite control. In effect, state power was replaced by advertising power, as cover prices were reduced and exclusion or adaptability awaited the radical papers. These had previously flourished by flouting the strict state laws, but as the market became more reliant on advertising they either folded, as they could not attract advertisers, or had to sufficiently alter to take advertising on board. It may be suggested that advertisers were actively prejudiced against radical papers. However, the main discrimination was motivated by expedience as these newspapers attracted poor audiences whose spending power was limited.[28]

The case of the *Daily Herald* is revealing. This originated as a strike sheet and became a weekly newspaper. When it achieved daily status and increased its circulation, its costs led to a financial collapse. Advertisers proved reticent and expenses could not be recouped by doubling the cover price. Finally, it was saved by the Labour party and Odhams. Yet as Curran claims: 'as a result, a genuinely radical, iconoclastic paper became the official mouthpiece of the moderate leadership of the Labour party . . . Lack of advertising tamed it by forcing it to become subservient to another form of moderating influence.'[29]

This argument not only contests the Whig histories but questions Habermas's theories. First, it challenges the concept of a rational bourgeois public sphere. Habermas celebrated newspapers which were selective in their interpretations. However, a significant radical press existed which allowed audiences to engage in a wider and more critical debate. Second, it illustrates that the establishment employed the market system to commercialize the radical press in order to retain social control. This shows that Habermas failed to include class struggle in his history of press representation. Moreover, it signifies an inadequate analysis of the market system's ability to filter 'social access to the public sphere'.[30] These perspectives, therefore, have argued that a free press eroded or failed to materialize. The arguments have fallen into several categories; Habermas's view of a replacement of a rational public sphere with a system of capitalist domination; a revisionist critique demonstrating that factionalism and political compliance existed in the eighteenth-century press; and Marxist accounts of the radical press's decline as economic controls subsumed political restrictions.

The Press in the Late Nineteenth and Early Twentieth Century

From 1855 to 1920 the press matured and may be considered under the following headings: manufacture, ownership, output and ideology.

Manufacture and the press market

Mass communications became industrialized due to the new technologies, lower cover prices and advertising. The press went from being printed on small-scale presses to becoming nationally circulated. The printing machinery increased in sophistication, alongside the emergence of an infrastructure of national delivery services. As advertising was unrestricted, cover prices were reduced and circulations were increased. However, the cheap daily papers sold at a figure far below their cost. The gap was closed by advertising which on smaller papers accounted for over half the income. Therefore, this income needed to be secure. Further, as advertisers were attracted by large daily circulations the pressure to expand increased, which in turn forced up fixed costs with the need for large presses and heavy labour. The small-scale, multiple structure of the press industry was replaced by an integrated, large-scale organization directed by unremitting market expansion.[31] In turn, manufacturing costs, profit margins and the need for national circulations meant that starting-up prices dramatically increased. For instance in 1837, the *Northern Star* was launched for £1000, by 1918 the *Sunday Express* cost £1 million to start.

Ownership: the partisan press

These manufacturing expenses, advertising and starting costs created a closed newspaper market-place. Owners had to be wealthy to run newspapers. This led to papers receiving financial backing from the political parties. The concentric circles arrangement went beyond editorials pledging political support, as parties indirectly funded newspapers. Throughout this period all the major editors were either obliged or formally committed to a party-political backer. By the early twentieth century, the press was firmly connected with political finance. There were several examples of political parties acquiring newspapers through front organizations. The *Standard* was subsidized by the Unionist Central Office and the *Daily News* was bought during the Boer War by a syndicate led by Lloyd George to expound anti-war feeling.

The outstanding example of political acquisition occurred when Lloyd George's supporters purchased the *Daily Chronicle* to propagate support for the First World War. The money was drawn from wealthy admirers who contributed £1,650,000 for the paper. In this case, Lloyd George attempted to obtain the print media's favour through his ownership of a paper. In a fit of pique the incumbent editor Robert Donald resigned and the deal was criticized by politicians and journalists. Whilst it was no better or worse than what had preceded, Lloyd George's actions served to make several factors conspicuous: 'this transaction "exposed the myth of the fourth estate" because it confirmed in stark fashion the well established close connections between press and politics. To many the existence of "concentric circles" meant abandoning the pretence that the press was the "fourth estate".'[32]

The press consequently served as an extension rather than a check or balance on political institutions because of these ownership affiliations. It failed to be an independent arbiter of information as its economic organization placed it firmly within the political elite.

Output and ideology

However, despite industrialization, commercialization and ownership changes, the press market remained relatively small. A new target audience, drawn from the prosperous lower middle classes, was identified. The papers were sold to the educated and the growing industrial bourgeois. Subsequently, the presentation, selection and editing of news stories altered. News was parcelled into short and easily digestible portions. The editorial judgements were driven by the desire to make profits and emphasized sensational stories such as murders and adulteries. Further, a different writing style entitled 'new journalism' developed in the 1880s.

Market forces not only changed newspapers' output but created a print media which emphasized the values of the economic, political and social elites. The press's incorporation into the political elite through the pressures of advertising and ownership meant that it became an agent of social reinforcement. The commercialization of the press led to the propagation of consensual values and dominant Victorian values. This reporting stressed cooperation within acceptable societal norms such as the 'national interest'. Mass labour as the source for wealth was supplanted by a depiction of profits as the fountain of prosperity. The entrepreneur became the midwife for Britain's affluence. Collectivism was replaced by an emphasis on individual self-improvement.

The focus was placed on single political issues rather than a class analysis of society. Class conflict became anathema to a press which maintained that political problems could be resolved by parliament and which mobilized working class support for an institution which was largely populated by aristocrats. This understanding of parliament was reflected in the development of the lobby system in the 1880s. The new forms of journalism now centred on the mainstream political parties. These changes affected the radical papers which continued to exist. For example, *Reynolds News* became a populist paper due to the pressures of advertising finance and ideological incorporation. To sustain profitability, it concentrated on the issues which united its indigenous readership to the lower middle classes. Whilst it pursued a radical agenda on some matters, it simultaneously articulated the individualistic values of its petit-bourgeois audience. Thus, emigration would solve unemployment; business monopolies and speculation rather than industrial capital were attacked, and the shopkeeper's values were celebrated.[33]

This variation can also be identified through a comparison of Queen Victoria's coverage from the pre- to post-Stamp Act press. Between 1837 and 1855 the radical papers were republican and the Queen was vilified as being politically partisan, a reactionary, the head of organized corruption, the relative of foreign tyrants, and the mother of a brood of royal cadgers. However, this portrayal altered from the mid-1870s when she was presented as a benign, dutiful and loving monarch. In effect Victoria became the embodiment of national unity and the papers mobilized the population to celebrate her Golden and Diamond Jubilees in 1887 and 1897.[34]

Despite these financial, structural and ideological constraints the press held on to the fourth estate principle. Its credibility was established by its apparent independence from the state. This was a vital means for self-justification. Yet between 1855 and 1920, the press was integrated into the political mainstream and largely failed to act as a neutral observer. Principally, advertising had transformed the press market and output. However, from 1896 when Alfred Harmsworth bought the *Daily Mail* and throughout the 1900s there were changes, as press ownership became concentrated into the hands of a group of powerful magnates who became known as the press barons.

The Press Barons

Several factors contributed to this transformation. After the First World War the partisan press totally declined, due to industrialization, commercialization and the explosion of advertising. As advertising increased, greater sums were spent on editorial and promotional activities. As a result, the political parties found that newspaper ownership drained their resources. The market also became characterized by the domination of a limited number of daily titles and the processes of chain ownership. Between 1890 and 1920 there was a rapid acceleration in press conglomeration within national and local titles.

The Press Barons had attained their wealth from industrial holdings.[35] By 1921, Harmsworth (Lord Northcliffe) controlled *The Times*, the *Daily Mail*, the *Weekly Dispatch* and the *London Evening News*, whilst his brother Harold (Lord Rothermere) owned the *Daily Mirror*, the *Sunday Pictorial*, the *Daily Record*, the *Glasgow Evening News* and the *Sunday Mail*. Max Aitken (Lord Beaverbrook) owned a smaller number of titles including the *Daily Express*, the *Sunday Express* and the *Evening Standard*. Additionally there was spectacular consolidation of regional titles owned by the Berry brothers, Lords Kemsley and Camrose.[36]

The press market during the inter-war years

Throughout this period a shift occurred from provincial to national titles. In 1921, there were forty-one morning provincials, by 1937 this had been reduced to seventeen.[37] As the national popular press expanded, it became dependent on advertising revenue which accounted for three-quarters of its income, and on large sales founded on low cover prices. Subsequently, the constant circulation wars led to new promotional gimmicks such as insurance schemes and gifts for subscription in order to gain a wider readership. Further, as newspaper staffing levels increased by 72 per cent, 40 per cent of the total staffs were canvassers.[38] Consequently, newspaper styles changed during the press barons' period of control. The circulation wars resulted in increased paging, new typographical formats, and innovations such as crossword puzzles.[39] The intense competition pressured for a more universal content to cater for a less differentiated readership. Market research showed that the most popular stories focused on crimes, accidents, divorce, sport and human interest. Popular tabloid journalism, drawn from American styles, was used extensively.

This drive to maximize audiences downgraded political stories. Between 1927 and 1937 the *Daily Mail*'s coverage of political, social and economic issues fell from 10 to 6 per cent of its total news content, whilst sport's coverage rose from 27 to 36 per cent. This was enhanced by the effects of target advertising as quality papers accessed wealthy groups, whilst popular papers were directed at a mass market. In this respect, profits were more important than politics for the press barons:

> Newspapers . . . resemble fashionable ladies of the West End, in that they are more concerned with their figures than with their morals.[40]

The press barons' control over their papers

The press barons controlled their newspapers like personal fiefdoms. Editors were undermined by their proprietors' commercial and political interests. The barons maintained their power with great ruthlessness. Northcliffe and Beaverbrook sacked a great number of their staff. However, they combined terror with generosity and were known to shower their employees with sudden gifts. Moreover, they had their own particular style of management which concurred with their personalities. Beaverbrook was noted for his aloofness. Conversely, Northcliffe bullied his employees on a daily basis. The press barons shaped the editorial content and layout of their papers; for example Beaverbrook sent 147 separate instructions to the *Daily Express* in one day. Their personal interests often determined the news values and the selection of stories. Northcliffe's lifelong obsession with torture was exhibited in the magazine *Answers* which printed enquiries such as, 'How long is a severed head conscious after decapitation?'[41] They also created a common language for newspapers and determined the reporting styles of their respective papers. Overall, the proprietors set the tone of their papers and targeted a perceived readership. For instance, Beaverbrook's *Daily Express* reflected his 'New World' (Canadian) ethic of the self-made entrepreneur.[42] He commented that his paper served every class whether rich or poor, barbarian and free.[43] In contrast, Northcliffe's *Daily Mail* had a hierarchical world view which corresponded to the proprietor's traditional brand of conservatism and was directed at the established middle classes.

The press barons' politics

The change from partisan control to the Beaverbrook, Rothermere and Northcliffe concentration of ownership was apparent in these proprietors' political campaigns throughout the inter-war period. They were aware of their influence over political communication, as the circulation of national titles increased from 3.1 million in 1918 to 10.6 million in 1939.[44] Their papers were often populist. Beaverbrook produced many manifestos in his leader columns. The first was published on 20 March 1919. It was unsigned and in italics and attacked the government's running of the economy. Beaverbrook quickly followed this with an assault on those who had made profits out of the First World War, although he was careful not to name any potential ally. Later that year, the *Daily Express* exposed a fraudulent land deal for non-existent plots at 'Anzac-on-Sea'! Beaverbrook's leaders were noted for their short declamatory sentences, lack of qualification and final exhortations.[45] In the early 1920s, Rothermere and Northcliffe campaigned against 'squandermania' and urged cuts in public spending and wartime planning controls. To this end, they supported the 1921 Anti-Waste Campaign.

The press barons were conservative in their societal views. Protests and strikes were reported as threats to law and order rather than being indicative of unemployment or social deprivation. They stigmatized the political opposition and were anti-Marxist. For example, in 1919 the *Daily Express* carried the headline 'Spectre of Lenin Alarms Paris'. This was followed by reports on the horrors of Bolshevism.[46] In 1924 the first Labour minority government was branded as being Communist and in the subsequent election campaign the forged Zinoviev letter to British Communists was used to attack Ramsay MacDonald's leadership. The *Daily Mail* claimed this revealed a Bolshevik plot to incapacitate the British armed forces and plunge the country into civil war. This marked the zenith of the barons' 'Red Peril' campaign and significantly influenced the outcome of the 1924 General Election.[47]

The press was intensely patriotic, xenophobic and often racist. Rothermere and Northcliffe were anti-semitic and the *Daily Mail* explained Nazism as reflecting Germany's attempt to rid itself of its alien elements. For Rothermere, the 'international Jewish conspiracy' had led to Israelites insinuating themselves into the German administration. His newspapers argued that the Weimar Republic had twenty times as many Jewish government officials than Imperial Germany. Rothermere also favoured appeasement policies for Hitler's Germany. In 1938, the cartoonist David Low produced a drawing of Rothermere alongside two other appeasers, J. L. Garvin, *Observer* editor, and *The Times's* editor Geoffrey Dawson, dressed in tutus made out of newspaper and being choreographed by Joseph Goebbels, the Nazi Minister of Propaganda.[48]

For a short time, Rothermere's papers supported Oswald Mosley's British Union of Fascists (BUF). The *Daily Mail* produced headlines such as 'Give the Blackshirts a Helping Hand' and 'Hurrah for the Blackshirts'. The *Evening News* even ran a competition for the best letter on the theme of 'Why I like the Blackshirts'. This gave an obscure organization publicity and increased its membership. However, after the débâcle of the BUF's 1934 Olympia meeting and Hitler's 'Night of the Long Knives', Rothermere withdrew his support and denied the BUF the legitimacy it desired.[49]

Beaverbrook's and Rothermere's interests went beyond newspaper coverage to placing themselves at the centre of the political mainstream. Beaverbrook backed several politicians: during the First World War, alongside Northcliffe, he had pressured for Asquith government's to be removed and be replaced by Lloyd George.[50] In the 1920s, he allied himself to the prime minister, Andrew Bonar Law.[51] This interest in the establishment led to Beaverbrook's ambition to enter into office himself.

However, there was a difference in outlook between these proprietors and the politicians, for their power was economic, accumulated through industrial holdings and the ownership of profitable newspapers. This was 'independent of either their (parliamentary) standing or political favours'.[52] Therefore, the press barons were to alter the relations between the government and the press. They employed their papers as levers of power against the political establishment. In this respect, it has been argued that they attempted to challenge the political elite so that the press could occupy the fourth estate.

The United Empire Party Crusade

Their peculiar position, as both actors within the political elite and outsiders, was apparent during the period 1929 to 1931 of the United Empire Party Crusade led by Beaverbrook and Rothermere. Their acts and the Conservative Party leadership's reaction illustrated the anomalous position held by the press barons *vis-à-vis* the political establishment.

First, it is necessary to understand the press barons' status within the Conservative Party. Beaverbrook, in particular, had attacked the government but made little headway within the party. He had been marginalized after the death of his friend and ally Prime Minister Bonar

Law in 1923. Subsequently, he was excluded by Bonar Law's Conservative successor Stanley Baldwin, who saw him as a danger owing to his previous association with Bonar Law and his stewardship of the *Daily Express*. He was treated with suspicion because of his role in unseating Asquith's government. Simultaneously, Beaverbrook distrusted Baldwin whom he perceived as being devious.

Beaverbrook's reputation was matched by that of Rothermere who was also deeply mistrusted in the Conservative Party. Concurrently, Rothermere's ire had grown when Baldwin had failed to reward his support with an earldom and his son Esmond, a Conservative MP, was by-passed for political promotion. These tensions demonstrated a wide gulf between these two elite groups:

> Individually unacceptable, together an anathema, Rothermere and Beaverbrook occupied similar positions in Conservative demonology. In a rhetorical milieu in which principle, character, party and honour were the prescriptive claims to political respectability, both were tainted by shifting principles, contempt to party loyalty and the irresponsible excesses of press power. (The) depiction of the press lords in 1924 as the 'Wicked Uncles' besetting Baldwin as a 'Babe in the Woods' became a pervasive metaphor.[53]

In 1929, Beaverbrook and Rothermere took exception to Baldwin's economic policy. In response they established the United Empire Crusade. This contended that Britain's problems could be solved by transforming the empire into a free-trade zone protected by a high tariff wall. However, this campaign was motivated by the press barons' own desire to gain political power in the Conservative Party. Throughout the crisis, accidental and deliberate misunderstandings affected the behaviour of both sides. The Conservative Party attempted to qualify the resonance of the political crisis and placed pressure on Beaverbrook and Rothermere to compromise. In turn, they decided to play a game of cat-and-mouse with the Conservative leadership.[54]

The affair reached a head when negotiations broke down between the Conservative Party leadership and the press barons. In 1930, Beaverbrook and Rothermere saw their chance to undermine Baldwin by creating the United Empire Party (UEP). Rothermere's *Daily Mail* hailed it as the 'Party of Prosperity' and Beaverbrook's *Express* castigated the established parties as 'slaves of tradition'.[55] Thus, a fighting fund was created, 173,000 members were enrolled and it was announced that fifty candidates would be run in the next general election.[56] The party ran a candidate, Vice-Admiral Taylor, and won a safe Conservative seat at Paddington. In a by-election in the Labour ward of East Islington, they pushed the Conservatives into third place. To gain support, the press barons employed their newspapers as propaganda

machines to articulate their criticisms of the government. The Rothermere press declared that Beaverbrook was the most likely future
prime minister.[57] In this way, the papers were employed as political
relays. This was a deliberate attempt to use the press to bring down
the government. Beaverbrook had concluded that press power:

> is a flaming sword which will cut through any political armour . . . That
> is not to say that any great newspaper or group of newspapers can
> enforce policies or make or unmake governments at will, just because
> it is a great newspaper . . . They are in themselves unloaded guns. But
> teach the man behind them how to load and what to shoot at, and they
> become deadly.[58]

The campaign meant that Baldwin's stock fell and his support within
the constituencies wobbled precariously. At one point, forty Conservative MPs informed the Chief Whip that a change of leadership
was inevitable. However two factors interceded to undermine the press
barons' pursuit of power. First, Beaverbrook was too hasty when he
ran a UEP candidate in St George's Ward, Westminster. This was the
safest Conservative seat in the country. As Neville Chamberlain, then
Party Chairman, was to lament:

> It is in accord with the irony of politics that just as I was about to
> take the step which must have resulted in the speedy retirement of SB
> (Stanley Baldwin) Max (Beaverbrook) comes in with a move which
> must cause him to dig his toes in and will rally to him many who wish
> for change. This is the 2nd time Max has spoiled his own game by his
> precipitation.[59]

Second, this imprudent intervention allowed Baldwin to fight a
rearguard action to this challenge. He shifted attention away from the
issue of trade tariffs to the unaccountable and unconstitutional power
of the press barons. He made it clear that the press could act as an
adjunct, mouthpiece or denouncer of the political parties, but could
not use its power to undermine the political establishment. Thus,
the press barons solved Baldwin's problems by allowing him to focus
on the issue of press dictatorship. If they lost, he was secure. However, he was equally safe if they won, as the Conservatives would not
oust him because of the apparent political influence of the unelected
press barons. On 17 March 1931, during the climax of the campaign,
Baldwin delivered an outstanding attack on the press (my italics):

> The papers conducted by Lord Rothermere and Lord Beaverbrook
> are not newspapers in the ordinary acceptance of the term. They are
> engines of propaganda for constantly changing policies, desires, personal

wishes, personal likes and dislikes of two men. What are their methods? Their methods are direct falsehood, misrepresentation, half-truths, the alteration of the speaker's meaning by putting sentences apart from the context, suppression and editorial criticism of speeches which are not reported in the paper. . . . What the proprietorship of these papers is aiming at is power *but power without responsibility, the prerogative of the harlot throughout the ages.* . . . (This is not) a contest as to who would lead the party, but as to who is to appoint the leader of the party. It is a challenge to the accepted constitutional parliamentary system.[60]

Beaverbrook and Rothermere had attempted, albeit for reasons of self-interest and by means of their own particular methods, to create a power block through their newspapers in order to produce 'a circle of press power of equal strength and significance to that of the political circle'.[61] They failed, as their power, founded on economic and propagandist capital, could not compete with the normative democratic practices. The fierce response to this defiance meant that newspapers would continue to work hand-in-hand with the political establishment. The incident showed how the press was constrained by political controls and was indicative of the difficulties that accompanied the promotion of an independent press. The press barons' challenge to the political elite was undermined by the interconnections of economic, political and social power. The common practices of procedure, order and democracy foiled this attempt to contest the politician's power.

The Press during the Second World War

Throughout the Second World War the press was subject to state intervention. First, circulations were pegged back as newsprint was rationed. The scarcity of paper had a knock-on effect as newspaper managements voluntarily reduced the amount of advertising with papers slimmed down by two-thirds. This meant that advertisers could no longer determine output as advertising space decreased and were forced to advertise wherever they could. This change meant that alternative editorial policies could be pursued:

> Economic pressures had restrained . . . papers moving to the left in the late 1930s. But the wartime liberation from advertisers meant that they could aim solely at a working-class readership. They could also develop clear political identities in keeping their more homogeneous audiences.[62]

Second, the government believed that the press could be employed for propaganda purposes, in order to encourage the war effort. During the early period of the war, the government privately expressed fears over public morale. This was due to Britain's military defeats and the mass devastation bombing and civilian death and injury which accompanied the development of Total War. Thus, the state was anxious about the dissemination of information. This led to a number of clashes between the government and the newspapers about the press's independence.

In 1940 the Home Secretary, Sir John Anderson, introduced several measures that would control the press. The most infamous was Regulation 2D which gave the Home Office the right to ban material seen to be against the government's interest. Subsequently, this resulted in tremendous opposition from the press and many members of the older political establishment such as Lloyd George. In the event, two concessions were made: that no amendment to the regulations would be made without parliamentary consultation and that the regulations would only apply to papers that were against the war. State censorship, therefore, was not exclusive to the left-wing press. However, these controls served to focus the press's attention, make it more responsive and better at defending its interests. The *Daily Mirror* and *Daily Worker* successfully campaigned against state repression. Therefore, as the press had fought back and had been able to address a wider audience due to the reduction in advertising, there was greater optimism. Some commentators argued that it had finally attained its fourth estate position. Concurrent with this development stood the decline of party attachments and less owner power over output:

> By 1947, the party attachments of papers – as they had been understood to operate over the preceding hundred years – were effectively abandoned . . . (thus) completing the halting transition from official to popular control.[63]

The Post-War Press: 1945–1968

From the 1940s to the 1960s the press remained secure in having a vital place in the British polity. This period was punctuated by Royal Commissions on the Press in 1947 and 1961. The 1947 Commission recommended the creation of the Press Council to act as an internal regulator of the press's output. In spite of the contradictions between freedom of information and the concentration of ownership and party affiliation which had dominated newspapers, these commissions avoided recommending any statutory regulation. Instead, they perpetuated the arguments concerning the retraction of state intervention and advocated that a free press could only be provided through an unfettered marketplace. As Stephen Koss commented:

The rhetoric was redolent of the nineteenth century, when Cobden and Bright had trusted implicitly to the purifying influences of *laissez faire*. To contemplate state intervention . . . was, in a way, to revive the debate of the 1850s over the 'taxes on knowledge'. The arguments of the mid-Victorians . . . died hard.[64]

Whilst the principal tenets of market enterprise (consumer choice leading to a plurality of opinions and diversity of ownership) remained fixed, there were significant changes. First, the press market shrank in the face of competition from television, radio, magazines and other areas of the leisure economy. This led to the shedding of some nationals and a decline in the Sunday, weekly and regional papers. Second, the power relations between owners, editors and journalists were reformulated. The domination of the old press barons declined as ownership changed and the former generation died out. Their successors were motivated more by profits and intervened less over the newspaper's editorial line. This viewpoint was summed up by Lord Thomson who informed the 1961 Royal Commission on the Press:

> My purpose is to run newspapers as a business. *Q* To make money? *A* To make money. That is what you do business for.[65]

The press market

In many respects, this commercial attitude was fostered by the dynamics of the British press market. Newspapers were subject to internal and external pressures throughout the post-war period. In 1955, the rationing of newsprint was lifted. This led to the major papers increasing their paging for editorial and advertising purposes. Therefore, readers bought fewer newspapers and tended to stick with their preferred choice. A stagnation in circulation meant that papers had to become more competitive in attracting readers from their rivals. Further, it has been suggested that the war and rationing of newsprint had created artificially high newspaper circulations in what, by the end of the 1930s, was already an over-saturated market. As a consequence, there were too many titles and not enough readers. Subsequently, a number of papers closed (the *Daily Chronicle*), were forced to merge (the *Daily Sketch* into the *Daily Mail*) or were relaunched (the *Daily Herald* as the *Sun*).[66]

A major factor in the press's postwar development was the introduction of television. First, newspapers were challenged for advertising revenues with the advent of Independent Television (ITV) in 1955. ITV quickly attracted advertisers who could directly target audiences through television. This led to a significant reduction in the newspaper's proportion of the total available advertising. Second, the press no longer acted as the principal means through which the public obtained information. The more immediate impact of television pictures and the intrusive nature of the medium meant that the press no longer broke the news. Further, television became the most direct conduit between politicians and the public through election campaigns and the establishment of news departments at the BBC and ITV. Consequently, the power exerted by the press barons during campaigns such as the United Empire Crusade was ameliorated as the news market expanded to incorporate the electronic media.

Until 1956, the press had been protected from broadcasting through the fourteen-day rule.[67] This meant that broadcasters had to withhold news stories for a fortnight. However, the removal of the rule on BBC radio and television output, and the competition for news provided by the fledgling Independent Television News (ITN) organization, resulted in greater competition from broadcast journalists with the press. The newspapers found themselves in a secondary position, being forced to comment on news which had appeared the previous evening on television bulletins. Consequently, the total sales of papers declined by approximately 30 per cent. However, this decline was unevenly distributed. The most affected area was the Sunday and weekly papers whose sales dropped by ten million. The provincial press also suffered, most especially evening papers. The national daily press market remained strong although it suffered from fluctuations inaugurated through competition, price increases and promotions.[68] In turn, this led to a more differentiated national broadsheet and tabloid market. This has meant that certain types of papers, in particular tabloids, identified that they should run different, more populist stories to find a market. This development was to grow more marked throughout the 1970s and 1980s. Thus, as Colin Seymour-Ure has commented:

> This survival reflects the extent to which the daily papers' contents and appeal tied in with . . . various alternatives: they were complementary more than competitive. . . . In the post-war period, the national dailies managed to adapt their appeal so that people continued to find them useful, and advertisers therefore went on providing the essential economic base for most of them.[69]

Ownership

Simultaneously, the post-war press marked a decline in the interventionist ownership of Beaverbrook and Rothermere. Their successors were motivated by profits and largely perceived themselves as hands-off owners. For instance, the second Lord Beaverbrook, Sir Max Aitken, was less politically motivated. Moreover, throughout the 1960s and

1970s, the *Daily Herald* was liberated from pursuing the Labour Party's arguments and David Astor's proprietor-editor regime at the *Observer* ended. However, the new lines of ownership-editorial demarcation were most conspicuously drawn when Lord Cecil King was removed from control of the *Daily Mirror* in 1968. He had commissioned a front-page article advocating the removal of the then Prime Minister Harold Wilson and the creation of a national government, without prior discussion with the paper's editor. As James Curran has commented: 'King's lordly action was in the seigneurial tradition of his uncle, Lord Northcliffe; his dismissal by his fellow directors in response to what they called his "increasing preoccupation with politics", seemed at the time, to signify the end of an era.'[70]

Curran has identified this reform as a shift from hierarchical management to the delegation of editorial power in the national and regional press.[71] The owner who characterized this change was Lord Thomson who acquired the Kemsley empire in 1959 and *The Times* in 1967. In the Thomson group of newspapers, the editor enjoyed considerable autonomy over the paper's content if he worked within the pre-agreed budget. Thomson was heard to declare:

> I do not believe that a newspaper can be run properly unless its editorial columns are run freely and independently by a highly skilled and dedicated professional journalist.[72]

The *Sunday Times* editor Harold Evans exemplified this shift in power. In his book, *Good Times, Bad Times*, Evans explains that whilst Thomson was, above all, a businessman, he celebrated his papers' editorial freedoms. Internal constraints were largely removed and the *Sunday Times* became synonymous with its investigative reporting. Under Thomson and Evans' tutelage the paper dealt with the publication of Richard Crossman's political diaries, an investigation of the design faults in DC10 aircraft, an exposé of the spy Kim Philby and publicized the irreparable physical damage done to children through the prescription of the Thalidomide drug to pregnant women.[73] For Evans:

> Lord Thomson was not a journalist, but he was the best friend journalism ever had. . . . (His) distinction (was) that he created a new kind of ownership. He never once imposed his opinions on *The Sunday Times*, nor, remarkably, ever once sought out a single editorial favour for himself, his friends or any of his companies. He was the antithesis of the bully or manipulator. He was a free trader in ideas and enthusiasms.[74]

Output and ideology

The imperatives of a reformed press market and the more relaxed form of ownership led some commentators to claim that the partisan attachments which had characterized press relations with the political elite had been removed. Stephen Koss has argued that newspapers became more catholic in their news coverage as their party affiliations declined. Throughout elections, papers would express a party preference, but largely with a pragmatic gesture, and often change their party loyalties from campaign to campaign. Assurances were sought and given by Thomson when he bought *The Times* and the *Sunday Times* in 1967 that the paper's editorial freedom would be retained.[75] In effect, corporate businessmen had replaced the politically motivated press barons. As we shall discover, Koss believes that the 1960s was only a precursor to later developments in the contemporary press.

This perspective has been challenged by James Curran who has argued that an underlying set of partisan attachments remained intact. Whilst admitting the press only became more partisan after 1974, he suggests that most papers (the exception being *The Times*) retained their party affiliations throughout the 1950s and 1960s. More pertinently, Curran argues that the interventionist trends associated with ownership and control over output never truly disappeared. Instead a small group of proprietors continued to control the industry through their personal values and philosophies, despite the undoubted changes in editorial and journalistic power.[76]

Moreover, it may be argued that the underlying structural characteristics of the press industry were subtly maintained rather than fundamentally reformed. Throughout this period the press was characterized by the overwhelming power of advertisers, closed market entry and concentration of ownership. To this end, the press did not achieve the diversity of production which has been deemed to be an essential aspect of press freedom. In many respects, the post-war British press is reflective of Habermas's view that newspapers became agents of propaganda as different elite groups interacted with one another to distribute information in their own interests. In this respect, we have identified a rehearsal of some of the arguments which would be associated with the greater concentration of ownership inaugurated by Rupert Murdoch and others throughout the modern period. The development of post-war press during the 1940s to the late 1960s provides us with the context for the imperatives which have dominated the industry throughout the last twenty-five years.

Conclusion

The historical development of the press demonstrates that information cannot be perceived as an agency in itself, but the dissemination of communication is conditional on the context of production and consumption. Thus, underpinning the press's institutionalization have been the associated aims of diversity of information for citizenship through the consumption of newspapers and diversity of ownership through their production. However, the British press's history has demonstrated that these aims have been problematic to achieve.

Throughout the years, press freedom has been contested. Formally, it may be argued that freedom was attained through reforms such as the repeal of the Taxes upon Knowledge. The Whig viewpoint suggests that once advertising financed the press and allowed cover prices to be reduced, the press market flourished with new titles and a diversity of opinions. Effectively, the free press was achieved as owners desiring profits had to respond to audience needs to maintain circulations. Therefore, this ensured that a plurality of ideas entered the public realm.

Conversely, many criticisms concerning the profit motive exist. Some Marxists would argue that as the press has been incorporated into capitalism, it acts in the bourgeois's interests to suppress the working classes. Therefore newspapers provide a slanted vision as they develop false consciousness. Political economists such as Habermas maintain that a free press has been undermined through the orchestration of publicity, advertising power, partisan attachments, ownership and industrialization. The repeal of the Taxes upon Knowledge and the introduction of advertising demonstrated that the individual's access to information was constrained rather than liberalized. At the point of production, controls were introduced, throughout the late 1800s and first half of the twentieth century, over entry, manufacture and distribution. As a result, press barons such as Beaverbrook, Northcliffe and Rothermere were able to dominate the market-place and use their papers as mouthpieces for their own political positions.

Between these opinions, the reality has proved to be rather more complicated and demonstrates how competing power blocks have existed within the political and social elites. For instance, the press has often enjoyed an antagonistic relationship with the political elite, most especially when the press barons used their papers, for selfish political interests, to challenge the politicians. Paradoxically, it may be suggested that the press stood against the political elite and attempted to dismantle the partisanship which had previously existed. However, Beaverbrook and Rothermere's ultimate failure and Baldwin's concept of 'power without responsibility' forced them back into the cultural and political norms. Throughout the post-war period, a retraction of proprietorial power occurred as businessmen motivated by profits rather than political power entered the industry. Yet as Curran has demonstrated, many of the underlying characteristics remained intact. Throughout the years, therefore, there has been an ebb and flow in press–state relations marked by periods of tension and accommodation.

It now remains to be seen how the press has developed in the last twenty-five years.

Further reading

Arthur Aspinall, *Politics and the Press, c.1780–1850*, Harvester, 1973.
George Boyce, James Curran and Pauline Wingate (eds), *Newspaper History: From the 17th Century to the Present Day*, Constable, 1976.
Anne Chisholm and Michael Davie, *Beaverbrook: A Life*, Pimlico, 1993.
James Curran and Jean Seaton, *Power without Responsibility: The Press and Broadcasting in Britain*, Routledge, 1991 (4th edn).
Peter Dahlgren and Colin Sparks (eds), *Communication and Citizenship: Journalism and the Public Sphere*, Routledge, 1991.
Harold Evans, *Good Times, Bad Times*, Weidenfeld & Nicolson, 1983.
Simon Jenkins, *Newspapers: The Power and the Money*, Faber & Faber, 1979.
Stephen Koss, *The Rise and Fall of the Political Press*, vol. 1, Hamish Hamilton, 1981, vol. 2, Hamish Hamilton, 1984.
Alan J. Lee, *The Origins of the Popular Press 1855–1914*, Croom Helm, 1976.
Ralph Negrine, *Politics and the Mass Media in Britain*, Routledge, (2nd edn), 1994.
Colin Seymour-Ure, *The British Press and Broadcasting since 1945*, Basil Blackwell, 1991.

Notes

1   James Curran, in George Boyce, James Curran and Pauline Wingate (eds), *Newspaper History: From the 17th Century to the Present Day*, Sage Publications, 1978, p. 51.
2   For details on the local press, see Bob Franklin and D. Murphy, *What News? The Market, Politics and the Local Press*, Routledge, 1991, or Bob Franklin, *Packaging Politics: Political Communication in Britain's Media Democracy*, Edward Arnold, 1994.
3   This perspective is presented in Arthur Aspinall, *Politics and the Press, c. 1780–1850*, Harvester, 1973 and Ian Christie, *Myth and Reality in Late 18th Century British Politics*, Macmillan, 1970.
4   Michael Harris, 'The Structure, Ownership and Control of the Press, 1620–1780', in George Boyce et al. (eds), *Newspaper History*, pp. 83–4.
5   *The Report of the Committee on the Financing of the BBC (The Peacock Report)*, HMSO, 1986, p. 5.
6   See Michael Harris, 'The Structure, Ownership and Control of the Press', pp. 84–5. Harris has shown that although the government intended to massacre the press, proprietors were able to utilize their resources to circumvent the worst scenario of the stamp taxes.
7   James Curran, 'The Press as an Agency of Social Control: An Historical Perspective', in George Boyce, James Curran and Pauline Wingate (eds), *Newspaper History*, p. 53.
8   Ibid., p. 58.
9   James Curran and Jean Seaton, *Power without Responsibility: The Press and Broadcasting in Britain*, Routledge, 1991 (4th edn), p. 14.

10 John B. Thompson, *Ideology and Modern Culture*, Polity Press, 1992, p. 250.

11 Alan J. Lee, *The Origins of the Popular Press 1855–1914*, Croom Helm, 1976, p. 279.

12 Ivor Asquith, 'Advertising and Press in the Late eighteenth and Early nineteenth Centuries: James Perry and the *Morning Chronicle*, 1790–1821', *Historical Journal*, xvii., 1975, quoted in James Curran and Jean Seaton, *Power without Responsibility*, pp. 7–8.

13 C. W. Crawley (ed.), *War and Peace in the Age of Upheaval (1793–1830)*, Cambridge University Press, quoted from James Curran in Peter Dahlgren and Colin Sparks, *Communication and Citizenship: Journalism and the Public Sphere*, Routledge, 1991, p. 39.

14 James Curran in ibid., pp. 38–9.

15 Ibid., pp. 39–40.

16 James Curran in Peter Dahlgren and Colin Sparks (eds), *Communication and Citizenship*, p. 39.

17 See E. P. Thompson, *The Making of the English Working Class*, Gollancz, 1963.

18 James Curran and Jean Seaton, *Power without Responsibility: The Press and Broadcasting in Britain*, Routledge, 1991 (4th edn), p. 14.

19 James Curran, 'The Press as an Agency of Social Control', p. 66.

20 James Curran, 'The Press as an Agency of Social Control', pp. 64–5.

21 Ibid., p. 65.

22 Ibid., p. 61.

23 James Curran and Jean Seaton, *Power without Responsibility*, pp. 14–15.

24 James Curran, 'The Press as an Agency of Social Control', p. 61.

25 J. F. Stephen in ibid., p. 59.

26 Ibid., pp. 59–60.

27 Ibid.

28 James Curran, in George Boyce, James Curran and Pauline Wingate (eds), *Newspaper History*, p. 69.

29 Ibid., p. 70.

30 James Curran, in Peter Dahlgren and Colin Sparks (eds), *Communication and Citizenship*, p. 41.

31 Alan Lee, 'The Structure, Ownership and Control of the Press, 1815–1914', in George Boyce et al., (eds), *Newspaper History*, pp. 118–19.

32 Ralph Negrine, *Politics and the Mass Media*, Routledge, 1994 (2nd edn), p. 47.

33 James Curran and Jean Seaton, *Power without Responsibility*, pp. 41–2.

34 Ibid., p. 46.

35 Ralph Negrine, *Politics and the Mass Media*, p. 48.

36 Simon Jenkins, *Newspapers: The Power and the Money*, Faber & Faber, 1979, pp. 21–7.

37 Graham Murdock and Peter Golding, 'The structure, ownership and control of the press, 1914–76', in George Boyce, James Curran and Pauline Wingate (eds), *Newspaper History*, p. 132.

38 Ibid., p. 131.

39 Anne Chisholm and Michael Davie, *Beaverbrook: A Life*, Pimlico, 1993, p. 211.

40 Colonel Lawson, quoted from Graham Murdock and Peter Golding, in George Boyce et al. (eds), p. 132.

41 A contributing factor to Northcliffe's ghoulish preoccupations may well have been his own oncoming death through syphilis – which was the most well-known best kept secret at the time. Apparently, when Northcliffe died, in a pique of syphilitic dementia, he was said to have attempted to strangle his doctor!

42 Fred Hirsch and David Gordon, *Newspaper Money*, Hutchinson, 1975, p. 70.

43 A. J. P. Taylor, *Beaverbrook*, Penguin Books, 1972, p. 489.
44 Ibid., p. 130.
45 Anne Chisholm and Michael Davie, *Beaverbrook*, pp. 209–10.
46 Ibid., p. 210.
47 Raymond Snoddy, *The Good, the Bad and the Unacceptable*, Faber & Faber, 1992, pp. 27–8.
48 Ibid., p. 31. For further details, see Colin Seymour-Ure, *The Political Impact of the Mass Media*, Sage Publications, 1974 (Chapter 3).
49 For further details, see Robert Benewick, *The Fascist Movement in Britain*, Allen Lane, The Penguin Press, 1972, pp. 98–104.
50 Anne Chisholm and Michael Davie, *Beaverbrook*, pp. 136–49.
51 Ibid., pp. 199–201.
52 Ralph Negrine, p. 48.
53 R. C. Self, *Tories and Tariffs: The Conservative Party and the Politics of Tariff Reform, 1922–1932*, Garland, London and New York, 1986, p. 513.
54 For further details, see ibid., pp. 499–586.
55 R. C. Self, *Tories and Tariffs*, p. 531.
56 Ibid.
57 Ibid., p. 522.
58 Beaverbrook in Anne Chisholm and Michael Davie, *Beaverbrook*, p. 276.
59 Neville Chamberlain's Diary, 1 March 1931, in R. C. Self, *Tories and Tariffs*, p. 581.
60 Stanley Baldwin quoted from Keith Middlemas and John Barnes, *Baldwin*, Weidenfeld & Nicolson, 1969, p. 598.
61 Ralph Negrine, *Politics and the Mass Media*, p. 49.
62 James Curran and Jean Seaton, *Power without Responsibility*, p. 81.
63 Stephen Koss, *The Rise and Fall of the Political Press, Volume 2*, Hamish Hamilton, 1984, p. 642.
64 Ibid.
65 Lord Thomson quoted from Graham Murdock and Peter Golding, 'The Structure, ownership and control of the press', p. 142.
66 Simon Jenkins, *Newspapers: The Power and the Money*, Faber & Faber, 1979, p. 32.
67 See Michael David Kandiah, 'Television enters British Politics: The Conservative Party's Central Office and Political Broadcasting, 1945–55', *Historical Journal of Film, Radio and Television*, Carfax, vol. 13, no. 2, June 1995, p. 279.
68 Colin Seymour-Ure, *The British Press and Broadcasting since 1945*, Basil Blackwell, 1991, p. 18.
69 Ibid.
70 James Curran and Jean Seaton, *Power without Responsibility*, p. 86.
71 Ibid., p. 85.
72 Ibid.
73 For further details, see Harold Evans, *Good Times, Bad Times*, Weidenfeld & Nicolson, 1983, pp. 1–79.
74 Ibid., p. 13.
75 Stephen Koss, *The Rise and Fall of the Political Press*, pp. 662–3.
76 James Curran and Jean Seaton, *Power without Responsibility*, p. 86.

3
The Contemporary British Press

The historical development of the press indicates that the fourth estate principles have proved problematic to realize. Instead of the broad range of views being orchestrated through a free market, the British press has been subject to the power of advertisers, ownership, proprietorial intervention over editors and the industrialized nature of the press market. However, during the post-war phase with the rise of the financial proprietor personified by Lord Thomson and greater editorial autonomy (personified by the *Sunday Times'* Harold Evans) it appeared that some of these constraints were offset. Newspapers were still run for profits, pursued high circulations through lower cover prices and advertising revenue, but it seemed that a wider variety of opinions could be expressed.

However, despite this appearance of change, many of the underlying structural characteristics of the press industry remained intact; advertising power, closed entry and a concentration of ownership. From the late 1960s, these latent factors became more conspicuous as press ownership changed. A new breed of press baron, notably Rupert Murdoch and the late Robert Maxwell, emerged. Other press magnates now include Lord Stevens, Conrad Black, and the third Lord Rothermere. Their concentration of ownership has obvious parallels with the previous press baron period. However, the modern proprietors have fostered greater corporation and diversification in their business empires. They have responded to the general economic patterns of conglomeration and internationalization within the global media system. Moreover, Stephen Koss in *The Rise and Fall of the Political Press in Britain* argues that owners such as Murdoch remain businessmen who are more concerned about profitability than politics.

This viewpoint has been disputed by others, notably Harold Evans, who clashed with Murdoch over the political stance of *The Times*. Therefore, it may be suggested that there has been a decline in editorial autonomy, as Murdoch and others have been interventionist or have appointed like-minded journalists to edit their papers, most notably the ex-*Sunday Times* editor Andrew Neil. In this respect, it has been noticeable that as Murdoch grew more right-wing his papers reflected his allegiance to Margaret Thatcher throughout the 1980s. Alongside this change in ownership has been the incorporation of new technologies into the manufacture of the press. Effectively, 'single-key stroking' meant that newspaper journalists could have their stories printed from their own computer terminals. The old processes of hot-metal, composition and the use of skilled printers were subsumed. This meant that the press industry became the battleground for some bitter industrial disputes throughout the 1980s. This was partly due to the closed shop practices of the printers and to the management's desire to increase profits by cutting labour costs. Simultaneously, technology has dictated the nature of the press market. Whilst many libertarians advocated that there would be an expansion of titles, encouraging a plurality of views, the reality has been one of increased concentration of ownership and market closure. Further, the impact of television news meant that the press no longer acted as the principal medium for disseminating information. As it was challenged for advertising by ITV, the press market has reorganized itself. Principally, a greater differentiation has taken place between the content of broadsheet and tabloid newspapers. The tabloids which have emphasized human interest, scandals and sex stories have increasingly been accused of sensationalism by focusing on the private lives of public and private figures. Subsequently, there have been increased calls for some form of statutory regulation.

Once again this returns us to the central dilemma of press freedom, as any form of regulation has been deemed to be regressive and stemming freedom of speech. Further, it calls into question the contemporary nature of the press as advertising and ownership pressures have often been cited as shaping its discourse, most especially on political issues. Therefore, it is the purpose of this chapter to analyse, assess and explain whether the contemporary press fulfils its fourth estate function or, as critics would claim, has been incorporated into the dominant political, economic and social order.

The British Press from 1968: the Rise of New Entrepreneurs

From the late 1960s, a new breed of press baron, notably Rupert Murdoch, emerged. At present, alongside Murdoch stands Lord

Stevens, the Chairman of the public company United Newspapers (which has recently merged with the broadcasting corporation MAI) which produces the *Daily Express*, the *Sunday Express* and the *Daily Star*; Conrad Black, owner of the *Daily Telegraph* and the *Sunday Telegraph*; and the third Lord Rothermere's Associated Newspapers which owns the *Daily Mail*, the *Mail on Sunday* and the *Evening Standard*. Until his mysterious death in November 1991, Robert Maxwell owned the Mirror Group responsible for the *Daily Mirror*, the *Sunday Mirror*, the *Sunday People*, the *Scottish Daily Record* and *Sporting Life*. Subsequently, the Group was taken over by a consortium who appointed the former editor of *Today*, David Montgomery, as the Chief Executive.

Murdoch had built up a successful chain of newspapers in Australia inherited from his father Sir Keith Murdoch. In Britain, his consolidation of titles started when he bought (in competition with Maxwell) the *News of the World* in 1968. A year later he fought off Maxwell to own the replacement for the *Daily Herald*, the *Sun*. This was understood by many as evidence of Murdoch's inability to understand the British press market as the paper had been a loss-maker for several years. However, through a shrewd marketing strategy directed by Murdoch and the editors Larry Lamb and Kelvin MacKenzie, he created a populist market-leader. The success of his tabloids enabled Murdoch to expand, incorporating the tabloid *Today*, which he has subsequently closed down for lack of profitability, and move into the broadsheet market. He was seen to have finally arrived when he bought the ailing *Times* and the *Sunday Times* in 1981.[1] To this end, he was indebted to the Thatcher government which decided that his monopoly did not contravene the rules of the Monopoly and Merger's board.[2]

Throughout the 1980s, the Big Five's dominance was awesome, accounting for the control of fifteen national titles and representing over 90 per cent of the national sales.[3] However, their power was challenged by Andreas Whittam Smith, who led a break-away from *The Times* and created (and edited) the *Independent* in the mid-1980s. This paper was owned by a trust that would not intervene over its editorial content. It was initially successful, establishing a clear position in the press market. However, due to a decline in circulation and advertising, the paper's profitability was reduced. Further, the circulation battles in the broadsheet market had a detrimental effect. This led to the paper's incorporation into the Mirror Group in 1994.

Finally, the *Guardian* is exempt from conglomerate power. It is owned, through its parent company the *Guardian and Manchester Evening News*, by the Scott trust. This was established in 1936 after the death of the paper's first editor C. P. Scott and is composed of ten trustees.

The editor, who is appointed by the board, has complete autonomy. More recently, in competition with the *Independent*, the *Guardian* bought the Sunday paper, the *Observer*, from 'Tiny' Rowland's company Lonhro.

This concentration of ownership compares with the previous press baron period. However, Peter Golding and Graham Murdock have shown that the modern proprietors have encouraged greater corporation and diversification in their business empires. They have been involved in the general economic patterns of conglomeration and internationalization within the global media system.[4] Rupert Murdoch has bought American newspapers such as the *New York Post*, owns the American Fox television network, the Hollywood studio Twentieth Century Fox and fifty per cent of the satellite broadcasting company Sky. In 1993, he exploited the potentially lucrative Asian market by purchasing Star Television. The new press barons use their papers' profits to provide the capital to invest in their other media interests and to gain sufficient credit from their bankers to aid greater corporate expansion. This produced financial difficulties for Murdoch's News Corporation and in 1990 it declared a short-term debt of 2.9 billion dollars. Murdoch had problems repaying his loans and the company nearly collapsed, with an eleventh hour agreement being reached.[5] However, Murdoch's problems were minuscule compared to his late rival Robert Maxwell.

The collapse of Maxwell Communications and the Mirror Group

Born Jan Ludvik Hoch in Czechoslovakia, Maxwell had made his fortune in book and periodical publishing with the Pergamon Press. In the 1960s, he had been a Labour Party MP for Buckingham. At his height he claimed to be worth £1000 million. However, before his death he was chased by the receivers. At the time, this fact remained obscured by Maxwell's propensity to serve libel writs on his detractors.

Throughout the 1980s, the Maxwell Communications Corporation (MCC) became overstretched, becoming reliant on bank loans, as Maxwell diversified his interests in the print and electronic media systems. After his mysterious death from his yacht the *Lady Ghislaine* in the Mediterranean, his debt was £2.7 billion.[6] Yet worse was to follow as it was revealed that he had illegally bankrolled his other companies by using the £526 million of the *Daily Mirror*'s pension funds. His theft led to his sons (not heirs, as Maxwell did not believe in inherited wealth) being bequeathed a bankrupt corporation with a tarnished reputation and being charged with fraud, as they were pension fund trustees. The problems were compounded as Maxwell's companies were formally registered in the tax haven of Liechtenstein. This meant that retrieving the debt would be almost impossible. Maxwell's former paper, which had recently praised its late proprietor, turned on his memory with venom:

> Maxwell's resting place is close by the Garden of Gethsemane where Judas Iscariot betrayed Christ for thirty pieces of silver. He should feel at home there.[7]

The manufacture of the press

The new press barons benefited from the development of the new electronic technologies. The old methods of print-room composition and typesetting could be replaced by 'single-key stroking'. This meant that journalists and advertising staff could set words in type without requiring the printers. An early proponent of this change was Eddy Shah, who directed his local Warrington paper to use the new technology. Shah's attempt was rebuffed by the print unions after a vicious industrial dispute. Similarly Marmaduke Hussey, then Chief Executive of Roy Thomson's *The Times*, tried to introduce these technologies and set off a one-year industrial dispute with the National Graphical Association (NGA). The subsequent crisis enabled Rupert Murdoch to buy the paper in 1981.

However, the full impact of the change occurred when Murdoch, needing to cut labour costs and wishing to quell the power of the print unions, moved all of his papers from their traditional Fleet Street base to a warehouse site in Wapping in 1986. This was equipped with computer technology so that the journalists could immediately have their words printed off. In one stroke, Murdoch had changed the nature of the national press industry. His use of secretive tactics and the deal he made with the Electricians' Union leader Eric Hammond enabled him to by-pass the Society of Graphic and Allied Trades (SOGAT) and the NGA. This dismantled the closed-shop arrangements and meant that employment practices were streamlined.

This was a painful process resulting in a bitter industrial dispute at 'Fortress Wapping'. Murdoch withstood the mass picket of the plant and the rail unions' refusal to ferry his papers by negotiating a deal with the transport company TNT. After a year, the battle of attrition was won by News International and the print unions were decimated.

For Murdoch the victory was significant as the printers had been a constant thorn in his side by increasing his expenditure through labour agreements, 'Spanish practices' and disruption. For instance, the 'inkies' had successfully stopped his most notorious paper the *Sun* from publishing its more virulent criticisms of the Labour movement.

The National Union of Journalists (NUJ) was equivocal about the move, feeling that the printers had been difficult and deserved their comeuppance.[8] Moreover, as the Wapping dispute followed on the 1984–5 miners' strike it was illustrative of the shift in political power from corporatism to Thatcherism. Murdoch received praise from the government for breaking union control and Wapping cemented his close relationship with the prime minister. To this end, he enjoyed support from the political establishment as the police were mobilized to protect his plant from the mass Saturday night pickets. It would be later discovered that they abused their powers on several occasions against the striking print workers.

However, it should be remembered that, despite the union over-manning, many skilled craftsmen lost their jobs. This form of 'industrial gangsterism' had tilted the industry's labour relations against the workforce and into the print management's hands.[9] For instance after Wapping, Robert Maxwell had no compunction in sacking his print staff. The assault broke the unions and led to the replacement of a high number of well-paid workers with a lower number of poorly paid employees. Moreover, this move eroded Fleet Street as the base of the national press and boosted the creation of giant plants in London's East End to produce papers.

The Press Market

The new technologies cut production costs and allowed several papers to be started, comprising the *Independent*, *Today*, *News on Sunday* and the *Sunday Correspondent*. Cento Veljanovski, a market-liberal economist, has argued that technological change, industrial relations reforms, lower production costs and manning have allowed for a wider plurality of views to be expressed through the introduction of a greater number of titles.[10] However, it should be noted that these new papers either collapsed or were incorporated into one of the conglomerates. *Today*, originally established by Eddy Shah (who had taken on the unions at Warrington), lost money and was bought out by Lonhro. In turn, Rupert Murdoch bought the paper, only to ultimately close it because of a decline in circulation in November

1995. That all suffered difficulties is indicative of the closed nature of the newspaper market.[11] In reality, technological changes have augmented the power of the dominant media barons. As Colin Sparks comments:

> It is virtually impossible to make a successful new entry without very substantial resources and prior experience of the industry. In effect, only those who are already in the industry, either in the UK or elsewhere, can hope to join it.[12]

The concentration of press ownership has produced greater monopolization. First, there are controls over entry. Despite the industry's computerization, the starting-up costs of a nationally circulated paper still remain prohibitive for prospective proprietors. Second, the overall press market has not grown and is declining. New papers have found it difficult to draw readers away from established titles. In this context, cover price reductions can squeeze out competition. As a result, the *News on Sunday* and the *Sunday Correspondent* folded as they were not allowed to find their readership. Constant circulation wars have affected both the tabloid and broadsheet market. Recently, Murdoch's *Sun* cut its cover price to 20p to undermine the *Daily Mirror*. The *Independent* had originally taken away readers from *The Times*. However, the increasing market pressures created by a spectacular price-cutting war between Murdoch's *Times* and Black's *Daily Telegraph*, meant that the *Independent* found that its circulation was drastically reduced. Although, as Roy Greenslade has commented, *Today*, owned by Murdoch, was an unwitting victim of its proprietor's tactics:

> It is not facile to view *Today* as a casualty of Murdoch's own price war. By pricing the *Times* well below its rivals its sales were boosted. By increasing pagination it took up more printing capacity. By accepting huge losses on *The Times*, Murdoch needed to save elsewhere. All these factors caused *Today* to close. It is also clear that *Today* never seriously challenged the *Daily Mail* in the middle market, nor looked more than being a mild irritant to the *Mirror*.[13]

Despite this overall decline, high circulations are still required to sustain the newspaper industry, most especially the tabloids. The leaders are the *Sun* and the *News of the World* in the tabloid market and the *Daily Telegraph* in the broadsheet market respectively:

Table 3.1 National newspaper circulation

	Sept 1994	Aug 1994	% change	Apr–Sept 1994	Apr–Sept 1993	% change
Dailies:						
Sun	4,140,980	4,183,047	−0.51	4,160,338	3,833,539	14.50
Daily Mirror	2,553,380	2,538,206	0.58	2,512,278	2,656,856	−5.51
Daily Record	772,867	782,691	−1.28	752,584	751,349	0.16
Daily Star	753,506	759,161	−0.74	743,501	775,096	−4.08
Daily Mail	1,778,751	1,763,678	0.85	1,759,744	1,744,030	2.62
Daily Express	1,320,060	1,328,117	0.22	1,335,933	1,470,594	−6.95
Today	611,993	656,705	−5.81	612,820	562,831	10.85
Daily Telegraph	1,091,622	1,091,658	0.00	1,039,266	1,017,291	2.16
Guardian	410,785	378,987	6.39	395,568	404,639	−1.50
Times	607,148	597,636	1.59	549,770	375,495	46.41
Independent	290,031	289,403	0.22	276,258	336,004	−17.78
Financial Times	290,284	272,161	5.55	290,016	285,203	1.69
Sundays:						
News of the World	4,856,102	4,865,855	0.22	4,803,665	4,619,518	3.99
Sunday Mirror	2,590,530	2,573,976	0.64	2,568,137	2,645,738	−3.01
People	2,022,658	2,050,637	−1.35	2,017,209	2,004,225	0.65
Mail on Sunday	1,921,629	1,904,590	0.89	1,952,644	1,951,743	0.05
Sunday Express	1,463,447	1,488,445	−1.68	1,506,747	1,694,770	−10.96
Sunday Times	1,233,231	1,165,333	5.83	1,196,710	1,218,112	−1.60
Sunday Telegraph	690,591	686,120	−0.81	656,172	584,625	12.24
Observer	477,093	460,000	3.72	487,800	497,124	−1.68
Independent/Sunday	316,735	313,511	0.71	318,722	370,395	−13.95

Source: *Guardian* 11 September 1995, p. 13

Advertising remains the other main source of revenue. Its importance varies: local free titles are dependent on advertisements as they sell products to consumers rather than provide stories for readers; the daily tabloids receive 30 per cent of their funding from advertisements, whilst the more expensive and smaller circulated broadsheets receive up to 70 per cent of their money from advertising.[14] The search for advertising in the broadsheet market has changed the papers' formats. This was tied to the technological revolution of 'single-key stroking' as lay-out changes could be introduced for relatively low costs. For instance, Murdoch's move to Wapping enabled Andrew Neil, the former editor of the *Sunday Times*, to increase the paper's paging, divide it into several sections and change the colour magazine. Increasingly, the other Sunday and, to a lesser extent, daily broadsheets have followed this lead. As Neil promised his advertisers:

> The *Sunday Times* is going to land on your doorstep with a thud from now on.[15]

Further, with the introduction of ITV in 1955, the press's monopoly of advertising revenue was undercut. Throughout the years, advertisers have diversified using television and commercial radio campaigns, alongside the press. In 1988, ITV received 31.4 per cent of advertising expenditure compared to the national newspapers' 16.2 per cent.[16]

More generally, television continues to be an important rival. The competition from broadcast journalists in news and current affairs programmes has increased from the 1960s to the 1990s. Indeed, the proliferation of new media' distribution techniques promoted through cable and satellite (allowing newspaper owners such as Murdoch entry into the television market) has meant that the terrestrial news services at the BBC and ITN now face severe competition. This has continued the trend that most people now receive their immediate news through the electronic media. Consequently, as the press no longer provides the public with direct information, its output has changed.

Output and Ideology

Subsequently, the broadsheet and tabloid markets have become differentiated. The following provides a humorous description of the British press:

The Times is read by the people who run the country.
The Guardian is read by people who would like to run the country.
The Financial Times is read by the people who own the country.
The Daily Telegraph is read by the people who remember the country as it used to be.
The Daily Express is read by people who think that the country is still like that.
The Daily Mail is read by the wives of the men who run the country.
The Daily Mirror (which itself once tried to run the country) is read by the people who think they run the country.
The Morning Star is read by the people who would like another country to run the country.
The Sun – well, Murdoch has found a gap in the market – the oldest gap in the world.

– An Advertising Copywriter[17]

The broadsheets supply a more analytical commentary on the news. They are aimed at a specific readership and, with the exceptions of the *Guardian* and the *Independent*, have a bias toward the Conservative Party. They are noted for their coverage of 'hard news' from the political or business sphere, for their editorial stances and the quality of their writing, often from named columnists. In the main, readers use these papers to supplement the information that they have received from the television news. However, they have still provided exclusives to break the news. In 1994, the *Guardian* investigated the financial irregularities of several government ministers and used the notorious 'cod-fax' (on House of Common's notepaper) in an attempt to expose the Chief Executive of the Treasury Jonathan Aitken.

Conversely, the press owners have identified that tabloids should run more populist stories to find a market based on celebrity gossip, sexual infidelities, human interest and sport. Feature articles often include the serialization of popular fiction and most recently the plethora of books on the collapse of the Prince of Wales' marriage. It should also be noted that the hard and fast lines between tabloids and broadsheets have dissolved with regard to royal scandals, as broadsheet editors have been willing to pay vast sums to authors for serialization rights. Further, television, which was ignored by the tabloids in the 1950s and 1960s, has been a staple source for stories in the most popular tabloids from the 1970s onwards. Articles on televized sports, soap operas and pop stars have become common-place. In particular, this formula, aimed at the section of the population advertisers called C2, was developed and refined by Rupert Murdoch and his editors Albert 'Larry' Lamb and Kelvin MacKenzie at the *Sun*. As the paper, along with its Sunday sister the *News of the World* (which over the years has shared many of the same editorial staff), proved to be a major success, eventually toppling the *Daily Mirror*'s circulation figures by the late 1970s, others were forced to follow suit. The *Mirror*, which had been prepared to provide detailed coverage of events such as the Vietnam War in the 1960s, became more down-market and has yet to recover from the ravages of its former owner Robert Maxwell. Maxwell saw himself as an modern-day Beaverbrook and devoted several pages in each issue to self-publicity. Roy Greenslade, a former editor of the *Daily Mirror*, has argued that since Maxwell's demise the paper has further declined. He blames the Mirror Group's Chief Executive David Montgomery for the dismissal of editor Richard Stott in 1992 and the inadequacies of Stott's replacements:

> Trivia has dominated the editorial content of all but pages six and seven. The *Mirror*, which had lost some of its political clout under Maxwell, has since forfeited all claim to being a serious paper. It is no longer regarded by Labour MPs as required reading . . . It is a sorry article, a moronic shadow of a newspaper which once had such credibility that it was quoted by angry Tory prime ministers.[18]

Lord Matthews (then chair of the United Newspapers) in 1978 created the *Daily Star*, whose content was defined by its first editor Derek

Jameson as 'tits, bums, QPR and roll your own fags', to challenge the *Sun*.[19] His successor Lord Stevens went as far as dealing with David Sullivan, the pornographer, who had entered the newspaper market with the *Sunday Sport*. However, from the 1970s to the 1990s the *Sun* remained the market leader.

The tabloid press: a case study of the Sun

Murdoch, Lamb and MacKenzie combined to create a specific type of tabloid. Throughout the 1970s and 1980s the *Sun* became synonymous with a brazen style which underpinned its layout, tone and content. The paper uses a typeface called 'Tempo' and has a famous red masthead. Throughout the years, it became associated with a particular writing style, with notorious headlines such as 'Gotcha' and 'Freddie Starr ate my Hamster' and its ability to set aside several pages to cover major events or 'earthquake stories'. Its titillating presentation of human interest stories, sports exclusives, regular topless female models on page three and serialization of popular novels such as Jacqueline Susann's *Love Machine* all served to increase its circulation.

Larry Lamb claimed that the *Sun*'s emphasis on sex reflected the permissive society of the late 1960s and early 1970s, although many feminists attacked the paper as being misogynist and sexist. However, Lamb and Murdoch argued that they were producing a paper which was: 'strident, campaigning, working class, young, entertaining, politically aware, cheeky, radical, anti-establishment, fun, breezy and, most of all, hugely profitable.'[20] Lamb, with the backing of Murdoch, shifted the paper's political allegiance. The *Sun*'s predecessor, the *Daily Herald*, followed the Labour party's line. However, throughout Lamb's editorship the paper moved steadily towards the right, eventually supporting Margaret Thatcher's Conservative Party. Thatcherism, with its strident political style and libertarian philosophy, appealed to the entrepreneurial working class that the paper targeted as readers. In 1979, Lamb produced this valedictory editorial:

> ...Why do we advise a vote for the Tories?
> Because *The Sun* is above all a RADICAL newspaper.
> And we believe that at this time the only radical proposals being put to
>   you are being put by Maggie Thatcher and her Tory team...
> ...*The Sun* says: Vote Tory, Stop the rot. There may not be another
>   chance.[21]

This editorial model and political output was refined throughout the 1980s when Lamb was replaced by Kelvin MacKenzie. MacKenzie proved to be far more brash than his predecessor. He was noted for his technical skills, outrageous editorial style, and his vehement disdain for his rivals, the unions and the political opposition. He derided the *Daily Mirror* for its humbug over the working classes and launched bingo to rebut the *Star*'s main selling point. Further he had a clear dislike of the 'quality' press and particularly despised the *Guardian* which he dubbed 'The World's Worst' and which:

> represented all the soggy pinko thinking many of his generation had fallen for in one way or another. He was proud that he had not fallen for the bullshit and he loudly rejected everything it stood for. More than this he hated it as a product, with its great rambling features, arty pictures and trendy design. He was sincerely convinced that it was the worst newspaper in the world.[22]

MacKenzie's populism dominated the editorial which overtly supported Margaret Thatcher's policies, blackened Labour councils (particularly the Greater London Council led by Ken Livingstone in the early 1980s) and mobilized against the miners during the 1984–5 strike. A chance picture of NUM leader Arthur Scargill appeared to show him raising his arm in a Nazi salute. MacKenzie provided a headline 'Mine Fuhrer'. However, the print-workers refused to touch the picture and the paper was forced to issue a blank front page.[23]

Further, as the circulation wars increased between the *Sun* and the *News of the World*, Maxwell's Mirror Group of papers and the *Star*, the tabloids became increasingly sensationalist. This has been apparent in their depiction of wartime news, tragedies, and scandal involving both public and private figures. On several occasions, Rupert Murdoch and the *Sun* took the lead. For example, the infamous 'Gotcha' headline which followed the sinking of the Argentinian battleship the *General Belgrano* during the Falklands conflict. The headline was made up by Mackenzie and Wendy Henry, who then felt that it should be withdrawn. However, Mackenzie was to be shocked when he was overridden by Murdoch. Peter Chippindale and Chris Horrie provide the following description of what took place:

> Mackenzie burst in, fired up with adrenalin and visibly shaken. 'I've had to change it all because there's a report that there may be 1,200 Argies dead' . . . Murdoch strolled out on to the editorial floor, where Mackenzie caught up with him. 'I wouldn't have pulled it if I was you' Murdoch said in a casual way. 'Seemed like a bloody good headline to me.' Mackenzie protested. 'A lot of people have died, boss' he said. 'Maybe our own people have been hurt. We don't know yet.' But Murdoch assured him: 'Nah, you'll be all right,' walking off apparently unconcerned.[24]

Throughout the 1980s, the paper ran reports on the sex lives of pop star Elton John and the dying television personality Russell Harty. In the former case, this proved to be expensive as John was awarded 1 million pounds in libel damages. However, MacKenzie overreached himself when his reporters covered the Hillsborough stadium disaster in which ninety-five Liverpool fans died. The paper produced gruesome pictures of the dead fans. Moreover, it claimed that fellow fans had robbed and urinated on those who had been crushed. Whilst this image of football hooliganism had been propagated throughout the 1980s in the tabloids, it was totally inappropriate for a disaster which had been fostered by poor policing and the instalment of fences at football grounds. In the resulting furore, the paper's circulation in the Merseyside area completely dropped, Murdoch apologized and MacKenzie was publicly castigated. Since MacKenzie's departure, the *Sun*, now edited by Stuart Higgins, still remains a byword for sensationalism.

Sensationalism

The *Sun*'s high circulations have influenced other proprietors. The competition for readers has produced a more sensational, tabloid press which has been prepared to run 'kiss and tell' stories about celebrities, private citizens, members of parliament and the royal family. Inevitably, in the cross-fire of these circulation wars, both public figures and private citizens have had their reputations severely damaged.

Considerable media attention has focused on the failure of the Prince of Wales' marriage to Lady Diana Spencer. The papers have published photos of Diana at her gym and extracts from respective books backed or written by both parties. In the world of politics, leading parliamentarians such as Cecil Parkinson were forced to resign due to sex scandals. The intrusions into the lives of public figures have been tempered by the arguments that many have courted publicity and should be prepared to deal with the price of fame. This appeared to be true when it was disclosed that the actor Hugh Grant had had a sexual encounter with the prostitute Divine Brown. Grant and his publicity-seeking girlfriend Elizabeth Hurley had to be prepared to face the music! In the case of the Waleses, both Charles and Diana have used the papers to propagate their antagonisms towards one another. For some public figures there are advantages in using the papers to publicize their problems. In particular, footballers and their agents often plant stories that they are considering transfer offers from other clubs in order to renegotiate their current contracts. Further, the tabloids' desire for scandal has produced an infrastructure of publicity agents such as Max Clifford, who hawk their clients from paper to paper to sell their stories to the highest bidder.

The papers themselves claim that they are pursuing stories about politicians and other major figures in the public interest. However, the invasion of a private individual's privacy is more complicated. Ordinary people are often thrown into the media spotlight through sheer chance, good luck or personal misfortune. These intrusions are difficult to sustain with regard to the argument of public interest. Most recently, these problems have been exacerbated with the advent of the British national lottery. As players have won enormous sums, they have been seen as fair game by the tabloids. The lottery company, Camelot, attempted to conceal the identity of the winners; however, the papers were able to gain the details and publish their names.

The activities of the sensational press have been subject to increasing outrage throughout the 1980s and 1990s. Public figures and private citizens have had their lives investigated for possible scandal and unsubstantiated claims have been published despite their fallacious nature. Often apologies and retractions only appear in small print and tucked well away in the paper. This has led to politicians renewing calls to increase the powers to regulate the press and possibly introduce statutory legislation to prevail in the tabloids. In 1989, the Labour backbencher Tony Worthington presented a Right of Reply Bill, whilst the Conservative MP John Browne attempted to introduce a Privacy Bill. Within the House there was considerable support for both bills, although neither received Royal Assent. The Thatcher government made clear its sympathy for the motions (although it was careful to reiterate the concept of a free press market to placate its political allies within the press) and its annoyance that the regulatory structure had failed the public.[25]

Press Commissions and Regulation

Throughout the post-war years Royal Commissions in 1947, 1961 and 1977 have reviewed the performance of the press. They attempted to square the imperative of a free press with unwarranted intrusion. All of these inquiries maintained that the press should have no special laws placed upon it and must be treated like any business, organization or citizen. Therefore, to monitor the press, the 1947 inquiry established the Press Council to self-regulate the papers' output. Throughout the years, the performance of this body was criticized as it was perceived as ineffectual and toothless. As Bob Franklin comments:

> The Press Council's ability to restrain tabloid excesses proved to be dismally limited for four reasons: the first related to problems of the council's remit. The council was unable to act on any issue of fabrication,

offence or misrepresentation unless it received an official complaint. . . . Secondly, the Press Council lacked effective sanctions. Council demands that its judgements should be published prominently were treated with contempt. Thirdly, the council lacked staff and resources. It adjudicated on only a handful of cases each year and often took up to six months to arrive at a judgement. Finally, but most significantly, the council could operate effectively only while it enjoyed the co-operation of the press; council credibility was undermined ultimately by the voluntarism on which it rested. . . . Self-regulation in the form of the Press Council proved no match for market forces.[26]

The Press Council's anachronistic position and failure to control the press led to the Thatcher government establishing a Committee of Inquiry, chaired by David Calcutt QC, to provide proposals concerning privacy and press intrusion. The 1990 Calcutt Report gave the press twelve months to clean up its act or face statutory controls far exceeding legal limits on taste, decency and libel. It recommended a new self-regulator with greater powers. With Calcutt, the government attempted to tread a delicate balance between the normative concept of a free press and the demand for interventionist legislation. As David Mellor, the then Home Office Minister with responsibility for the media, aptly commented:

> On the one hand the government is very reluctant to interfere, certainly by way of statute, knowing it [the press] to be one of the foundation-stones of a free society. But equally government has to be aware of the widespread detestation in Parliament at some things that have been happening in recent years in the popular press. I do believe the press – the popular press – is drinking in the Last Chance Saloon.[27]

In response, the Press Complaints Commission (PCC), initially chaired by Lord McGregor, replaced the Press Council. This drafted a new code of conduct which comprised four main clauses: newspapers should only publish reliable information and apologize for inaccuracies; there should be a right to reply; editors needed to discriminate between conjecture and fact; and press incursions into private citizens' lives were unacceptable.[28] In practice, the PCC was less than successful. Bob Franklin argues that it was doomed, as it did not conform to Calcutt's recommendations for a self-regulatory organization.[29] The PCC was composed of a panel of editors who operated a loosely drawn code and would only adjudicate on complaints from aggrieved readers. They also rejected a proposal to provide a hot-line to assist those fending off invasions of privacy. Throughout the early 1990s, a sensational press continued to thrive and treated the PCC with contempt.

Calcutt's 1992 official review of the press's response provided three main recommendations. First, that a statutory Press Complaints Tribunal, chaired by an independent judge, be created. Second, three criminal offences should be introduced to outlaw the entrance into private property without permission, the use of surveillance devices on private property and the taking of photographs on private property. Third, a civil tort would protect any infringement of privacy.[30] Ironically, the publication of Calcutt's second report coincided with the press achieving its most spectacular political scalp. The *Daily Mirror* revealed that David Mellor, the first National Heritage Secretary and former Home Office Minister, had been engaged in an extra-marital affair and had received presents from the daughter of an eminent PLO leader. Some conspiracy theorists might suggest that the Heritage Ministry's renewed investigation into press ethics and Mellor's forced resignation were more than coincidental!

In response to Calcutt, the press argued that any regulation or statutory provision would open the floodgate for intervention. At the more populist end, Kelvin MacKenzie provided a predictably vigorous defence of journalistic integrity and press freedom in front of the Parliamentary Select Committee on National Heritage which followed on from Calcutt. He alleged that he was privy to information about several MPs' sexual peccadillos and their appearance in the files of the prostitute Linzi St. Clair. Others have argued that if statutory codes were introduced, then investigative journalism, deemed to be a key feature of a free press, would be stymied and the press would fail as public watchdog over the political, social and economic elites.

Despite the calls for statutory privacy legislation, Calcutt's recommendations and a select committee inquiry, the Department of National Heritage (responsible for the media since 1992) remained equivocal. In her first action as Secretary of State for National Heritage, Virginia Bottomley announced that legislation would not be required. Publicly, the free press argument continues to be articulated:

> A free press is vital to a free country. Many would think the imposition of statutory controls on newspapers invidious because it might open the way for regulating content, thereby laying the Government open to charges of press censorship.
>
> The Government does not believe it would be right in this field to delegate decisions about when a statutory remedy should be granted to a regulator such as a tribunal.
>
> For both reasons, the Government does not find the case for statutory measures in this area compelling. It believes that, in principle, industry self-regulation is much to be preferred.[31]

To this end, the government decided to drop Calcutt's recommendation for a statutory tribunal, ombudsman and right to privacy.[32] A hidden agenda may also be suggested, as governments of all political complexions understand the dangers of antagonizing the press. Peter Preston, Editor-in-Chief of the *Guardian* and the *Observer*, and a member of the Press Complaints Commission said: 'They [the government] backed off . . . which is what was always going to happen. Especially this close to an election, with the Leader of the Opposition on the other side of the world talking to Rupert Murdoch.'[33]

The political debate which surrounds press sensationalism has been shaped by the concentration of press ownership and the government's continued reliance on the 'threadbare and tattered ideology of the free (press) market'.[34] Royal Commissions on the press and inquiries such as Calcutt have received attention, yet their influence has been limited. Underpinning their investigations there exists a contradiction. They perpetuate the belief that press liberty can be maintained through a free press market and controls over government intervention. They contend that commercial enterprise, market dynamics and individual private property rights allow for free information. However, this *individualistic* attitude refers to the pre-industrial conception of the polity. It does not address the highly integrated and oligopolistic patterns of ownership and control which exist in the press.

The recent problems concerning sensationalism turn our attention back to the press as a fourth estate and whether a free press market has affected greater political liberty. The failure of governments to address and reform the underlying structural characteristics of the press supports Jürgen Habermas's view that the political economy of the press has been characterized by the power of advertisers, greater concentrations of ownership and political clientelism. It remains to be seen how the modern press barons have exerted their political power in the late twentieth century.

The Political Power of the Modern Press Barons

The modern press barons may be compared to their inter-war predecessors – Northcliffe, Beaverbrook and Rothermere. Some commentators believe that modern press owners have been *financial proprietors* rather than *political actors*. They have been more pragmatic and less doctrinaire. However, others argue that the modern proprietors have reduced internal democracy, reinstated hierarchical controls and intervened in political affairs. Whilst Rupert Murdoch and most of the other press magnates (the exception being Robert Maxwell who was a largely unsuccessful Labour MP in the 1960s) have not aspired to political office, they persist in challenging the constitutional norms of elective representation by using their papers to support political parties and express certain ideologies at the expense of alternative viewpoints.

Financial proprietors

Undoubtedly, the modern set of owners are different from their predecessors. Simon Jenkins, the former editor of *The Times*, noted that the new proprietors were required to keep their eyes fixed on the balance sheet. If their papers fell below the normal standards of profitability they would be dealt with ruthlessly. Further, unlike their predecessors, they did not court the influence of the high and mighty.[35] As Raymond Snoddy has commented there was a perceivable difference in attitude and ambition:

> None of the Big Five is as mad as Lord Northcliffe, who launched the *Daily Mail* in May 1896 and died in August 1922 suffering, at least towards the end of his life, from paranoid megalomania. None is as manipulative or mischievous as Lord Beaverbrook of the *Daily Express*, or as politically unbalanced as the first Lord Rothermere who admired Hitler.[36]

This change in attitude led to Stephen Koss arguing that the press's affiliations with the political parties have declined. Koss believes this emerged when Roy Thomson controlled *The Times* and has continued into the modern era:

> newspapers grew steadily more catholic and less partisan in their ordinary news coverage. When confronted by a general election, they usually expressed a party preference, but always with at least a gesture of pragmatism and often for a different party from the one they had previously endorsed.[37]

Stephen Koss has identified Rupert Murdoch as the personification of this shift from political actor to businessman.[38] Accordingly, Murdoch appeared to be immune and indifferent to political controversies. Whilst politicians attempted to court him, especially during elections, he remained impervious to their solicitations.[39] His papers would change their partisan attachments for commercial rather than political reasons. Moreover, in spite of the *Sun* shifting its party allegiance from Labour to the Conservatives in 1979, over half of its readers ignored its editorial advice.[40]

Proprietorial intervention

Although Stephen Koss has been correct in stressing that Murdoch and others are businessmen who will deal with amenable host regimes, their analysis may be criticized as being either mischievous or misleading. As Raymond Snoddy has commented: 'All the . . . members of the Big Five (apart from Maxwell) are not just supporters of the Conservative Party: they were, and almost certainly still are, unambiguous admirers of Mrs Thatcher and what she stood for.'[41]

As Snoddy indicates, the majority of the press owners shifted to the right and fervently supported Margaret Thatcher's government. Therefore, it can be suggested that ownership power has been restored and that the modern proprietors are *interventionists*. Whilst Murdoch and most of the other press magnates have limited political aspirations (Maxwell being the exception), they have challenged the constitutional norms by using their papers to express certain ideologies and to support political parties. Thus, Koss's analysis is mitigated on several counts. At one level, it dismisses proprietorial interference in business or economic activities. A number of businessmen, including Victor Matthews at Trafalgar House and James Goldsmith, have seen the inclusion of a newspaper as a natural part of their financial empires. On several occasions, a conflict of interests between journalistic responsibility and the demands of the owners has been apparent. This was illustrated by two events at the *Observer*. First, a row brewed up in 1984 between 'Tiny' Rowland, then owner of Lonrho and the *Observer*, and his editor Donald Trelford over an exposé of Zimbabwean President Robert Mugabe's Fifth Brigade which had brutally subjugated dissidents in Matabeleland. Rowland, who had invested in Zimbabwe, threatened to either close the paper, sell it off or sack Trelford. He publicly attacked the paper and apologized to Mugabe, whilst the staff supported Trelford. Eventually, Trelford was accepted back after he had written a letter of resignation. This was seen as an outstanding example of journalistic integrity defeating ownership power. However, the same cannot be said when Rowland and Trelford employed the paper to condemn the business activities of the Al-Fayed brothers in 1991. On this occasion, Rowland was in competition with the Al-Fayeds to buy the department store Harrods. The resulting controversy tarnished Rowland, Trelford and the *Observer*.

Further, as the modern press barons have diversified their business interests, they have used their papers to orchestrate promotional campaigns for their other media interests. Julian Petley has identified several linkages between cross-media ownership, publicity campaigns and the ideological subtext of the newspapers' output.[42] First, newspapers can be used to advertise television events. In particular, Rupert Murdoch's papers have lobbied for their owner's Sky Television. Columnists often refer to the benefits of satellite television and the sport's pages have built up audiences for events exclusively carried on Sky Sports. Second, at a more serious level, such self-promotion is reflective of vested interests. When Associated Newspapers, who own the *Daily Mail* and the *Daily Express*, launched Channel One on cable, they promoted it extensively in their papers. The hype included an attack on the terrestrial broadcasters for their restrictive practices and ancient regulatory structures.[43] Third, it is representative of the political alliances made between newspaper owners and governments. Throughout the 1980s, Murdoch's papers attacked the BBC and ITV as he attempted to launch a satellite station, often with the backing of Margaret Thatcher. To some extent, this was part of Murdoch's campaign to undermine terrestrial television in order to expand his own media interests. However, the close allegiance which he enjoyed with Margaret Thatcher on a personal, political and ideological level meant that such actions were politically motivated. The support provided by his papers to the Thatcher revolution invariably meant that the government turned a blind eye to his economic ambitions and often lauded him as a model of entrepreneurship.

This web of political and economic interests was apparent when Andrew Neil employed the *Sunday Times* to criticize the BBC over the programme *Real Lives: At the Edge of Union* which interviewed IRA suspect and Sinn Fein spokesman Martin McGuinness. In many respects, the Thatcher government's condemnation of the programme and the BBC Governors' intervention to have it removed were instigated by the paper's reporting. More explicitly, Neil seized upon the controversy engendered from the fall-out from the Thames documentary *Death on the Rock*. The programme reported that three IRA suspects had been subject to a 'shoot-to-kill' policy in Gibraltar. Through its use of eye witnesses it challenged the official explanation, and became subject to an extensive blackening campaign run by the *Sunday Times*.

In all these cases, an undermining of journalistic values can be detected. Instead of providing free and accurate information, business and political pressures shape the output of newspapers. Simultaneously, journalistic and editorial autonomy has been challenged by the return of hierarchical owner control over the newspaper industry. When the late Robert Maxwell bought the Mirror Group for £113 million in 1984 (a figure that stood well above the group's true worth) he intended to use the papers to pursue personal and political power:

> Maxwell was preoccupied, an informed guess suggests, by his image as the new Beaverbrook. He would become a great newspaper tycoon, leading from the front, inspiring great feats of reportage. The *Mirror* would once again become a great newspaper with unbridled influence. He, Robert Maxwell, would be the modern colussus, bestriding Fleet Street, Westminster and the City. Like the 'Beaver', his counsel would be sought from politicians, financiers and even trade unionists. All would

seek his advice and help, and eagerly await his judicious opinions on solving Britain's major problems. Daily, his newspapers would disseminate his views to the world in what he would publicly describe as 'a small contribution'.[44]

There are also clear parallels between Rupert Murdoch and Beaverbrook. First, both were foreigners who established major newspapers in Britain. Murdoch, an Australian, shared the Canadian Beaverbrook's 'New World' values and has championed entrepreneurship as the foundation for national prosperity. Second, Murdoch, despite the size of News International, like Beaverbrook, believes in having a hands-on role in the running of his newspapers. When he first arrived in 1968, in a scene akin to Orson Welles's *Citizen Kane*, Murdoch outlined his proprietorial role to the *News of the World* editor Stafford Summerfield. He informed the long-serving editor that he had not come all the way from Australia 'not to interfere'.[45] To his dismay, Summerfield found that Murdoch read proofs, wrote leaders if he wanted, instructed the staff and changed the paper. Such intervention soon led to Summerfield's resignation.[46] Third, this has led to a decline of internal democracy. Journalistic freedom has been stymied and editors have been undermined. With the exception of the *Guardian*, in which the editor is selected by the Scott Trust board with some journalistic input, editorial appointments are made by owners. In the main, Murdoch appointed compliant editors who followed his general principles. Those who did not follow the party line were quickly removed.

This occurred most spectacularly in the early 1980s when Murdoch gained control of *The Times*. To edit the paper, and appease his opponents, he appointed the *Sunday Times* editor Harold Evans, who, for many, had come to symbolize editorial autonomy within newspapers. The two rapidly fell out. On commercial grounds, Murdoch wanted to recoup his investment although *The Times* had been an ailing paper and he had guaranteed that it would not be taken down-market. However, he reneged on these promises, undermined Evans's control of the paper's costs, slashed editorial budgets and finally accused his editor of being a spendthrift.[47] The principal difficulty occurred over *The Times*'s political stance. Again, Murdoch had made guarantees to John Biffen, the Conservative Trade Secretary, that the editor would control the paper's political policy. Again, he reneged on these commitments. Murdoch wanted to remove his editor as he objected to the editorial's centrist nature. In early 1982, the government was remarkably unpopular and Murdoch felt an obligation to support Margaret Thatcher. Throughout the year, Evans and Murdoch fought battles over the Social Democratic Party (SDP), the virtues of monetarism and the support of the journalistic staff. Eventually, Murdoch used his political allegiances to force Evans's resignation in 1983.[48] Evans commented:

> It's just like the 1930s again . . . And the political reality is that the press barons are seeking to use newspapers not simply for money-making but for exercising personal power.[49]

Thus, Murdoch's editorial stance has proved to be a key factor in the running of his papers and developing their political affiliations. As he has grown more right-wing, so have his papers. This reached its apotheosis in the late 1980s, as Margaret Thatcher's position was strengthened.

Therefore, whilst the new press barons are less overtly motivated than their predecessors in not aspiring to high office, the contemporary press is reflective of their political ideologies. Editorial power has waned in the face of proprietorial power. The owners determine the editorial policies of their newspapers. Further, Murdoch has placed allies such as Andrew Neil and Kelvin MacKenzie in positions of power. Throughout the 1980s and early 1990s, this led to a press with an undoubted Conservative Party bias. However, as Harold Evans aptly comments:

> Murdoch's conservatism has nothing to do with a homely philosophy of self-reliance; its wellsprings are the retention of power and money, its methods are manipulation and the adroit manufacture of alliances. It has a wider political expression, but it is for all that less deep-rooted; it can be jettisoned at any moment for advantage. Politicians are endorsed when the calculation is that they will win power and patronage. A newspaper independent of the proprietor's needs at any moment has no place in such a scheme of things. It is a personal tool.[50]

The partisan attachments and political clientelism of the press

On a broad level, therefore, the modern press barons have been important political actors. However, one also needs to address the partisan nature of their papers. Colin Seymour-Ure has developed the concept of *parallelism* to examine how the newspapers respond to the political parties. He has defined three major links: organizational, loyalty to party goals and the reader's partisanship, in order to determine whether newspapers' political affiliations have paralleled the interests of the parties.[51] Theoretically, the parties' relative strength should exactly parallel their press support. However, newspapers' affiliations have confounded this principle, as they have made a virtue of being *political* rather than *partisan*.[52] Invariably, the papers do not enjoy direct organizational links with the parties and they often provide a critical discourse of those in power. However, as Ralph Negrine has commented, they do align themselves to certain parties and provide support for their programmes and policies:

> This support is rarely total but undoubtedly some newspapers, e.g. the *Daily Mail* and *Sun*, are more ready than others to support wholeheartedly the political party of their choice. Such a connection between newspapers and political parties is only to be expected; newspapers have traditionally wished to play a part in the political system.[53]

Throughout the 1980s and early 1990s, the papers predominantly supported the Conservative Party, apart from the Mirror Group's tradition of supporting the Labour Party. During Robert Maxwell's tenure, however, Neil Kinnock was backed against the more radical elements of the party and he used the *Daily Mirror* to falsely accuse the NUM President Arthur Scargill of the fraudulent use of union funds. The ultimate irony of this gesture should not be underestimated!

In particular, Rupert Murdoch's papers fervently supported Margaret Thatcher's government. Murdoch used his newspapers to attack the government's political opponents such as the NUM and the so-called 'Loony-Left' Greater London Council (GLC) led by Ken Livingstone. Murdoch was closely associated with Thatcher on a personal level and enjoyed monthly meetings with the former prime minister. For Thatcher, Murdoch was the epitome of the entrepreneurial class she believed would sustain the national economy.

Alongside this partisan attachment existed a mutual form of political clientelism. As Evans suggests, Murdoch's political patronage was pragmatic. As long as he continued to support the Thatcher government, it did not interfere in his business affairs by introducing any form of cross-media ownership legislation. This support for the Conservative Party continued when Thatcher was forced to resign in 1990. Notably, the newspapers galvanized an otherwise disastrous 1992 election campaign helping John Major to return to office. In particular, the Labour leader Neil Kinnock was castigated in the *Sun*:

> We don't want to influence you in your final judgement of who will be Prime Minister! But if it's a bald bloke with wispy red hair and two K's in his surname, we'll see you at the airport.[54]

However, since 1992 the relationship between the Conservative Party and Murdoch has become extremely hostile. In part, this has been due to John Major's poor performance and his perceived moderation of the Thatcherite agenda. However, serious problems have surrounded the possible introduction of privacy legislation as the government has accused the press of 'chequebook' journalism. Further, the Major government intends to impose cross-media ownership controls on the press barons' media empires in Britain. Therefore, the fall-out which has characterized the relations between the present Conservative government and Murdoch's papers has been promoted by the proprietors' belief that the government has stolen from the hand that feeds it.

Events reached a head in June 1995, when John Major announced that he would resign and contest a leadership election. Many Tories believed that this action had been forced on Major due to the poor press he received from Murdoch papers and Conrad Black's *Daily Telegraph*. Moreover, these papers mobilized around the challenge made by John Redwood, the former Welsh Secretary and leading Thatcherite, to Major's leadership. In the event, Major won in a reasonably convincing manner. However, Patrick Wintour comments:

> Many Major loyalists in the lobbies were furious at the Tory press including Conrad Black's *Daily Telegraph*, for trying to throw out Mr Major this week. They were especially angry at the press claim that Mr Major would not be able to stay on if he lost the support of more than 100 MPs, an artificial barrier they claimed had been erected by Mr Major's sworn enemies. Some in Downing Street also blame the Murdoch press for initially destabilising his leadership so he was forced to resort to the re-election ploy.[55]

Simultaneously, Murdoch has intimated that he is considering supporting Tony Blair's reformist Labour Party at the next general election. Consequently, the new Labour mandarins have fallen over themselves to court Murdoch. Fifteen years' worth of rancour between Murdoch and the party, punctuated by the 1984 miners' strike and the year-long dispute at Wapping, have been put on hold. Blair, alongside the former Australian Labour Party Prime Minister, Paul Keating, was only too happy to accept Murdoch's invitation to address a conference of News International's senior management held in July 1995. The winds of change had now apparently tilted full course:

> The invitation to Mr Blair follows a rejection of Mr Major by each of the Murdoch titles in Britain – *The Times, The Sunday Times, The News of the World, The Sun,* and *Today.*
>
> The costs of Mr Blair's trip, to the Hayman Island, off Queensland, are to be paid for by News Corporation. The trip was personally proposed by Mr Murdoch three weeks ago.
>
> Labour officials justified acceptance of the invitation on the basis that it is a platform to put over Labour's views to the world's single biggest media outlet. No policy concessions would be made to Mr Murdoch by Labour as a consequence.[56]

From this evidence, it would be a mistake to suggest that the modern press owners have relinquished their political ambitions. However, it may be ascertained that the nature of their political power has changed. Instead of actively engaging in Britain's parliamentary parties, they are far happier to direct their support at compliant politicians. They manipulate politicians for several reasons. To some extent Stephen Koss is correct; the modern press barons are pragmatic businessmen intent on enlarging their interests. However, more importantly, they use their influence to shape the political and ideological agenda. Consequently, they can enhance their power and prestige in the British polity.

Conclusion

This chapter has identified that the structure of press ownership and control changed from the late 1960s with the arrival of modern proprietors such as Rupert Murdoch. The modern press barons have been motivated by several imperatives: first, they have used their papers to create *profits*. They have exacerbated the press market's 'closed' nature by increasing starting-up costs and pursuing circulation wars. Moreover, instead of widening choice through provision, the new press technologies have allowed proprietors to reduce their production costs and to dismantle the power of the print unions. Further, as we shall discuss in chapter 7, the press has become a part of the larger corporate development of media diversification and conglomeration.

In their pursuit of profits, the modern press owners have employed *sensationalism* to increase their circulations to attract advertisers. Consequently, there has been a growing distinction between tabloid and quality papers. These down-market trends have created a political furore with the government considering the introduction of privacy legislation alongside the reform of the Press Council and the introduction of the Press Complaints Commission. However, the Major government has remained equivocal about establishing any form of press regulation, preferring to limit its attention to controls over telephone bugging and the use of the telephoto lens. The government's reluctance to intervene has been motivated less by the traditions of press freedom and more by the clientelism which has been established between proprietors and politicians over the years.

This turns our attention to the second major trend – the press barons have employed their papers to *increase their own power*. Through their patronage of the political parties, they have enjoyed an advantageous position within the British polity. This has meant that governments have been willing to turn a blind eye to the expansion of their media assets. However, they have not simply pursued these political alliances in order to gain favourable business conditions. They have sought to use their newspapers to exercise personal and political power. The major press barons still have a considerable stake and say in who will run the country, as exemplified by the events of summer 1995.

These forms of proprietorial power return our attention to the central dilemma surrounding a free press. Formally, a free press should disseminate a plurality of views through a free market of providers. State regulation has been deemed to be regressive and stemming freedom of speech. However, the press barons have monopolized their power and have used their papers to establish the political discourse. Ultimately their actions are anti-democratic as they advance specific elite positions to the detriment of alternative viewpoints. The contemporary nature of the press has also been determined by advertisers, who will deploy their economic power to have articles removed or to promote an uncritical view of their own activities. Throughout the British press there are notable conflicts of interest. Therefore, in this climate, it is difficult to sustain the belief that the press acts as a fourth estate responsible for highlighting abuses and checking the power of political and economic elites. Increasingly, it has failed to perform its democratic functions and has been incorporated into the dominant political, economic and social order.

Further Reading

Tom Bower, *Maxwell: The Outsider*, Mandarin, 1991 (2nd edn).
Peter Chippindale and Chris Horrie, *Stick it up Your Punter: The Rise and Fall of the* Sun, Mandarin, 1989.
James Curran (ed.), *The British Press: A Manifesto*, Macmillan, 1978.
—— and Jean Seaton, *Power without Responsibility: The Press and Broadcasting in Britain*, Routledge, 1991 (4th edn).
Peter Dahlgren and Colin Sparks (eds), *Communication and Citizenship: Journalism and the Public Sphere*, Routledge, 1991.
Department of National Heritage, *Privacy and Media Intrusion: The Government's Response*, HMSO, 1995.
Harold Evans, *Good Times, Bad Times*, Weidenfeld & Nicolson, 1983.
Bob Franklin, *Packaging Politics: Political Communication in Britain's Media Democracy*, Edward Arnold, 1994.
Roy Greenslade, *Maxwell's Fall: The Appalling Legacy of a Corrupt Man*, Simon & Schuster, 1992.
Fred Hirsch and David Gordon, *Newspaper Money: Fleet Street and the Search for the Affluent Reader*, Hutchinson, 1975.
Simon Jenkins, *Newspapers: The Power and the Money*, Faber & Faber, 1979.
Stephen Koss, *The Rise and Fall of the Political Press in Britain*, vol. 2, Hamish Hamilton, 1984.
Larry Lamb, *Sunrise: The Remarkable Rise and Rise of the Best-selling Soaraway* Sun, PaperMac, Macmillan, 1989.

George Munster, *Rupert Murdoch: A Paper Prince*, Penguin, 1985.

Ralph Negrine, *Politics and the Mass Media in Britain*, Routledge (2nd edn), 1994.

Colin Seymour-Ure, *The Political Impact of the Mass Media*, Sage Publications, 1974.

———, *The British Press and Broadcasting since 1945*, Basil Blackwell, 1991.

William Shawcross, *Rupert Murdoch: Ringmaster of the Information Circus*, Chatto & Windus, 1992.

Raymond Snoddy, *The Good, the Bad and the Unacceptable: The Hard News about the British Press*, Faber & Faber, 1992.

Jeremy Tunstall and Michael Palmer, *The Media Moguls*, Routledge, 1991.

Notes

1 For further details on Murdoch see William Shawcross, *Rupert Murdoch: Ringmaster of the Informational Circus*, Chatto & Windus, 1992.

2 Tom Baistow, 'The Predators' Press', in Norman Buchan and Tricia Sumner, *Glasnost in Britain?*, 1989, p. 59.

3 Raymond Snoddy, *The Good, the Bad and the Unacceptable: The Hard News about the British Press*, Faber & Faber, 1992, p. 117.

4 Graham Murdock and Peter Golding, 'The structure, ownership and control of the press, 1914–1976', in George Boyce et al. (eds), op. cit., pp. 144–6.

5 See William Shawcross, *Rupert Murdoch*, pp. 1–19.

6 For further details see Roy Greenslade, *Maxwell's Fall: The appalling legacy of a corrupt man*, Simon & Schuster, 1992.

7 Ibid., p. 379.

8 For a critique of the printers' working practices see Simon Jenkins, *Newspapers: The Power and the Money*, Faber & Faber, 1979, pp. 48–61.

9 Eric Butler quoted in Peter Chippindale and Chris Horrie, *Stick it up Your Punter: The Rise and Fall of the Sun*, Mandarin, 1989, p. 189.

10 Cento Veljanovski, *The Media in Britain Today*, News International Plc, 1990, p. 13.

11 See Colin Sparks, 'Concentration and Market Entry in the UK National Press', *European Journal of Communication*, 1995, Sage, vol. 10(2), pp. 180–206.

12 Ibid., p. 193.

13 Roy Greenslade, 'For whom the bill tolls', *Guardian*, Section 2, 20 November 1995, p. 14.

14 For further details see Bob Franklin, *Packaging Politics: Political Communication in Britain's Media Democracy*, Edward Arnold, 1994, pp. 42–4.

15 Andrew Neil quoted in George Munster, *Rupert Murdoch: A Paper Prince*, Penguin, 1987, p. 265.

16 Ibid., p. 42.

17 Taken from the cover of Fred Hirsch and David Gordon, *Newspaper Money: Fleet Street and the Search for the Affluent Reader*, Hutchinson, 1975.

18 Roy Greenslade, 'Distorting Mirror', *Guardian*, Section 2, 18 September 1995, p. 14.

19 Peter Chippindale and Chris Horrie, *Stick it up Your Punter!*, p. 70.

20 Ibid., p. 12.

21 Larry Lamb, *Sunrise: The remarkable rise and rise of the best-selling Soaraway Sun*, Papermac, 1989, pp. 155–7. For his troubles, Lamb was rewarded by Thatcher with a knighthood. This apparently increased Lamb's pomposity and was the

source of mirth in the paper's newsroom. See Peter Chippindale and Chris Horrie, *Stick it up Your Punter!*, pp. 62–3.

22   Ibid., p. 83.
23   Peter Chippindale and Chris Horrie, *Stick it up Your Punter!*, pp. 175–6.
24   Ibid., pp. 118–19.
25   Raymond Snoddy, *The Good, the Bad and the Unacceptable*, p. 95.
26   Bob Franklin, *Packaging Politics*, p. 45.
27   David Mellor in Raymond Snoddy, *The Good, the Bad and the Unacceptable*, p. 101.
28   Ibid., p. 47.
29   Bob Franklin, *Packaging Politics*, p. 47.
30   David Calcutt, *Review of Press Self-Regulation*, Cmnd. 2135, Department of National Heritage, HMSO, January 1993.
31   'Government rules out legal moves on media intrusion', *The Herald*, 18 July 1995, p. 4.
32   Department of National Heritage, *Privacy and Media Intrusion: The Government's Response*, Cm 2198, HMSO, 1995, p. 23.
33   John Diamond, 'Bottomley lets off the long-lens brigade'; Media and Marketing, *The Times*, 19 July 1995.
34   James Curran, introduction to James Curran (ed.), *The British Press: A Manifesto*, Macmillan, 1978, p. 8.
35   Simon Jenkins, *Newspapers: The Power and the Money*, Faber & Faber, 1979, p. 50.
36   Raymond Snoddy, *The Good, the Bad and the Unacceptable*, p. 120.
37   Stephen Koss, *The Rise and Fall of the Political Press in Britain* (vol. 2), Hamish Hamilton, 1984, p. 667.
38   Ibid.
39   Ibid.
40   Ibid., p. 668.
41   Ibid., p. 118.
42   Julian Petley, paper given at 'Media Versus the People: Media Ownership and Democracy', Campaign for Press and Broadcasting Freedom Conference, 18 March 1995.
43   Ibid.
44   Tom Bower, *Maxwell: The Outsider*, Mandarin, 1991 (2nd edn).
45   James Curran and Jean Seaton, op. cit., p. 87.
46   Ibid., p. 87.
47   Harold Evans, *Good Times, Bad Times*, Weidenfeld & Nicolson, 1983, p. 304.
48   Ibid., pp. 318–51.
49   Ibid., p. 7.
50   Ibid., p. 6.
51   Colin Seymour-Ure, *The Political Impact of Mass Media*, Sage, 1974, pp. 173–4.
52   Colin Seymour-Ure, *Changing Partisanship in the British National Press*, paper presented at the ECPR Workshop: New Developments in Political Communications, 1996, p. 3.
53   Ralph Negrine, *Politics and the Mass Media in Britain*, Routledge, 1994 (2nd edn), p. 53.
54   Quoted from Michael Leapman, 'Supping with the Devil', *Independent*, 7 January 1995, p. 25.
55   'Blair to talk at Murdoch conference', *Guardian*, 7 July 1995, p. 2.
56   Ibid.

4
The British Public Service Broadcasting System

On one level, British broadcasting's political independence is tied to the press's liberty. Formally, it is committed to the tenets of accuracy, impartiality and objectivity. However, unlike the press, broadcasting has demonstrated significant governmental intervention since the advent of radio in the 1920s. Although they remain constitutionally independent from the state, the British Broadcasting Corporation (BBC) and, to a lesser extent, Independent Television (ITV) have been regulated by and organized as public bodies. This has been justified by:

1 Broadcasting's power to shape opinions over newspapers. Sound and pictures have greater influence over the public than the printed word. In particular, television dominates the private space and is less escapable than the press.
2 The technical qualification of a limited spectrum of airwaves. Until the 1980s, domestically available radio and television broadcasts were restricted to a narrow band of nationally available frequencies. This reduced the number of possible channels and determined broadcasting's organization, as it was deemed to be a limited resource. Such a dissemination of information provoked a political question. Could the state's legitimate concern to utilize a vital national resource be accommodated with the principles of free choice and the broadcaster's freedom of expression within a limited number of outlets?[1]

In responding to this conundrum, British policy-makers and broadcasting chiefs, notably the first BBC Director-General John Reith, established the public service model. Initially, broadcasting was organized as a public monopoly. The BBC established a dominance over national and local radio which was only to be challenged in the early 1970s when

Heath's government established the framework for local commercial radio. With regard to television, from the 1950s until the late 1980s, it has comprised of a public broadcaster, the BBC, funded through a licence fee, and private channels (ITV and Channel Four) funded through advertising. These organizations competed for audiences rather than revenues. They are responsible for providing a mixed schedule built on the programming trinity of educating, informing and entertaining.

Thus, the British broadcasting system, comprised of a public and commercial sector, evolved in an integrated, rather than competitive fashion.[2] Different financial arrangements, channels, ideas and structures were incorporated into a cohesive order initiated by the first BBC Director-General John Reith during the 1920s and 1930s. The introduction of Independent Television (ITV) did not herald a break from this tradition. Instead, this followed the prescribed pattern and the commercial companies' supervisory body, the Independent Television Authority (ITA, later IBA) was a complementary regulator to the BBC Board of Governors.[3] Further, broadcasting has been contingent on the support of the political elite. Therefore, as broadcasting is a social as well as an economic commodity, its political position has been important.

This chapter's purpose is to assess the dynamics which have defined the course of British broadcasting. It will consider how a unitary system emerged and determined how political relations between the state and broadcasting have been conducted. Important areas comprise: the basic tenets and institutions of public service broadcasting; the regulation of these broadcasting organizations and their political position *vis-à-vis* the state. The survey will extend from the creation of the British Broadcasting Company in 1922 to the late 1970s. These dates refer to the establishment and perpetuation of a Public Service Broadcasting system (PSB).[4] As we shall discover, Channel Four's creation in 1982 and Margaret Thatcher's election in 1979 challenged the groundrules which had previously demarcated state–broadcasting relations.[5]

Two qualifications are required. First, many measures were pursued due to short-term political requirements rather than being developed to create an overall framework for broadcasting. Second, because of this lengthy time-scale it would be impossible to cover all the important areas. Thus, it has been necessary to place a number of limits on this study. Inevitably such qualifications are, to some degree, arbitrary; however, a judicious selection of material will prove to be useful in aiding our understanding. Jeremy Tunstall suggested that broadcasting legislation follows a twelve-yearly cycle and this model may be employed to outline issues, trends and themes from the evidence.[6] In the conclusion to this chapter we will address the following questions: how valid have the assumptions of unitary expansion been? What does this material demonstrate about the relationship between the state and broadcasters?

The Limited Spectrum of Airwaves

Until the last decade, domestically available radio and television broadcasts were only obtainable on a limited spectrum of airwaves. This stemmed the number of channels. The experience of the early American radio system, in which competing radio stations interfered with each other's frequencies, demonstrated the practical need for a regulated system. However, it was realized that broadcasting raised political as well as technical questions. For British policy-makers this meant that a limited resource had to be utilized in the citizens' interest and for broadcasters to provide a wide range of views.[7]

The solution arrived at should be a temporary one. This is due to constant societal changes which demand alternative responses at different times. At best, a solution can only partially solve the dialectic between the state – broadcasting – and the audience. Yet the British system has been defined by agreements reached in the early mid-1920s with the creation of the BBC as a public corporation. Whilst the societal demands of the 1920s were resolved, it does not follow that this conception should be fixed. That such a perspective has defined British broadcasting from this period to the late 1970s is not so much a measure of its correctness, but an indication of how broadcasting cannot be divorced from the political and national interests. Although the BBC represented a solution to a technical problem, it was a sociological invention of profound importance involving a consortium of different interests including manufacturers, broadcasters, politicians and civil servants.

Two factors dominated the government's concern over broadcasting. First, the government did not want to involve itself in programme-making nor the commercial costs of radio. Second, its actions were defined by post-war interventionism.[8] Although the British economy was market-led, the market was not seen as the most effective method to manage a limited national resource such as broadcasting. As the First World War increased state power over health, insurance, coal and food-rationing, the political elite's conception of state intervention had expanded. A regulated order was deemed to be desirable.[9]

Consequently, when the Marconi Company applied to broadcast, fears were raised about the free-market exploitation of a valuable national resource by a private monopoly. This concern, tied with the technical qualifications of the limited spectrum, pressured the government into taking an interventionist role in broadcasting. Thus a bargaining process between public and private forces to find a solution occurred. Underpinning this process was the public utility ethos which channelled the government's approach. In 1922, a publicly organized company – the British Broadcasting Company (BBC) – was created to provide a public service. It was jointly financed by the rival manufacturers. By 1927 the British Broadcasting Company was replaced by the British Broadcasting Corporation. A Royal Charter governed the corporation for a ten-year period and established the basic tenets of public service broadcasting (PSB). This response to a technical issue demonstrated a number of features which have characterized British broadcasting policy. Throughout broadcasting's development, it has been conceived as a vital national resource which would be regulated in the public's interest. Further, this was indicative of an understanding of the social purpose of broadcasting:

> the concept of social communications, and thus broadcasting, is closely linked to the more general notion of culture. . . . The (British) definition points back to the nineteenth century, to Matthew Arnold's moralistic conception of culture as exposure to 'the best that has been thought and felt', to his horror of bad taste and vulgarity. Philistinism and parochialism were the enemies. The function of cultural institutions was to embody the 'collective' best-self.[10]

Public Service Broadcasting

An incremental television duopoly developed. The BBC and ITV were not identical structures. There were significant differences in funding, regional composition, institutional ethos and regulation. However, a convergence between the public and commercial sector occurred, underpinned by the concept of public service broadcasting. This was defined by the following principles:

- geographic universality – everyone should have access to the same services;
- catering for all interests and tastes;
- catering for minorities;
- catering for 'national identity and community';
- detachment from vested interests and government;
- one broadcasting system to be funded directly from the corpus of users;
- competition in good programming rather than numbers; and
- guidelines to liberate programme makers and not to restrict them.[11]

These tenets determined the duopoly's growth and programming output. The British system has evidenced the contribution of the national economic and political culture. Its development was associated with state statutes, committees, reports and regulations. Broadcasting policy approximately occurred in twelve-year cycles, centred on committees of inquiry which promoted important debates about the key issues.[12] Indeed, some commentators have deemed it as the most regulated television system in the world.[13]

The creation of a duopolistic structure

Effectively, the BBC and ITV became two halves of the same system which derived from a 'single root and . . . these branches, instead of diverging over the years . . . stabilised their concentration more or less in parallel'.[14] Unlike other broadcasting systems (for example, those in the United States) the British broadcasters have competed for audiences rather than revenues. This was mutually beneficial as it channelled a substantial amount of revenue into the system. It produced a circumscibed form of competition as BBC and ITV producers have vied for their reputations, critical renown and audience approval.

Several policy cycles have marked the development of British broadcasting. The first marked the transition between the BBC as a company to a corporation. The corporate development of the BBC was sustained through the principle of universality of provision. To create a national, centrally scheduled output, John Reith argued for assured sources of funding and the brute force of monopoly. To this end, he achieved support from the 1926 Crawford Committee. The committee approved a broadcasting monopoly, and stated that the British Broadcasting Company should be replaced by a 'Public Commission operating in the national interest'.[15] It recommended that the BBC should not be divorced from vested interests and involve 'persons of judgement and independence, free from commitments . . . men and women of business acumen and experienced in affairs'.[16] The BBC was publicly funded by an annual, national poll-tax – a licence fee – raised from the population and collected by the Post Office.

The second policy cycle challenged the BBC's monopoly. After its Charter had expired in 1946, the Corporation expected that its licence would be automatically renewed. However, parliament felt that the war had made the BBC an instrument of the state.[17] In 1949, the Labour government created a committee chaired by Lord Beveridge, famous for his recommendations for health and welfare reforms, and including the then Conservative backbencher Selwyn Lloyd. Although it argued that the public monopoly remained the most effective way to organize broadcasting, it was highly critical of the system. The report recommended that the licence should be renewed, yet felt that the BBC was not publicly accountable. The governors, who acted as public trustees, were ill-equipped. The Beveridge committee recommended a number of safeguards to stem 'the four scandals of monopoly: bureaucracy, complacency, favouritism and inefficiency'.[18]

As the report was published in January 1951, its recommendations were largely ignored due to the general election. Instead, the Conservative Party's victory focused the debate upon commercialization.[19] Selwyn Lloyd's dissenting minority report provided the platform for this approach. He disagreed with the public service broadcasting monopoly and felt that it should be challenged by competitive commercial stations. Sponsorship could fund this service and would stem the monopolization. The debate highlighted the BBC's bureaucratic rigidity and its possible acquiescence to an 'extreme' government who, during crises, might take control of the corporation's output. Consequently, it was argued that a commercial service should compete with the BBC to stem monopolization, to provide popular programming and to promote greater political liberty. *eg : worldwide.*

In contrast to the BBC, the ITV system was financed through advertising revenues. The government preferred to raise money through spot advertising rather than sponsorship. This meant that television companies would retain programme responsibility whilst agreeing to commercial breaks, at specific points, in return for advertising revenues. However, throughout the 1954 Television Act's committee stage an important provision emerged; the public regulation of a private enterprise. This represented a compromise between the traditionalist Conservative lobby (influenced by Lord Reith), who feared that broadcasting would go down-market, against the commercial lobby. This underpinned the 1954 Act and the interpretation of its recommendations during the founding of Independent Television (ITV):

> The public service conception of broadcasting was thus substantially maintained in a compromise mediated between the State's claim to regulate and the claims of free enterprise. The Government congratulated itself with the thought that such a combination of effective control on one hand, and greater freedom on the other, was a typically British approach to this new problem.[20]

The Act licensed a new service comprising regional contractors who would provide both local and network programming. Elaborate regulations stemmed any form of commercial vulgarization, with instructions to maintain impartiality, restrictions on taste and decency, a quota of British originated production designed to stop the proliferation of American imports, and limitations controlling the advertiser's power over the schedule and programming. To maintain these arrangements, a public regulator – the Independent Television Authority (ITA) – was created.[21]

Thus, ITV was fashioned in the BBC's image. It was regulated by an interventionist body which had licensing and programming powers. Moreover, due to its five-yearly licence renewal, it was subject to parliament in the same way as the BBC, whose charter was granted on a ten-yearly basis. Indeed, the Act legitimized a confusion by calling the commercial broadcaster 'Independent Television'. As Gerald Beedle, a future director of BBC Television, ascertained it was 'intended to imply independence from the BBC . . . but was taken to mean independence from the government'.[22]

The early development of the commercial network enhanced convergence with the public broadcaster. ITV was a plural system designed to promote competition and regionalization. However the subsequent crisis in profitability (due to the inequity of advertising revenues throughout the regions) meant that the ITV companies centralized their organization to minimize the financial risk. Each contractor contributed to the network's total output at an agreed rate of payment proportional to its wealth. Therefore, smaller regional companies could enjoy the fruits of nationally syndicated programmes which would attract audience and advertisers. Simultaneously, the larger contractors could cover their costs by selling their programmes nationally. The commercial carve-up indicated that cartelism was to become the key organizing principle for commercial television. The plural system was replaced by a unitary order, in which the 'Big Four' (Rediffusion, ATV, ABC, Granada) dominated the network's institutional (for example, control boards) and programming (for instance, national schedules) affairs. The smaller companies occupied a non-competitive subsidiary role chiefly providing local programmes.[23] The commercial system which took root, with its compromise between the free market, a centralized schedule and control structure, and the public service, became a complementary service to the BBC.

The movement toward duopoly suffered from a formative tension. By 1960, the financial inequity between the BBC and ITV had grown, with ITV's advertising revenue totalling £60 million against the BBC's paltry £15 million from the licence fee. In response, the Conservative government established the Pilkington Committee to review broadcasting. This included Richard Hoggart, who had written *The Uses of Literacy*, and the 1962 report reflected Hoggart's concern over the erosion of working class values through the industrialization of leisure practices. Television could profitably or detrimentally influence the masses.[24] Its purpose was to enlighten through raising educational standards and moral awareness. The committee praised the BBC for performing this task. Conversely, it felt that ITV had produced worthless populist programmes aimed at the lowest common-denominator. The ITA was an impotent watchdog and it recommended that the commercial sector should be reformed.[25]

The report's arguments were largely ignored by the government, which was selective in its interpretation. For instance, it supported the introduction of the 625 line system and the creation of BBC2. Revealingly, the key proposals to be found in the 1963 and 1964 Television Acts were those which, when removed from the report, laid the foundation for a planned co-existence between the BBC and ITV.[26] The 1963 Act increased the ITA's scheduling powers. The ITA would agree the schedule with the contractors through a series of network and regional committees. Further, the authority could mandate a quota of documentary and current affairs programmes during peak hours. More importantly, Section 7 of the 1964 Act placed a levy on ITV contractors to stem excessive profits. This was an additional payment over the rentals paid to the ITA. The proceeds went into the Exchequer depending on the contractor's advertising revenues. For the first £1.5 million of revenue there was no taxation; on the next £6 million the rate stood at 25 per cent, and companies receiving receipts above £7.5 million were levied at a level of 45 per cent. In such a manner, it was posited that the financial inequity between the BBC and ITV could be partially eradicated.[27] Although these measures were *ad hoc*, they added up to more than the sum of their parts. Taken together, the levy and the increase in the ITA's interventionary powers meant that the ITV companies were forced to reinvest their profits in programming (to avoid excessive taxation) and to conform to greater public service commitments. These could be seen as a prescription from government for the running of a national broadcasting service.[28] The legislation had settled a framework for integration and the television duopoly had been firmly established.

'Peaceful co-existence'

During this period of 'peaceful co-existence' a number of features became apparent:[29] first, the duopoly was the sole supplier of programmes due to the limitations of technology and market entry. This meant that the BBC and ITV had a monopoly over production resources, creative talent and the output of their product. A vertically integrated broadcasting system emerged in which the public and commercial sectors acted as programme-makers and broadcasters. This developed out of a command economy, in which the money received from the licence fee and advertising entered the broadcasting market to be spent as the broadcasters pleased. Moreover, the national interest obligation secured a home production quota to control foreign programming on the channels.

The BBC and the ITV network increased their output, enlarged their labour force, and widened their activities. Their growth was underpinned by an incremental increase in broadcasting finance. The BBC's income was enhanced by the turnover from black and white to colour licences. ITV's growth was heightened by the ITA's re-allocation of the company franchises in 1968 and the general increase in advertising expenditure:

> Throughout the sixties and seventies there was tremendous expansion within both the BBC and ITV. These were the 'Fat Years'. There were increases in real terms within the licence fee which was then negotiated every year . . . and the advertising market for the ITV. The BBC and ITV could afford to be lavish. During this period, labour practices were relaxed and agreements grew up.[30]

The financial controls were designed to enhance new programmes. The hourly costs for original programming were high due to the labour in writing, producing and developing a production. In 1984–5, the average expenditure for a first-run production was £52,000 per hour. The following table indicates the total amounts required by the broadcasters to schedule new programmes, either home-initiated or acquired:

Table 4.1 Costs of new television programming, 1984

	£ (Million)
BBC (network only)	329.9
ITV	375.0
Channel Four	95.4
SC4	24.6
Total	824.9
Total TV expenditure	1,359.2
New TV programmes as percentage of total TV expenditure	59.1%

Source: Richard Collins et al., *The Economics of Television*, 1988

Second, the industry became unionized as the unions made agreements with willing managements over wages, working hours, security of tenure and craft specialization. To gain employment, a technician had to be a member of the ACTT or BETA. These closed shop practices secured the labour market and, along with the general expansion, created an intensively manned labour force.

Third, broadcasting exhibited the growth of professionalism as cultural practices evolved. The broadcasters shared similar backgrounds, values and attitudes. Invariably they were male, white, middle-class and

Oxbridge educated. This ethos was enhanced through the seepage of personnel from the BBC to ITV during the 1950s. For instance, throughout a six-month period between 1955 and 1956 nearly 500 BBC staff members left to pursue careers in ITV. Moreover, due to the craft specialization required in broadcasting, individuals with residual talents in presentation, management and production could weave a career path between the BBC and the ITV companies. The alumni have included Paul Fox, Melvyn Bragg and Michael Grade. These factors served to establish a core broadcasting elite. This linkage contributed to a standard set of shared internal conceptions and practices, mediated through the ideology of public service broadcasting. In many respects, this has been a self-fulfilling process. Nicholas Garnham describes it as follows:

> Broadcasters have been induced to underwrite the legitimising myths of our broadcasting institutions because those myths have in part been designed precisely to maintain the internal cohesion of the institutions and control those at the top by flattering the broadcasters. Isolated from his audience by the nature of the medium, the broadcaster has allowed professional standards, validated by the judgement of his peers, to become an end in themselves and a very real barrier between him and the public.[31]

Fourth, the programming principles of educating, informing and entertaining remained at the core of the public service system. This concept of broadcasting demonstrated that elite groups felt that British broadcasting should have a social rather than economic value. The duopolistic period marked a streamlining of Reithian standards with programming to encourage cultural diversity, regionalism and entertainment.

Reith had felt that broadcasting should be educational to train character and promote a sense of moral obligation. A paternalistic attitude was introduced to authorize cultural values rather than represent listener interests. A mixed programming policy was employed to cover a wide number of subjects, whether they be trivial or serious. To be 'educated' the audience had to encounter everything that could be heard. Therefore, radio was to act as a disseminator and filter for accepted values. Reith stated in 1924 that 'It is occasionally indicated to us that we are apparently setting out to give the public what we think they need – not what they want . . . But few know what they want and very few know what they need.'[32]

The BBC's programme policy, from the 1920s until the late 1950s, reflected an assumption of national cultural homogeneity which perceived culture as an undifferentiated force.[33] It was challenged by the advent of ITV whose mix included action series, comedies and quiz shows which were popular ratings winners. Its success meant that the BBC's audience share had been reduced to 28 per cent by 1957. Theoretically, the corporation could afford to ignore ITV as it continued to receive a secure income through the licence fee.[34] Yet the BBC understood that such a drop in audiences could be disastrous for the licence fee which was a legally binding poll-tax. Thus, it realized it would have to develop popular programming to attract half of the national audience and significantly adapt Reithianism. Under the leadership of Director-General Hugh Greene the BBC moved in this direction by producing new or alternative work such as *Face-to-Face*, *That Was the Week that Was* (*TW3*), innovative drama, and the coverage of general elections, alongside a staple diet of popular light entertainment situation comedies and musical shows such as the *Black and White Minstrel Show*.

This was a two-way process. Whilst the BBC had been forced to alter, it was argued that the quality of ITV programmes was raised through this competition for audiences. This shared outlook was reinforced as Independent Television was arranged to keep outright commercial values distinct from the programming. Therefore, there were no sponsored programmes and the companies were required to conform to the tenets of public service broadcasting. Although it was not immediately apparent, the monopoly within ITV secured this, as it created a cohesive system which was easier to regulate. Competition meant convergence in practice.[35]

Throughout the 1960s and 1970s self-regulating programme codes were developed. For instance, complementary scheduling arrangements were built up between the BBC and ITV companies. Gradually the two sectors stemmed the competition for audiences as nightly schedules were orchestrated to ensure a parity of viewers. Current affairs programmes were twinned. BBC Director of Television Huw Weldon explained that 'if Panorama ran opposite a movie on ITV, and if World in Action ran opposite a comedy show on BBC1, the audience of both Current Affairs programmes would drop steeply'.[36] This created a rigged market and enabled advertisers to target their audience. Further, both sides conformed to a 9:00 pm watershed, after which more adult programming would be shown.

Therefore the duopoly was a great success as it assured that money was directed into programming and talent. This resulted in higher technical standards and quality in content. The 1960s and 1970s were a 'golden age for British broadcasting' as innovative programmes were backed and series, which if not initially successful, were allowed to find their audiences. The British broadcasting system held a position in the national mythology, receiving praise from the public and the conditional support of the political elite. It was argued that the licence fee was relatively inexpensive and provided good value. Simultaneously, ITV's public regulations meant commercialism had been contained. The duopoly was perceived as an intrinsic 'part of (the) national anatomy . . . (a) part of (the) social system and (a) part of the national way of life'.[37]

The regulation of British broadcasting

Constitutionally, the BBC governors were public trustees whose responsibilities included reviewing the corporation's output, representing it to parliament and ensuring public accountability. Thus, the board guaranteed that the corporation pursued public service programming strategies, remained accountable to its audience, maintained editorial independence and deflected state intervention.[38] In day-to-day terms the governors' power has been circumscribed. The board members were part-time laymen who were responsible for general rather than detailed policy. They have been dependent on the full-time secretariat for their working knowledge of the corporation. Their functions were defined by Reith and BBC Chairman John Whitley in the 1931 Whitley Document. This limited the governors by delineating their role as guardians of the national interest. Real power was vested in the corporate executive:

> The suggestions sometimes made that the Governors should be appointed as experts or specialists in any of the activities covered by the Broadcasting Service is not regarded as desirable. . . . With the Director-General they discuss and then decide upon major matters of policy and finance, but they leave the execution of that policy and the general administration of the Service in all its branches to the Director-General and his competent officers.[39]

Conversely, the ITA (later the IBA after the launch of independent radio in 1973) has had a more hands-on role in the public regulation of the ITV sector. Whilst its board was composed of part-time members, the authority has been serviced by a full-time management headed by a Director-General. Since its powers were enhanced in the 1964 Act, it has licensed the programme contractors and advertisers, whilst applying prohibitory regulations when required as the legal broadcaster. As the IBA was the broadcaster, which transmitted the ITV companies' programmes, it was an interventionist body which could dictate programme schedules in accordance with public service criteria. The IBA's programming and scheduling powers enabled it to commit the contractors to providing minority programmes during peak periods, as one-third of the total output should be of a documentary or factual nature. It had the power to revoke the contractor's licence if it did not conform. This safeguard was designed to mediate the commercial imperative of advertising revenue.

As a consequence, the British broadcasting system has been supervised by interventionist regulators in relation to programming, scheduling and financial affairs. However, the formal elements provide a limited amount of information about the regulation of British broadcasting. The minimalist broadcasting policy indulged in by governments has meant that regulation has not so much been a legally defined framework as a practice which established by precedent. This form of regulation has been termed 'private interest government' characterized by the invisibility of government intervention, a secretive regulatory process, clientelism, establishment politics and self-restraint.[40] For instance, the relationship between the IBA and the ITV companies has been criticized for exhibiting elements of regulatory capture in which the regulator has acted in the industry's rather than the public interest. Moreover, this may promote covert manoeuvres between professional broadcasters, amateur regulators and politicians:

> *Defacto* the BBC developed a system of self-regulation, underwritten by state power, a form of royally-chartered arrangement for professional self-regulation. . . . This system was overlain and indeed sustained by discrete, informal political pressures from ministers; the threat of political intervention served to tighten self-regulation. The BBC was effectively licensed as a 'closed shop', treated by the state as the sole representative of British broadcasting (until 1954) and enabled to control who broadcasts what, with legal rules kept to a minimum.[41]

Throughout the years, the BBC governors' and the IBA's accountability to the public, rather than to the broadcasters or the political elite, has been questioned. They have either been understood as providing a buffer between state and broadcasting, or seen as a mechanism through which state control may be covertly exerted. For instance, a series of 'informal linkages' have been constructed to allow for several forms of 'dealing' to occur.[42] Therefore, the regulator's position provides questions about the relationship between broadcasters and the state, and turns attention back to the central dilemma of broadcasting; is it possible to resolve within a limited number of outlets the demands of the state, the citizen's freedom of choice in his/her search for personal satisfaction and the broadcasters' desires to express the truth as they perceive it?

The Political Position of British Broadcasting

The broadcasting institutions argue that they are free to broadcast within the confines of the law. This liberal-pluralistic position contends that through legal, institutional, and funding devices the external pressures of government intervention have been resisted.

The BBC was described by Reith as an 'institution within the constitution'.[43] It was subject to the Crown and was required to follow the pluralism of parliamentary democracy. The BBC was governed by a Royal Charter which enabled it to be resistant to overt state pressures as an 'arms-length' relationship existed. Whilst the licence fee has provided assured funds for programming requirements, it has preserved the corporation's political independence from the state. It meant that the BBC was not dependent on state revenues and could fulfil its role as an independent broadcaster.[44] The corporation has been guided by the notion of impartiality in its representation of political affairs. However, whilst the BBC rejects any control of content, its accountability is mediated by its acceptance of parliament's definition of political behaviour. It has understood that it should represent the parliament's discourse. Broadcasting provides an impartial brokerage of information in the predominant political system.[45]

The ITV system's independence has been ensured through a mixture of advertising revenue and regulatory control. Its finances were indirectly drawn from the public rather than the state. As we have seen, it has been argued that this produced a free press in Britain.[46] The IBA's position as a broadcaster meant that if the state attempted to intervene, the regulator would act as a cushion between the government and the programme-makers. Thus, in any court case the IBA would be the responsible party instead of the regional contractor. As with the BBC, the IBA saw parliament as its natural pole and has understood that it should provide impartial information within the dominant political system.

Minimalist broadcasting legislation (meaning that the BBC Board of Governors and the IBA had a relatively free hand in how they interpreted directives), was consciously developed to stem state intervention and enhance broadcasting freedoms. Further, supporters of this position would argue that as the Home Secretary has never technically employed his veto power over broadcasting; democracy has been served. Alternatively, it may be argued that the Home Secretary has never had to effect such powers due to the inbuilt self-restraint and ideological adherence of the broadcasting institutions to the dominant political culture.

Alternative Perspectives on the Political Position of Broadcasting: the Case of Broadcast Journalism

The pluralistic model of the relationship between broadcasters and the state has been subject to several critiques. In particular, the liberal interpretation has been criticized from Marxist interpretations of the media. The neo-Marxist critique has evolved from the theory of false consciousness and belief that capitalism not only owns the means of production, but the cultural means of production. Broadcasting is judged as an agent for consensus, producing the mass acquiescence to practices which operate against the proletariat's interests.[47]

However, there is no single Marxist approach to broadcasting. Traditional Marxists conceive the public sphere as an arena for capitalist class domination in which elites (political or economic) may disorganize opposition through ideological indoctrination. Therefore, the public duopoly was seen to have been structured, controlled and located within the dominant framework of capitalist class interests. Conversely, Gramscians such as Stuart Hall have determined that the ruling class is an alliance of competing social strata and that its ideology has been subject to tensions because of this unstable constellation of forces. Although the Marxist approach has been extensively criticized, it draws attention away from the traditional paradigm of a broadcasting system upon which political forces are exercised. It is no longer perceived as existing in a vacuum but is understood to interact with the political elite. Consequently a more complicated variant emerges. For example, Stuart Hall has commented upon the 'external pressures-resistance model':

> The question of 'external influence' (on broadcasting) is a thoroughly inadequate way of framing the problem. It is predicted on a model of broadcasting which takes at face value its formal and editorial autonomy: external influences are then seen as illegitimately encroaching upon this area of freedom . . . the real relationship between broadcasting, power and ideology is thoroughly mystified by such a model.[48]

A variation on Hall's analysis has appeared in the diverse works on British broadcasting, such as Michael Tracey's *The Production of Political Television*, Anthony Smith's *Television and Political Life*, Ralph Negrine's *Politics and the Mass Media in Britain* and Philip Schlesinger's *Putting 'Reality' Together*. Although these academics do not constitute a particular 'school' of criticism, throughout their work broadcasting is seen neither as 'a temple of liberty nor as a cudgel of oppression but an instrument of political negotiation, neither good nor bad, to be used or abused by those who seek to influence public opinion'.[49] Therefore, although they share Hall's interest in exploring the relations between the broadcasters and the state, they are not driven by his assumptions of class, ideology and indoctrination. Instead, their analysis is concerned with the practicalities of the broadcasting system's position in the body politic. Anthony Smith has shown how an informal nexus of like-minded individuals have been appointed to regulate and manage television. He comments that political leaders may employ television as a 'megaphone' to propagate their interests, yet the medium itself is not inherently structured to be monolithic or persuasive in itself.[50]

From this perspective, broadcasting's political position is contingent on institutional practices, varying understandings of accountability and liberty, periodic tension and accommodation with particular constituencies of the political elite (by passing partisanship), contradictions, and compromises. In particular, a paradox has informed the practices of broadcast journalism and has led to a number of crises in which broadcasters have attempted to reconcile their commitment to balance and objectivity, alongside their obligations to the national interest. Whilst the broadcasters claim to be impartial and objective, they have acknowledged that they are oriented towards the hegemony of the state and have willingly accepted the notion of parliamentary democracy. Roger Bolton has commented:

> The BBC itself has no opinions on matters of public debate but it does demand of its employees professional adherence to certain principles. It supports parliamentary democracy, for example, it opposes racial discrimination, it defines objectivity and balance and requires both of its journalists. . . . Those who do not believe in these things will believe that the pursuit of them involves censorship of other ideas and beliefs, will believe that the organization recruits in its own image, and perpetuates 'bias'.[51]

This was evident during the BBC's response to the 1926 General Strike. As the sole national source of information about the disorder, the BBC stood in a powerful position. Principally, it decided to provide the nation with an impartial account of the strike under the aegis of the law.[52] This meant that the BBC excluded anti-governmental support, as the High Court had declared the strike to be illegal. Reith argued that 'There could be no question about our supporting the Government in general, particularly since the General Strike had been illegal in the High Court. This being so, we were unable to permit anything which was contrary to the spirit of that judgement and which would have prolonged or sought to justify the strike.'[53]

Therefore, instead of overtly supporting the status quo through propaganda or open censorship, the broadcasters employed more subtle techniques such as selection, presentation and omission to tacitly aid the government. For instance, the BBC acquiesced to the government's demand to exclude all forms of oppositional political leadership. The Labour Party leader Ramsay MacDonald and other trade union leaders, despite requesting appearances on the radio, were refused any opportunity to broadcast.[54] Another speaker who was rejected was the Archbishop of Canterbury and news editorials reiterated constant calls for calm.[55]

The BBC's ambiguous position in the General Strike was heightened through the organizational links which were created between its employees and the government who jointly formulated news strategies and shared offices in Admiralty House.[56] Philip Schlesinger has noted:

> In effect the BBC's personnel were mobilized, with the Company itself being declared an 'essential service' by the government 'so that no member of staff could volunteer for other duties'.
>
> But the connection between the BBC and the state went further than discernable organizational links. There was also an ideological consonance between the views of Reith and those of the 'moderate' members of Baldwin's Cabinet. Reith, like the government, took the view that the Strike was a threat to the Constitution.
>
> The BBC was politicized by making it into an emergency service, and incorporating its top echelons into the government information machine ... There was nothing as crude as planting a censor in the makeshift newsroom. It simply was not necessary as Reith and his staff knew what had to be done, and moreover, fully accepted its propriety.[57]

Throughout the strike, the contradiction between impartiality and the national interest meant that the BBC was forced to pass off government intervention. It declared that these decisions were taken in the public interest. This was apparent in 1935 when the BBC proposed a series on the British Constitution to include interviews with the Fascist, Oswald Mosley and the Communist, Harry Pollitt.[58] The Foreign Office objected to Pollitt's involvement as he was a revolutionary. The BBC claimed that these speakers could not be muzzled under the terms of the Charter but only through state intervention. The Foreign Office responded that the question could be resolved if Mosley's anti-democratic undesirability was made the central issue. This proposal was unsatisfactory until the the Postmaster General reminded Reith of the licence's renewal and that it would be wise to comply with the government. The series was dropped and there was no mention of government interference.[59]

Alternatively, the dilemma between serving the principles of impartiality or the national interest has led to the BBC resisting state pressure. For example, during the 1956 Suez crisis the BBC withstood direct governmental pressure by broadcasting critical reports of Anthony Eden's governmental policies. Moreover, when Eden requested a ministerial broadcast, the BBC allowed Labour leader Hugh Gaitskell to reply for the opposition. The severity of Gaitskell's criticisms led Eden to request that the transmission should be toned down.[60] The BBC, however, rejected this proposal. Whilst this may be seen as an example of broadcasting asserting its independence from the state, Negrine has commented that the BBC was duplicating the concerns of parliament as the 'national interest' was unclear, as the government's wider motives were generally being questioned, and as:

> The BBC's handling of the Suez crisis . . . was in line with its own practices; practices it had helped to formulate many decades earlier. Clearly, had there been no political party in opposition to the Government's actions, or widespread disquiet nationally and in the press, the BBC would have found it much more difficult to pursue an impartial line. The reproduction of the Parliamentary struggle, though it does expose broadcasting organizations to numerous threats, does not ultimately place it in mortal danger since it is only balancing competing and legitimated parliamentary views. So long as it employs those general principles which had been established in order to govern the relationship between broadcasters and the political parties in Britain, its independence is secured.[61]

Whilst the the Suez crisis may be perceived as an example of the broadcasters asserting their autonomy from the state, it was apparent that the absence of a defined argument by the government and the political furore that existed, enabled the BBC to be critical of Eden. Elsewhere, throughout its history, broadcasting's political position has been complicated by its accommodation of the national interest during periods of crisis, most notably during the General Strike. In that climate of political turmoil, in which Winston Churchill advocated the commandeering of the BBC for crude propaganda purposes,[62] Reith seized the opportunity to demonstrate to Baldwin's government how broadcasting could be advantageously employed for state interests.[63]

Throughout its history a close relationship between politicians, civil servants and the BBC's management has continued to define relations. Therefore, internal and external constraints have governed the broadcasting institutions' approach to political issues. Consequently, the location of the BBC and ITV in the political system is paradoxical. On one side, state intervention has been aided by the system's minimalist legislation, regulation, and governing ideologies. However, whilst underlying structural characteristics may be seen to be apparent, a number of complexities are present. Many broadcasters believe that they are constitutionally independent from the political elite. Moreover, *de facto* powers have produced an environment that exhibits shared aims, continuity and tension. It is now necessary to consider how the relationship between broadcasters and the political elite has evolved.

Broadcasting's Relations with the Political Elite

The principles of public service broadcasting were drawn from a concordance of interests between broadcasters and politicians which had
evolved in the mid-1920s. An expedient bargaining process defined
relations. Raymond Williams outlined three factors which underpinned
the British broadcasting system. These comprise: the nationalization of
culture fomented through Britain's early industrialization and the small
geographic area for communications; the easy assimilation of public service values, based upon paternalism and responsibility, by broadcasters
due to an established version of the national culture perpetrated through
an unusually compact ruling class;[64] and:

> the character of the British State which, because of the compactness of
> its ruling class, proceeded in many matters through appointment and
> delegation rather than by centralised state administration. This permit-
> ted the emergence of a state-regulated and state-sponsored public cor-
> poration which was yet not subject to detailed state control. The flexibility
> which was latent in this kind of solution, though continually a matter
> of dispute, permitted the emergence of an independent corporate broad-
> casting policy, in which the independence was at once real, especially
> in relation to political parties and temporary administrations, and quali-
> fied, by its definition in terms of pre-existing cultural hegemony.[65]

As a consequence, the system's realities contrasted with its formal
objectives. Whilst British broadcasting acquired a prescriptive set of
legislative and regulatory rules over the years, state power has been
characterized as being minimalist. Throughout this period, there was
no media department of state and regulations were left to be interpreted by the regulatory bodies. However, it was through this apparently loose form of political organization that state power was exercised.
Broadcasting reflected the British political tradition of an unwritten
constitution whereby authority has been applied through the informal
practices of precedence, bargaining and dealing.[66] The private nature
of the relationship between broadcasters and politicians meant that the
system proved to be more responsive to discreet pressure than legal
intervention. In turn, the broadcasting institutions' freedoms have been
defined in a set of parameters. A number of understandings have underpinned British broadcasting.

The concept of balance provided a core understanding to the relationship between broadcasters and politicians. This led to shared aims
and a concurrence on what is politically acceptable. Balance has extended beyond party politics, as it has structured the whole system 'as
a direct restriction on programme output; between public service and
commercial impetus; between centre and periphery; professionalism

and accountability; integrity of broadcasting and access'.[67] This has meant that impartiality and objectivity are to be contained within the dominant political consensus. In turn, this principle has been enhanced by the BBC's, and later Independent Television News' (ITN), practice of recruiting from a narrow strata of university graduates, in particular Oxbridge, whose class background made them predisposed to established standards. Further, institutional practices have tended to reinforce this ideological adherence to the normative practices. The BBC News and Current Affairs departments have employed a 'referring up' system in which the individual maintained autonomy as editorial independence was devolved and s/he was expected to only take orders from his/her immediate superior. This centralized chain of command has served a political purpose by enforcing conformity within the corporation.[68]

This has contributed to the doctrine of 'self-censorship'. Both the BBC and ITN are aware that they must operate in acceptable norms. As they conform to parliamentary democracy, broadcasters are loath to propagate extra-parliamentary positions and morally objectionable positions such as racism in spite of proclaiming impartiality. However, self-censorship has extended to politically sensitive subjects in which the national interest has been perceived as overriding impartiality. In particular, the BBC's coverage of Northern Ireland has been closely guarded by editorial control, managerial intervention and an, albeit sometimes reluctant, acceptance of the British state's position.[69] However, state power can be exercised through more tangible, if similarly covert methods of control, as follows.

The state has had a direct and indirect control over broadcasting's financial structure. The government has exercised its power through the annual setting of the licence fee and was instrumental in channelling these central funds to the BBC. For many years, the government was only prepared to relinquish a small part of the licence fee. Although the BBC argued that it was directly funded by its listeners and viewers, in reality, governments have effectively directed the flow of money raised by the fee.[70] This economic control has been tacitly employed to gain a financial leverage over the BBC. Political control has been mediated through the appointment process. The BBC governors and IBA board members have been state-appointed, first by the Postmaster General, and later by the Home Secretary. These individuals are usually drawn from the narrow strata of the great and good (public figures, industrialists, academics, trade union leaders) and their social composition would indicate that state interests would, at the very least, be complemented. Moreover, throughout the development of British broadcasting governments have attempted to place political allies and sympathizers in important positions.

Most notably, Harold Wilson attempted to force his will upon the broadcasters through the politicization of the appointment process. During the late 1960s and early 1970s broadcasting's relations with the Wilson government (and his Opposition) were strained. The Labour government felt that the BBC had been infiltrated by Conservatives and distrusted the Director-General Hugh Greene. This led to Wilson appointing Lord Hill, the former Conservative MP and chairman of the ITA, to the chairmanship of the BBC Board of Governors, in order to temper Greene.[71] After Greene's retirement this came to a head, when the BBC showed a programme in 1971 entitled *Yesterday's Men* concerning Wilson's shadow cabinet. Wilson claimed that he had been the victim of the BBC's political bias and as a result the BBC reformed its institutional practices.[72] Hill, in his capacity as chair, intervened to judge upon the editorial content of the programme, forced the BBC to apologize and took on an executive role.[73] This marked the first intrusion of the governors in the domain of management.[74] Hill's actions may be seen to have had an overtly political purpose by taming the BBC.

The British broadcasting system has been structured, therefore, through a mixture of legal rules, regulation and precedence, so that political power might be covertly exercised. It should be remembered that both the BBC and ITV enjoyed tacit support from the political elite. Ultimately, the state's influence over broadcasting demonstrates a deficiency in the notion of an independent public service broadcasting system.[75] Instead political interests have channelled through a concordance of ideologies, purpose, and consensualism. This was made inadvertently conspicuous by the 1936 Ullswater Committee:

> Where the interests of the State appear to be at all closely involved, it is open to the Corporation to consult a Minister or Department informally and of its own accord. This method leaves decision and discretion in the hands of the Corporation.[76]

Within these unwritten rules a number of ambiguities exist. Politicians have been ambivalent towards television. All politicians enjoy using televison to propagate their messages. However, it can expose their weaknesses and flaws to the general public. This has promoted a series of political tensions when governments have felt that their interests have been undermined.

Conclusion

The British broadcasting system has evolved in an incremental fashion through a mixture of political negotiation, interventionist regulation, precedent and institutional development. Underpinning these factors has been the concept of public service broadcasting. This concept emerged from the compromise between manufacturing and state interests and resulted in the British Broadcasting Corporation. It was seen as the most socially useful mechanism to utilize efficiently a vital national resource which was limited to a narrow band of airwaves. The first BBC Managing Director and Director-General John Reith tapped into a series of arguments, supporting the 'public service utility' concept, which had curried favour amongst the contemporary political elite. In spite of the commercial push that gave rise to ITV, the 1954 Television Act created an interventionist regulator, the ITA (later IBA), and used normative methods of control to shape the independent system. The authority had the power to enforce public service schedules on the contractors. Although ITV is strictly composed of private companies who are funded by advertising, the system has retained many of the public sector's characteristics.

This development was mediated by the cultural concerns of the 1962 Pilkington Report, which resulted in a levy being placed upon the ITV companies to stem excessive profitability and direct money into quality programmes. It was exacerbated by the cartelism which accompanied the introduction of networking. This was later enhanced in the complementary schedules between BBC and ITV. Moreover, as the BBC became the training ground for ITV executives, technicians and administrators common ideologies relating to programme output and the worth of the public service broadcasting institutions were promoted. Indeed, institutional practices, as much as programming, defined the meaning of the public services. The regulatory bodies also strengthened the trend toward convergence.

These developments have a political dimension. When broadcasting's growth is viewed through the perspective of its central dilemma – the rights of the individual to access information, from a limited national resource, against the needs of the state to regulate that resource to maximum efficient potential – it is apparent that the public service resolution has remained contingent on the goodwill of the political elite.[77] This illustrates that a subtle form of state hegemony has been negotiated through British broadcasting's ideological, cultural and institutional practices. Although political disputes have occurred between broadcasters and the government, a number of informal linkages between broadcasting and political elite were manufactured, alongside a series of ground-rules which were demarcated through practices such as self-regulation. This understanding harks back to the crucial phase of negotiation between Reith and the government to transform the BBC from a company to a corporation, which coincided with the 1926 General Strike. Throughout this strike the BBC demonstrated its worth to the government by providing a national information service which was legitimized through the concept of impartiality. The strike also demonstrated that the company would provide tacit support to the state through its belief in parliamentary democracy, the law and its constitutional position. Further, the BBC, in particular, has been subjected to the government's ability to set the licence fee.

The British broadcasting system was founded upon public service principles. It has been governed by interventionist regulators and organized as a duopoly. The BBC and ITV competed for audiences rather than funds, as their finances were assured by the licence fee and advertising. The broadcasting institutions were independent, although political power was mediated through an informal system based upon consensualism. The system appeared to be secure. However, as we shall see, alternative models for broadcasting were to become more prevalent. These coincided with several developments; the rise in new technologies, financial inequity between the public and commercial sector, a political climate characterized by conflict rather than consensualism and the development of an ideological position which questioned the integrity of the public service model.

Throughout its history broadcasting did not alter due to societal needs. Instead of a dialectic between the public and broadcasting, a compact between the state and the broadcasting institutions has defined their growth. Due to the lack of social adaptability the institution's values became an end in themselves and the system became removed from the dilemma it was meant to resolve. As we shall discover, several variations of this critique became apparent throughout the Annan and Peacock debates.

Further Reading

Asa Briggs, *The History of Broadcasting in the United Kingdom: Volume I, The Birth of Broadcasting; Volume II, The Golden age of Wireless; Volume III, The War of Words; Volume IV Sound and Vision*, Oxford University Press, 1961, 1965, 1970 and 1979.

——, *Governing the BBC*, BBC, 1979.

——, *The BBC: The First Fifty Years*, Oxford University Press, 1985.

Broadcasting Research Group, *The Public Service Idea*, BRU, 1985.

Tom Burns, *The BBC: Public Institution and Private World*, MacMillan, 1977.

R. H. Coase, *British Broadcasting: A Study in Monopoly*, Longmans Green, 1950.

James Curran and Jean Seaton, *Power without Responsibility: The Press and Broadcasting in Britain*, Routledge, 1991 (4th edn).

Kenneth Dyson and Peter Humphreys, with Ralph Negrine and Jean-Paul Simon, *Broadcasting and New Media Policies in Western Europe*, Routledge, 1988.

LIVERPOOL JOHN MOORES UNIVERSITY
LEARNING SERVICES

Goldie, Grace Wyndham, *Facing the Nation: Television and Politics 1936–1976*, The Bodley Head, 1977.

Peter Golding, Graham Murdock and Philip Schlesinger (eds), *Communicating Politics: Mass communications and the political process*, Leicester University Press, 1986.

Ian McIntyre, *The Expense of Glory: A Life of John Reith*, Harper Collins, 1993.

Ralph Negrine, *Politics and the Mass Media in Britain*, Routledge, 1994 (2nd edn).

Jeremy Potter, *Independent Television in Britain, Volume 3: Politics and Control 1968–90*, MacMillan, 1989.

J. C. W. Reith, *Broadcast over Britain*, Hodder & Stoughton, 1924.

J. C. W. Reith, *Into the Wind*, Hodder & Stoughton, 1949.

Paddy Scannel and David Cardiff, *Serving the Nation: Public Service Broadcasting before World War Two*, Open University Press, 1982.

Philip Schlesinger, *Putting 'Reality' Together*, Routledge, 1987.

Bernard Sendell, *Independent Television in Britain, Volume 1: Origin and Foundation*, MacMillan, 1982; *Volume 2: Expansion and Change*, MacMillan, 1983.

Colin Seymour-Ure, *The British Press and Broadcasting since 1945*, Basil Blackwell, 1991.

Anthony Smith (ed.), *British Broadcasting*, Sources for Contemporary Issues, David & Charles, 1974.

Anthony Smith (ed.), *Television and Political Life: Studies in Six European Countries*, MacMillan, 1979.

Charles Stuart (ed.), *The Reith Diaries*, Collins, 1975.

Michael Tracey, *The Production of Political Television*, Routledge, 1978.

Jeremy Tunstall, *The Media in Britain*, Constable, 1983.

E. G. Wedell, *Broadcasting and Public Policy*, Michael Joseph Books, 1968.

H. H. Wilson, *Pressure Group: The Campaign for Commercial Television*, Secker & Warburg, 1961.

Notes

1   Nicholas Garnham, *Structures of Broadcasting*, BFI, 1980, p. 15.

2   E. G. Wedell, *Broadcasting and Public Policy*, Michael Joseph Books, 1968, p. 51.

3   This reference does not apply to any one single perspective, for instance, neo-Marxist, pluralistic etc. It can be determined from commentators such as Wedell, *Broadcasting and Public Policy*, 1968, to the Marxist (either Althussarian or Gramscian) accounts of the 1970s and from the political economist Nicholas Garnham. See for example *Structures of Television*, BFI, 1980 or Stuart Hall *'External Influences upon Broadcasting'*, Birmingham Occasional Paper, 1972, to the less implicitly moral and more quizzical approaches of Anthony Smith in 'Mysteries of the Modus Vivendi' in Anthony Smith (ed.) *Television and Political Life*, MacMillan, 1979.

4   Jeremy Tunstall, 'Media Policy Dilemmas and Indecisions', *Parliamentary Affairs*, vol. 37, no. 3 Summer 1984, p. 315 which states, '1982 saw the birth of the fourth major policy-making cycle in the British media since 1945.'

5   The rise of new or different British broadcasting issues has occupied the concerns of many commentators. See, for instance Ralph Negrine, *Politics and the*

Mass Media in Britain, Routledge, 1988; Raymond Kuhn (ed.), *The Politics of Broadcasting*, Croom Helm 1986; Stuart Hood and Garret O'Leary, *Questions on Broadcasting*, Methuen, 1990; Kenneth Dyson and Peter Humphreys, *Broadcasting and New Media Policies in Western Europe*, Routledge, 1988 etc.

6 See Jeremy Tunstall, 'Media Policy Dilemmas and Indecisions', op. cit., pp. 310–26.

7 Nicholas Garnham, *Structures of Broadcasting*, p. 15.

8 See James Curran and Jean Seaton, *Power without Responsibility: The Press and Broadcasting in Britain*, Routledge, 1991 (4th edn), p. 120.

9 Ibid.

10 Kenneth Dyson and Peter Humphreys, *Broadcasting and New Media Policies*, p. 64.

11 Broadcasting Research Unit, *The Public Service idea in British Broadcasting – Main Principles*, 1985/6.

12 Kenneth Dyson and Peter Humphreys, *Broadcasting and New Media Policies*, p. 100.

13 See for instance Grace Wyndham Goldie, *Facing the Nation: Television and Politics 1936–1976*, The Bodley Head, 1977.

14 E. G. Wedell, *Broadcasting and Public Policy*, p. 51.

15 James Curran and Jean Seaton, *Power without Responsibility*, p. 133.

16 Asa Briggs, *The BBC: The First Fifty Years*, Oxford University Press, 1985, p. 89.

17 H. H. Wilson, *Pressure Group: The Campaign for Commercial Television*, Secker & Warburg, 1961, p. 35.

18 Beveridge Report, in James Curran and Jean Seaton, *Power without Responsibility* (3rd edn), p. 132.

19 Stuart Hood, *On Television*, Pluto Press, 1987 (3rd edn), p. 63.

20 Stephen Lambert, *Television with a Difference?*, BFI Publishing, 1982, p. 9.

21 James Curran and Jean Seaton, *Power without Responsibility* (3rd edn), p. 179.

22 Gerald Beedle, in Burton Paulu, *British Broadcasting: Radio and Television in the United Kingdom*, Macmillan, 1981, p. 156.

23 This was eventually replaced by the 'Big Five' (Thames, LWT, Granada, Yorkshire and ATV) after the 1968 reallocation of franchises.

24 James Curran and Jean Seaton, *Power without Responsibility*, pp. 185–93.

25 Ibid., p. 187.

26 Bernard Sendell, *Independent Television in Britain: Volume 1 Origin and Foundation 1946–62*, MacMillan, 1982, p. 63.

27 It should be noted that the levy system had obvious attractions to the Treasury, who had been unable to gain a hold on the companies' money.

28 Bernard Sendell, *Independent Television in Britain: Volume 2: Expansion and Change*, Macmillan, p. 172.

29 Christopher Dunkley, *Television Today and Tomorrow*, Penguin Books, 1985, p. 80.

30 Interview with Towyn Mason, Deputy Secretary to the BBC Governors, 28 July 1992.

31 Nicholas Garnham, *Structures of Broadcasting*, p. 32.

32 Charles Stuart (ed.), *The Reith Diaries*, Collins, 1975, p. 125.

33 In this respect, Reith was influenced by elite group fears that traditional high culture, the domain of artistic endeavour, was being subsumed by popular culture. Therefore, it may be argued that the BBC's programming principles referred to an agenda set out in Matthew Arnold's 1867 book *Culture and Anarchy*, London: Cambridge University Press, 1960 (repr.).

34 There are a number of distinct parallels between the BBC's position in the late

1950s and the issues it has faced, and continues to face during the 1980s and 1990s. The BBC's audience share is predicted to drop to 23 per cent by the end of the decade. The current Director-General John Birt's response has been to define the BBC as a specialized public service broadcaster, providing programmes which could not be made in the increasingly commercial ITV sector or on satellite services.

35 Ralph Negrine, *Politics and the Mass Media*, p. 101.
36 Huw Weldon, in Tom Burns, *The BBC: Public Institution and Private World*, MacMillan, 1977, p. 55.
37 Harold Wilson, in E. G. Wedell, *Broadcasting and Public Policy*, p. 52.
38 See Asa Briggs, *The BBC: The First Fifty Years*, p. 17. For further details see Asa Briggs, *Governing the BBC*, BBC, 1979.
39 The Whitley Document quoted from Anthony Smith (ed.), *British Broadcasting*, David & Charles Sources for Contemporary Issues, 1974, pp. 60–1.
40 Kenneth Dyson and Peter Humphreys, *Broadcasting and New Media Policies*, p. 255.
41 Ibid., pp. 257–8.
42 See for instance Anthony Smith (ed.), *Television and Political Life: Studies in Six European Countries*, MacMillan, 1979, pp. 1–40.
43 See for instance Philip Schlesinger, *Putting 'Reality' Together*, Routledge, 1987.
44 Raymond Kuhn (ed.), *The Politics of Broadcasting*, p. 6.
45 Ralph Negrine, *Politics and the Mass Media*, pp. 120–1 with additional quotations from Anthony Smith, *Television and Political Life*, p. 21.
46 See for instance ibid., pp. 78–83.
47 Jean Seaton and Ben Pimlott (eds), *The Media in British Politics*, Avebury, Aldershot, 1987, p. ix.
48 Stuart Hall, *External Influences upon Broadcasting*, p. 8.
49 Jean Seaton and Ben Pimlott, p. ix.
50 For further information, see Anthony Smith, *Television and Political Life*, Ch. 1.
51 Roger Bolton, in Peter Golding, Graham Murdock and Philip Schlesinger (eds), *Communicating Politics*, Leicester University Press, 1986, p. 97.
52 See Asa Briggs, *The BBC: The First Fifty Years*, pp. 364–6.
53 John Reith, in Tom Burns, *The BBC: Public Institution and Private World*, MacMillan, 1977, p. 17.
54 Philip Schlesinger, *Putting 'Reality' Together*, Routledge 1987, p. 17. Reith disagreed with these tactics of omission, but complied with the government's wishes. For further reading, see James Curran and Jean Seaton, *Power Without Responsibility*, Routledge, (4th edn), 1991; Ralph Negrine, *Politics and the Mass Media in Britain*, Routledge, (2nd edn), 1994; Asa Briggs, *The Birth of Broadcasting*, Oxford University Press, 1961; Michael Tracey, *The Production of Political Television*, Routledge Kegan Paul, 1975 and in particular Ian McIntyre, *The Expense of Glory: A Life of John Reith*, HarperCollins, 1993, pp. 141–8.
55 Ibid., p. 17.
56 Ibid.
57 Ibid., pp. 17–18.
58 James Curran and Jean Seaton, (4th edn), p. 143.
59 Ibid., pp. 143–4. A Cabinet minute stated (p. 144): 'It would be neither true nor desirable to state publicly that the talks would be an "embarrassment to the Government" at the present time. But it would be true to say that they would not be in the national interest.'
60 For more details see Ralph Negrine, *Politics and the Mass Media* (1st edn), pp. 125–8.

61   Ibid., p. 128.

62   Philip Schlesinger, *Putting 'Reality' Together*, p. 18.

63   The strike occurred during a delicate phase in the negotiations transforming the BBC into a corporation. See Ian McIntyre, *The Expense of Glory*, p. 147: 'Reith's performance during the nine days of the General Strike cannot be judged in a vacuum, because he knew throughout that he had unfinished business with the government. The strike took place after the publication of the Crawford Report but before it had been debated in Parliament, and there was still much to be done if the Post Office was to be won over to his way of thinking on a number of outstanding issues.'

64   Raymond Williams, *Television: Technology and Cultural Form*, Fontana, 1974, pp. 33–4.

65   Ibid.

66   Tim Madge, *Beyond the BBC: Broadcasters and the Public in the 1980s*, MacMillan, 1989, p. 36.

67   Ibid., pp. 38–9.

68   For further details see Philip Schlesinger, *Putting 'Reality' Together*, pp. 163–204.

69   For further details, see ibid., pp. 204–43 and Liz Curtis, *Ireland: The Propaganda War*, Pluto Press, 1984.

70   Stuart Hood and Garrett O'Leary, *Questions on Broadcasting*, Metheun, 1990, pp. 11–12.

71   For further details, see Michael Tracey, *The Production of Political Television*. Tracey, in an interview with Dr Ralph Negrine for City of London Polytechnic Media Services (unpublished circa 1989), has also suggested that a lot of this tension was manufactured by the personal political style of Harold Wilson, who resented his treatment. After his electoral success in 1966, Wilson agreed to be interviewed by the BBC on the train from Liverpool (where he held his constituency) to London. At great cost, the BBC had arranged for an outside broadcast interview (the first from a moving train). However, at the last moment, Wilson reneged and refused to be interviewed by the BBC. Instead, he gave an interview to ITN, who had a film crew on the train, thereby giving them the scoop. The BBC was left with a large cost and no interview with the then Prime Minister. Lord Hill's appointment is also commented on in some detail in Grace Wyndham Goldie, *Facing the Nation: Television and Politics 1936–1976*, The Bodley Head, 1977, pp. 306–7.

72   For further details see Michael Tracey, *The Production of Political Television*, Chapter 10. Tracey provides a detailed study of the creation and development of this programme, the subsequent furore, the negotiations between the Director-General, Charles Curran and Harold Wilson, and reforms in Current Affairs programme practices.

73   Ibid., p. 195.

74   Ibid.

75   See Ralph Negrine's chapter in Raymond Kuhn (ed.), *The Politics of Broadcasting*.

76   *The Report of the Broadcasting Committee (Ullswater Committee) 1936*, in Tom Burns, p. 20.

77   See Nicholas Garnham, *Structures of Broadcasting*.

5

Whither Public Service Broadcasting?

Part One: British Broadcasting from the late 1970s to the 1990 Broadcasting Act

Introduction

Public service broadcasting incorporated many strengths and weaknesses. The positive principles of educating, informing and entertaining underpinned the system. Concurrently, the BBC and ITV competed for audiences rather than revenues. Thus, programmes were often of a high quality. Further, British broadcasting was seen to withstand governmental interventions through the licence fee, advertising, regulatory buffers and the commitment to impartiality.

Conversely, broadcasting's public accountability has been questioned. Due to its duopolistic structure it has been closed to new entrants, thereby upholding the status quo. Moreover, the broadcasters' professionalism produced an impervious attitude, principally in the BBC, which took no account of the audience. Although broadcasting was founded on freedom, independence and impartiality, its democratic role was criticized. In particular, the BBC, an 'institution within the constitution', has been subject to overt and tacit political pressure.

Left- and right-wing critics accused the BBC and the ITV companies of being closed institutions who under-represented many societal groups. From the perspective of the left, broadcasting was an agent of subtle propaganda. The gap between left-wing analysis and the construction of an anti-statist, liberal broadcasting system, was filled by the writings of Raymond Williams and Anthony Smith. Both argued for a public service system which encouraged greater access and openness. We will consider how this critique affected the debate engendered by the 1977 *Report of the Committee on the Future of Broadcasting (The Annan Report)*.

By the 1980s, as the radical right-wing predominated, the market-liberal critique of British broadcasting became prevalent. This was 'pushed' by the introduction of new technologies (cable, satellite, tele-communications), market-liberal ideologies and political will. The 1986 *Report of the Committee on the Financing of the BBC (The Peacock Report)* was underpinned by Adam Smith's concept of the market providing political liberty. It recommended electronic publishing and consumer sovereignty. Further, it argued that citizenship could be exercised through consumerism. Whilst citizenship presupposed collective action in the quest for equality, fraternity and individual liberty, consumerism advocated that individuals should pursue 'private solutions to public problems by purchasing a commodity'.[1]

In this chapter we will discuss how these theories were implemented through British broadcasting policy and will assess whether Channel Four, built on a publishing model funded through advertising revenue and the ITV companies' support, proved to be innovative and representative of minorities. Further, we will consider how certain market-liberal ideas entered terrestrial broadcasting through the 1990 Broadcasting Act. We will determine whether the policy process became compromised by the competing interests of economic liberalization and political authoritarianism. Moreover, we will ask if the 1990 Act was responsible for broadcastings' commercialization rather than any outright reform.

Further, we will consider whether alternative agendas have been pursued through these models or if they restricted public choice. Finally, the chapter will establish the context for the current developments affecting public service broadcasting into the second millennium. Presently, the imperatives of privatization, deregulation and consumerism are impacting on mass communications: we will bridge the gap between the traditional media paradigms and the explosion of communication technologies and their impact on citizen's rights in the late 1990s.

The Annan Debate and Channel Four

Throughout the 1970s, the fourth channel debate illustrated the major issues in broadcasting policy including editorial control, funding, structure and the broadcasters' relationship with the state. This was partly due to the political climate, as the debate occurred during Labour's period in power. However, primarily it reflected the increased concern over broadcasting's organization.[2]

Broadcasting and anti-statist liberalism

The growth of media studies during the 1970s subjected broadcasting to extensive criticism.[3] First, the system was accused of insularity due to its closed nature and lack of independent producers. Second, there were complaints about broadcasting's public accountability. The BBC and ITV companies were accused of being monopolistic and unrepresentative. In effect, public service broadcasting had failed to resolve the dilemma between governments' desires to control information and the public's democratic rights. Although broadcasting was a scarce national resource, state interests had outweighed the citizen's freedom of choice and the broadcaster's need to express his/her perception of the truth.

Such thinking was heavily influenced by Raymond Williams who argued that mass communications should enhance the learning process and restrict elitism. As broadcasting represented social rather than fiscal capital, he rejected the market. Rather, he suggested a cooperative trust which would encourage communal broadcasting and democracy. Consequently, different broadcasting models were proposed to encourage pluralism, diversity and viewer choice. They were shaped into a coherent perspective by the Standing Conference on Broadcasting (SCOB) who campaigned for a central funding scheme, increased worker participation, and a school for research. In particular, SCOB member Anthony Smith advocated an 'open access policy' in which contracted freelance broadcasting groups would produce their alternative programmes with the appropriate technical back-up:

> What (has) to be achieved is a form of institutional control wedded to a different doctrine from the existing broadcasting authorities, to a doctrine of openness rather than balance, to expression rather than neutralization.[4]

The Annan Report

Whilst the Annan Report supported the public service system, it concurred with the reformers over the fourth channel. It felt that Anthony Smith's National Television Foundation provided the institutional framework to encourage plurality. Annan replaced this with the Open Broadcasting Authority (OBA) in order to exercise some form of editorial and regulatory supervision over 'publishing on the airwaves'.[5] The OBA would operate like a publisher by broadcasting programmes made by independent companies, rather than producing them. The OBA's liabilities would be limited to interventions over libel, incitement to riot and obscenity. This light-touch authority should have enjoyed as much freedom as Parliament deemed possible.

In contrast to ITV's vertical integration, the fourth channel would transmit either programmes made by the ITV companies or, more importantly, contract independent producers to encourage community access. It should be financed through a mixture of sponsorship, interest groups and block advertising. Further, it decided that the OBA would sell spot advertising space rather than the ITV companies. This multiplicity of funding was conceived to ensure political independence. The OBA broke away from the traditional mode of broadcasting regulation. It appeared to be a desirable model, encouraging diversity on the new station. However, those who favoured it remained doubtful about its practical application due to 'the difficulty of persuading any government to relax its controlling powers over broadcasting'.[6]

The Channel Four policy process

Throughout the policy process, Annan's more radical recommendations were diluted through political will, lobbying and compromise. Initially, the Labour government was split between Home Secretary Merlyn Rees, who rejected the proposals as being unnecessary, impractical and too expensive, and the Prime Minister James Callaghan who favoured reform. In the event, this dispute was forgotten with the installation of Margaret Thatcher's government in May 1979. The Home Secretary William Whitelaw had opposed the OBA whilst in opposition, agreeing with the IBA that it could not sell advertising against the ITV companies if it was required to be innovative. He favoured Jeremy Isaacs' (then Director of Thames Television) compromise, in which the fourth channel would be an electronic publisher of a distinct service, but be regulated by the IBA.[7] Moreover, the ITV companies would sell the channel's advertising and support it through a levy, thereby securing its innovative status. The fourth channel would be different, but not that different:[8]

> We want a fourth channel that will neither simply compete with ITV-1 nor merely be complementary to it. We want a fourth channel that everyone will watch some of the time and no-one all of the time.[9]

The 1980 Broadcasting Act created a fourth channel regulated by the IBA in which the ITV companies would sell its advertising. It would commission programmes from independent companies who, through favourable financial rules, were to increase their output. The channel was required to be educative, innovative, experimental and to cater for minority audiences by providing a diversity of programmes, thereby ensuring a multiplicity of voices. Accordingly, the IBA established Channel Four, a corporate body consisting of a chair, board and Chief Executive who formulated policy, commissioned programmes, acquired programmes, planned the schedule and appointed the staff. The board consisted of twelve directors, of whom four came from ITV and five from the independent sector. Its membership included the former Trade Secretary Edward Dell as chair and film-maker Richard Attenborough as deputy-chair, and ironically Anthony Smith himself. Managerial positions were occupied by experienced and new broadcasters including Chief Executive Jeremy Isaacs and Controller of Programmes Paul Bonner. The channel was largely autonomous, although the IBA set the annual budget, intervened by appointing non-executive board members, and could determine the schedule between Channel Four and ITV. The programming policy was to commission alternative, minority programmes and encourage new talent, whilst complementing the ITV service. The IBA maintained that:

> This means not only that it [Channel Four] will provide as far as possible a choice at any one time between two programmes appealing to different interests, it means also that both the fourth channel and the present ITV service will be able to schedule programmes with less concern than is possible on only a single channel without the potential loss of a majority of the audience.[10]

Channel Four

Channel Four slotted into a unique, but complementary, position within public service broadcasting. Under Isaacs' leadership, it commenced operations in 1982. A wide variety of programmes were commissioned which proved to be popular, innovative and different. It courted political and popular controversy. It also boosted the British film industry by funding projects to be shown in the cinema and on television. Moreover, as the channel was guaranteed its funding, it did not have to chase ratings. Thus, minority interest programmes could be scheduled at peak times.

Isaacs left in 1987, to be replaced, surprisingly, by the then Head of BBC programming Michael Grade. Grade had a populist track-record and there was disquiet about his appointment. However, whilst modifying and commercializing Isaacs' approach, he continued to commission and schedule innovative programmes. These have sometimes been controversial but often popular. Further, he proved to be a successful politician, stemming any proposed privatization of the channel, and has recently become the spokesman for public service broadcasting. Yet, as we shall see, Channel Four's financial position was to alter substantially as a result of the 1990 Broadcasting Act. Moreover, some critics have suggested that the channel became more conformist and marginalized minority groups through its scheduling practices.

Ultimately, Channel Four marked a compromise between greater pluralism and regulatory order. The fourth channel policy cycle and subsequent development of the channel demonstrated how informal pressures and precedent could stem outstanding reform. Annan's pluralistic model had challenged the traditional public service tenets.

It considered broadcasting's social purposes through the provision of freedom of choice and speech. It was reflective of Locke and Mills's anti-statist, liberal-democratic arguments. In some respects, these ideas would be echoed in the market-liberal model advocated by the 1986 Peacock Report. However, a substantive difference existed between Annan and Peacock, as the latter would argue for the *market* as the provider for a plurality of voices.

The Peacock Debate and Report

The Peacock Report was *the* libertarian document to question public service broadcasting. It believed that consumer preferences were served through a competitive market.[11] Thus, it provided market-liberal recommendations based on Peter Jay's concept of electronic publishing. The report marks the point at which previously peripheral market-liberal arguments challenged the status quo.

The market-liberal approach towards broadcasting

The market-liberal interpretation of broadcasting originated with the libertarian concept of society as a competitive market in which individuals are the source of enterprise and wealth.[12] State powers are limited to sustaining individual welfare. As political elites qualify the individual's rights, policy can only be warranted if its benefits outweigh the costs to the individual. In turn, social communication must satisfy individual preferences, rather than exist as an unprovable public service good. Individual economic liberalization equates with societal benefit. Thus, the main objective for broadcasting was maximum consumer welfare. As programmes constituted leisure or luxury goods, alternative funding methods were necessary. Successful broadcasters combined sound commercial judgement with cost-efficient programming.

If public service tenets do not impinge upon the individual's right to choose, they are acceptable. However, this was not the case in British broadcasting, as regulation had inefficiently allocated resources. Broadcasting was unfavourably compared to the press. In the free newspaper market anyone could buy and launch a paper. Conversely, in the closed world of broadcasting, opportunities were restricted by the narrow range of frequencies and the duopolistic structure. Whereas the press was accountable through the market, broadcasting was regulated and controlled. Television, therefore, had been subject to regulatory capture. For instance, as the IBA enforced franchise agreements on the concept of *quality*, its monitoring of the franchisees had been weakened due to the absence of explicit performance criteria. This made it impossible to judge the regulator's accountability. It meant that the IBA was susceptible to clientelism as it had taken on the industries' assumptions of 'quality' and 'taste'. Thus it has 'no option other than to rely upon information supplied by (the) broadcasting organization which they are responsible for regulating'.[13]

However, regulators were not only captured but were responsible for broadcasting cartels. For instance, as the IBA imposed public service commitments on the network, it inadvertently let the powerful ITV companies 'carve up' the system through networking agreements to meet their obligations. This was mutually beneficial for the regulator and for the larger companies who sold their programmes to the smaller groups. In turn, the minor regional franchisees benefited as they kept their running costs down by not providing networked programmes. Consequently, the companies enjoyed healthy profit margins and thwarted any commercial competition. Cento Veljanovski comments:

> It was essentially a 'cartel-within-a-cartel' backed and enforced by the IBA which happened to be officially 'the broadcaster'. No one contractor could shirk, deflect or renege because the regulator enforced the cartel.[14]

These arguments questioned the financial structure and philosophy of public service broadcasting. R. H. Coase suggested that chance circumstances surrounding the early development of broadcasting had established the BBC's monopoly.[15] He attacked the Reithian belief that the BBC should be a public corporation founded on the 'brute force of monopoly'. The Institute of Economic Affairs (IEA) was critical of the lack of competition for revenues between the public and commercial broadcasters.[16] The Institute of Economic Affairs's Hobart Papers argued that television could be funded through subscription or pay-per-view programmes, the BBC should incorporate advertising to replace the licence fee, new channels should be utilized and governmental powers must be reduced. Therefore, through market-sensitive practices greater *choice* would be exercised:

> Governments ought to organize as much competition as can be crammed into the present wavelengths, and welcome any technical developments in broadcasting or wire that may enlarge the scope for still more competition in the future.[17]

Sir Robert Fraser, the first Director-General of the Independent Television Association (ITA), proposed a people's television in which the key principles would be 'popular pleasures and interests'. He argued that broadcasting should not be controlled by rigid institutions providing a mix of morally enlightening programmes. Instead, it should be lightly regulated and composed of private contractors. Programming should respond to popular choice rather than the imposed views of the broadcasting elite.

From the 1950s to the 1970s, the market model remained confined
to policy cells. The market had been restricted due to technical qualifications, financial restrictions and elite consensualism. However, due
to the new media technologies, by the mid-1980s broadcasting was ripe
for reform.

Market liberals and the new media technologies

In 1983, Cento Veljanovski and W. D. Bishop argued that cable systems, funded through subscription, could publish diverse, independently produced programmes. This would establish a *private* relationship
between the operators and subscribers. Consequently, these services
were leisure goods and free from the public interest. Therefore, they
contended that the public provision or regulation of the cable industry would restrict expansion. Competitive market practices would encourage a flexible response to changing demands, individual initiative,
and experimentation. To minimize the need for regulation and ensure
the efficient use of resources British Telecom should be devolved and
broadcasting deregulated.[18]

In turn, the Adam Smith Institute's 1984 *Omega Report* developed
a privatized model for British broadcasting. It recommended that BBC1
be funded through advertising; the IBA should be more commercially
aware and less dogmatic; and that BBC TV News should be separately
funded through a levy on BBC services and from subscriptions taken
by cable operators. Although this was an unofficial report, it articulated
a populist antipathy for the broadcasting elite's power to determine
the public's viewing habits. Commercialism and market forces became
the criteria for quality.[19]

Peter Jay's 'electronic publishing'

The economist Peter Jay argued that broadcasting's quality would be
indicated by the *access* it afforded to the consumer to determine what
s/he wanted to watch. Therefore, as the new technologies (cable, satellite) provided a wider number of channels, the viewer might fully participate in a form of electronic publishing. A nationally integrated cable
system could be developed through a mixture of public and private
funds. As it would be universally available, consumers could subscribe
to view individual programmes. In a true market-place the consumer
would dial for a programme and pay an appropriate charge in relation
to the programme's popularity. The television set (or radio) would be
like a telephone as the user selected the connection s/he wanted. Just
as 'electronic publishing' would revolutionize the individual's access
to programmes, it meant that the production and regulation of broad-

casting would be transformed. The broadcasting economy would no longer be vertically integrated. Instead, it would respond to new, independent production companies. They could produce anything they liked for cable in exchange for a transmission fee.[20]

To create a free broadcasting market in which the individual exercised not only his/her economic but also political freedoms, the BBC would be dismantled. Further, the ITV network which had also suffered from the public broadcaster's faults – monopolization, centralization, inefficiency, closed entry, a lack of public choice in programming, and an overbearing regulator (the IBA) – would have to be reformed. Essentially, the public and commercial sectors acted as a comfortable duopoly. In some respects, Jay concurred with Anthony Smith's pluralistic view as he stood against the elite's paternalism and corporatist disposition.[21] However, he employed the market as the provider of economic pluralism and political liberty. Consumer sovereignty would underpin the new broadcasting order as consumer preferences would dominate the producers' decisions and programming.[22] In addition, he argued that the British broadcasting system had been susceptible to political interference. However, once the technological, financial, institutional and public service barriers were overcome, the regulators, who had censored the individual's freedoms, would become an anachronism. Jay contrasted the state's control over broadcasting with the freedom and liberty of an independent press. The press had overcome state restrictions due to the introduction of eighteenth-century libertarian ideologies. Its freedom was a sacred political liberty, yet broadcasting had been closely and minutely controlled by accountable public bodies. There was no technical pretext for government-appointed regulators to apportion the air-waves. In turn, governmental interference in electronic publishing should be limited to the general laws of blasphemy, libel and obscenity.[23]

For Jay, electronic publishing would reflect the consumer's needs. Subscription services demonstrated the efficient management of resources, saved on advertising costs and the expenses incurred by the licence fee's collection. Ultimately, this would reform a system which had been dominated by political interference, favouritism, corruption and a metropolitan bias.

The Peacock Committee

The Home Office did not expect the Peacock Committee to recommend any major broadcasting reforms. Peacock had been called because the BBC had fallen foul of the Thatcher government who distrusted its corporate status, bureaucracy and ideology. It had a narrow remit: to assess the effects of the introduction of advertising or sponsorship on the BBC if they were to replace the licence fee.[24] Several reasons for this may be cited.

The Conservative Party felt that the licence fee was a regressive tax which penalized those who rarely watched the BBC.[25] It was not only unpopular, but difficult to collect due to public resistance. This made it inefficient as resources were set aside for reminder notices, home visits, detector vans and public prosecutions. Moreover, the fee had failed to stay on a par with ITV's advertising revenues. It had been cut by the government and was undermined by a decline in viewers switching from black and white to colour television receivers. In 1984 the BBC's income stood at £700 million in contrast to ITV revenues of approximately £1000 million. Further, Channel Four had cut the BBC's viewing figures. Thus, the commercial sector finally had the edge over the BBC's ratings and forced the corporation to chase ratings in order to preserve its funding, rather than act as a public service broadcaster.

Simultaneously, the political environment had changed. Thatcherism, conceived as an amalgam of market-liberal economic theories and libertarian political values, challenged the economic and political consensus. In many respects, Thatcher and her more ideologically motivated allies (such as Keith Joseph) were influenced by F. A. Hayek's libertarianism and Milton Friedman's monetarism.[26] Therefore the BBC was a collectivist vestige which was overmanned, hierarchical, bureaucratic and publicly unaccountable. However, the Thatcher government was most distressed by the BBC's political behaviour. Thatcherite authoritarianism deemed that the *British* Broadcasting Corporation had a national duty to support the government during crises. The BBC, in its ambiguous position as 'institution within the constitution', was again faced with balancing the national interest against the legal requirements of impartiality. As it adhered to the traditions of political neutrality, it stood in the firing line. In particular, Margaret Thatcher had been appalled when the BBC had interviewed an INLA spokesman after the group's assassination of her close ally Airey Neave in 1979. Throughout the 1980s, tensions increased (before, during and after Peacock's investigation) through incidents such as the BBC's coverage of the Falklands War, the reporting of the United States's bombing of Libya, the *Real Lives* interview with Martin McGuinness – which the governors withdrew over the head of the management – and Special Branch's seizure of the programme tapes concerning the Zircon Spy satellite.[27]

Thus, the Home Secretary Leon Brittan 'stacked' the committee with market-liberals who would favour advertising on the BBC. The libertarian economist Professor Alan Peacock chaired the committee, whilst the other leading member Samuel Brittan (the Home Secretary's brother) had advocated market-liberalism, deregulation, state retraction and individualism as Deputy Editor of the *Financial Times*. For political balance, Alastair Hetherington, former Controller of BBC Scotland, appeared to support the licence fee. However, after a row he had ended up running the BBC's smallest local radio station, Radio Highland and had left the BBC acrimoniously. Moreover, the government did not include any Labour MPs or trade union representatives.[28] Finally, Peacock's chairing of the committee and its focus led to accusations that he had confined the investigation to economic rather than social issues.[29]

The Peacock Report

Due to its narrow remit, it appeared that the Report would introduce advertising on the BBC. However, it rejected the adoption of advertising over the licence fee, as it considered that the BBC could not generate the required revenue without detrimentally affecting the ITV companies' profits and the presses' advertising market.[30] Further, as the BBC and ITV would sell audiences to advertisers rather than programmes to audiences, they might be driven into a ratings war to attract advertisers. Subsequently, range and quality for the viewer/consumer would be constrained.[31]

The report did not, however, advocate the licence fee's retention, as governments had used it as a political lever. On the contrary, its removal could hasten direct consumer choice. The new technologies were crucial. Jay's 'electronic publishing' model was desirable because a fibre-optic grid could provide an unlimited number of channels, be funded through subscription, encourage independent producers and be lightly regulated.[32] Thus, the consumer could have the widest range of choice and determine the merits of programming through his/her subscription:

> British broadcasting should move towards a sophisticated market system based on consumer sovereignty. That is a system which recognises that viewers and listeners are the best ultimate judges of their own interest, which they can best satisfy if they have the option of purchasing the broadcasting services they require from as many alternative sources of supply as possible. . . . The fundamental aim of broadcasting should in our view be to enlarge both the freedom of choice of the consumer and the opportunities available to programme-makers to offer alternative wares to the public.[33]

Peacock proposed a three-stage plan to encourage individual economic choice and the citizen's political liberty. A first stage of eighteen, immediate recommendations entitled 'The Preparation for Subscription' would dismantle the duopoly and establish the new technologies to create a free broadcasting market. Peacock determined that all new television receivers should include a peri-television socket to provide access to encrypted services and that a national cable grid be established through public funds. Once these reforms were established, in stage two or 'strategic potential', subscription would become the BBC's primary funding source and a more competitive environment would emerge. Finally, a multiplicity of subscription-based channels would promote a full consumer market. Broadcasting regulators would be replaced by a light-touch Public Service Broadcasting Council (PSBC).

Of the eighteen first-stage recommendations, those concerning broadcasting's financial structure and regulation would intensify competition in terrestrial broadcasting. First, the licence fee should be linked to the Retail Price Index (RPI) so it would not be set annually by the Home Office. This would secure the BBC's income and enforce efficiency, as the corporation had to spend on core rather than marginal activities. It could reduce governmental interference and lead to the fee's replacement by subscription. Second, Independent Television franchises should be auctioned. Competitive tendering would counteract the IBA's regulatory capture, as the 1981 franchise round had exhibited clientelism between the larger ITV companies and the IBA, at the expense of smaller franchisees.[34] Within the auctioning process the IBA would merely enforce rules governing quality, range and scheduling. When the bidders had satisfied these criteria, the franchises would go to the highest bidder.[35] Third, the BBC and ITV were subjected to a 40 per cent quota of independent productions. This allowed independent producers to circumvent the duopolistic barriers on entry. Fourth, Channel Four should sell its own advertising, thus divorcing it from the ITV companies and the IBA.

For Peacock, these reforms established a free broadcasting market to service consumer preferences. Further, economic changes altered relations between broadcasters and the state. Previously, citizens' rights had been undermined as the regulators had been captured by the broadcasters and the government. A complacent broadcasting clique had conformed to 'interest group pressures on moral legitimacy, practical effectiveness and ultimately the very stability and sustainability of liberal democracy'.[36] Samuel Brittan argued that the BBC Governors and the IBA were pre-publication censors. Whilst accusations of censorship were normally confined to controversial programmes which displeased governments, Brittan argued that the IBA, who vetted schedules and could withdraw franchises, was a covert censor.[37] Thus, alternative voices, that might be included in a market-based system, were excluded. Regulation should be light-touch and broadcasting subject to the general laws of taste, decency, defamation, sedition and obscenity.[38] The report proposed a Public Service Broadcasting Council (PSBC) to be financed by the broadcasters. It would be structured like the Arts

Council and would allocate funds to the respective station owners or programme-makers who had applied for bids. It was to protect the small public service element, although it would set aside consumer rights to general legislation.

In this way, the over-centralized, bureaucratic public service institutions would be replaced by a multiple-source market system promoting consumer choice. The committee believed that it had maximized the consumers' right by linking the recommendations to the tradition of 'Western writing (from Milton to Mill and beyond) in favour of freedom of expression'.[39] In 1694 Parliament had abolished pre-publication censorship, now a broadcasting system utilizing the new technologies could extend the citizen's liberty and freedom of speech.[40] The Peacock committee conceived a 'free broadcasting' system which was emancipated from state regulation, should only conform to the print media laws, was privately owned and funded through consumer subscription.

Critiques of the Peacock Report

The committee's rejection of advertising on the BBC appeared to be the key recommendation. The BBC congratulated itself, maintaining that only a minority had advocated advertising. This 'minority' included Margaret Thatcher who was disappointed with the report. Her government believed that the BBC was now impervious to reform as Peacock had linked the fee to the RPI.

For the broadcasters, Peacock was part of the government's attack on the BBC. They claimed that its market principles were foreign to the industry's finances.[41] Channel Four believed that it could not sell its own advertising whilst retaining its distinctive remit. The independent production quota would undermine regional production, create union problems, stem training and subsume creativity. Similarly, ITV was outraged by the franchise auction. The IBA would be unable to choose between the highest bid and a lower one which could ensure quality, and competitive tenders would remove money from the system forcing mergers or take-overs. Andrew Ehrenberg also suggested that internal competition existed for funds, airtime, audiences, viewer appreciation and critical renown.[42]

Therefore, they felt that Peacock attacked the system's cherished principles and opened it up to media barons such as Rupert Murdoch. As subscription undermined the traditions of *programme diversity* and *universality of service*, national public service broadcasting would be ghettoized and standards lowered in the chase for ratings. Peacock's central tenets of greater freedom for independent productions and consumerism conceived broadcasting as an economic commodity rather than as a socio-political entity.

Peacock's libertarianism could also be attacked on broader philosophical grounds. Markets provide consumers with a variety of rival commodities. Therefore, individuals may use private solutions to public problems through the purchasing of commodities. People will spend their way out of trouble rather than demand social change and improved provision. Consequently, they are not bestowed political participatory rights. The citizen is excluded from the redistribution of wealth and from the income allowing entrance to the market. Therefore, if material inequalities stem the individual's access to services which are required measures for citizenship, political rights are sacrificed. There is little real choice and empowerment.

Further, the return to individualism failed to address the highly integrated and oligopolistic patterns of media ownership. Channel proliferation and subscription did not necessarily promote consumer sovereignty or citizenship. Instead of a diversity and multiplication of ideas, the market could concentrate ownership and increase advertising or sponsor power. Finally, governmental responses have often been founded on an imperfect rendition of market-liberalism, owing as much to policy networks, political will, compromises and vested interests.

The 1980s Broadcasting Policy Cycle

Despite its unpopularity with broadcasters and politicians, the Peacock report influenced the broadcasting debate. Ostensibly, public service values were criticized and consumerism became the key criterion. Further, the government aimed for the free development of the new media channels. The technological push allowed it to attack the terrestrial system's vested interests. However, throughout this confused policy-making phase it is difficult to determine where the ideology ended and the politicking began. The government's decisions were indecisive and inconsistent. Further, there were political pressures from interested groups. The legislation emerged through political bargaining, will and pragmatism. Consequently, a substantive change in the emphasis of the recommendations occurred (see table 5.1). Ironically, the eventual Act reformed ITV, with the BBC being largely left alone as the politicians attempted to resolve the imperatives of deregulation, commercialization and the public service:

> The 1990 Broadcasting Act was a ragbag of different ideas and ideologies which in part related to Peacock, the industry, the Number Ten policy office etc. Whilst all legislation is imperfect and subject to political pressures, it has produced a number of inconsistencies and genuine problems.[43]

Table 5.1 The main recommendations of the political phase

Recommendation	The 1986 Peacock Report	The 1988 White Paper	The 1990 Broadcasting Act
The licence fee	The licence fee to be pegged to the Retail Price Index (RPI) by 1 April 1988 and collected by the BBC.	The licence fee's pegging to the RPI was noted. The BBC was the 'cornerstone of British Broadcasting'.	
ITV franchises	The competitive tendering of the ITV franchises.	A franchise auction in which the bid plus a profits levy is paid annually to the exchequer. The applicant was required to pass a quality threshold which would satisfy 'consumer protection' targets, positive programme requirements and ownership rulings.	A two-stage franchise auction including a 'quality' hurdle. The applicant provided programme and business plans, with a sealed annual bid based on advertising revenue for the next decade. The highest bid could only be considered on passing the quality hurdle. An 'Exceptional Circumstances' clause for companies with an outstanding record.
Channel Four's funding and programme output	Channel Four should sell its own advertising in competition with ITV and would no longer be funded through the ITV companies' subscriptions.	Channel Four to sell its own advertising, whilst simultaneously remaining an innovative broadcaster. A minimum level of income to be drawn from the ITV competitive tender and levy proceeds.	Channel Four to continue as an innovative broadcaster whilst selling its own advertising in competition with ITV. A levy drawn from the ITV companies.
Independent producers	The introduction of a 40% quota for original programmes commissioned from independent producers upon the BBC and ITV channels over a ten year period.	It was noted that Peacock's initial 40% quota had been reduced to 25% of the BBC's and ITV's output by the end of 1992.	The maintenance of the 25% quota on BBC and ITV channels.

Table 5.1   Cont'd

Recommendation	The 1986 Peacock Report	The 1988 White Paper	The 1990 Broadcasting Act
The New Media and subscription based services	All television receivers should incorporate a peritelevision socket allowing for subscription. The installation by British Telecom of a national fibre-optic grid for cable services.	A rejection of peritelevision sockets and of the national fibre-optic cable grid. The expansion of cable was left to the Cable Authority and the operators themselves. Similarly low or medium powered satellite services were left to the market. Some content regulations were included.	The Independent Television Commission (ITC) became responsible for licensing cable, domestic and non-domestic satellite services. The Cable Authority was abolished.
Regulation	The replacement of the traditional regulators with a 'light touch' omni-competent Public Service Broadcasting Council (PBSC).	The IBA to be replaced by a Radio Authority and the Independent Television Commission (ITC), responsible for supervising company licences, advertising and maintaining decency. Transmission services to be privatized. The legitimization of the Broadcasting Standards Council (BSC).	A corporate ITC as a *regulator* rather than a *broadcaster* to license ownership, programming, advertising and sponsorship. Previewing powers were removed, whilst programming and scheduling powers went to the ITV Network Centre. Further, the ITC would not represent the ITV companies in law courts. The ITC supervised the franchise auction. Transmission services were privatized and taken over by National Transcommunications Ltd. Radio services were hived off to the Radio Authority. Measures concerning the BSC and the Broadcasting Complaints Commission (BCC) were recommended.

The Thatcher government's response to the Peacock Report

As Peacock had found against the introduction of advertising, the government's attention to the BBC waned. Moreover, relations with the BBC improved due to the politicization of appointments and the corporation's caution. The BBC chairman Stuart Young's death in 1986 led to Marmaduke Hussey's installation. He dismissed Director-General (DG) Alasdair Milne who was replaced by Michael Checkland, the accountant Deputy DG. Whilst Milne had been the 'Editor in Chief', Checkland distanced himself from news and current affairs. This was covered by John Birt, the new Deputy DG, who amalgamated the two departments. Through such centralization he reinforced the 'referral' system as producers had to refer stories to editors, thereby exercising control over controversial items. Thus as the BBC began, in Margaret Thatcher's word, to 'put its house in order',[44] the licence fee was set by the Retail Price Index (RPI) from 1 January 1988.

In the aftermath of its immediate disappointment, the government perceived that consumer sovereignty might facilitate a more competitive market by opening it up to new entrants. In particular, the government and the Department of Trade and Industry (DTI) hoped that British Satellite Broadcasting (BSB) would succeed as a commercial enterprise.[45] However, as we shall discuss in chapter 6, the 1990 Act did not respond to satellite broadcasting's regulatory or ownership issues. Instead, its liberalization aided Rupert Murdoch, who had failed in his bid for the IBA-regulated D-MAC channels. The government's hands-off approach eventually allowed Murdoch to circumvent monopoly restrictions and gain sole control. Subsequently, he benefited from Margaret Thatcher's political patronage and her unwillingness to legislate for satellite broadcasting. Greg Dyke commented:

> A major factor . . . was the leeway they (the government) gave to Murdoch because he was their friend. This was purely patronage. When I complained about Murdoch's control I was told under no circumstances are we interested in doing anything. 'He won us the election'.[46]

The broadcasting policy was also reflective of the Prime Minister's interests, circles of influence, departmental positions, and the infiltration of a business elite into senior cabinet posts. After her 1987 electoral victory, Margaret Thatcher dominated the cabinet and the broadcasting sub-committee chair, shaped the policy as much as any ideology.[47] Her close ally was the businessman Lord Young, the Secretary of State for the DTI. As the DTI licensed broadcasting technology, it argued that the new media provided more competitive opportunities.

Therefore, radical solutions such as privatizing the airwaves, BBC2 and Channel Four were required.[48]

From 1986 to 1988, the DTI contested broadcasting with the Home Office. Whilst the Home Office conceded that consumer reforms were needed, it saw broadcasting as a public good. Alternatively, the DTI stood at the Thatcherite vanguard due to its privatization of utilities and industries. Although the 1988 White Paper marked a compromise between the Home Office and the DTI, the joins were conspicuous. For instance, Channel Four remained a public service broadcaster whilst competing with ITV to sell its advertising. As Steven Barnett comments:

> The White Paper is full of contradictions between the liberal establishment versus the Thatcherite business ethos. . . . Lord Young had the ear of Margaret Thatcher and Douglas Hurd, the Home Secretary, whose interest in broadcasting was minimal, was fighting a rearguard battle. The DTI, under Young, received patronage from Margaret Thatcher . . . In its departmental briefs it was looking to be the lead department related to broadcasting. . . . The shift back to the Home Office coincided with Young's removal.[49]

Throughout these complexities, the government hoped to open up broadcasting to competition. In particular, Margaret Thatcher, the Chancellor Nigel Lawson, the DTI and even the Home Office favoured the ITV franchises auction, believing the commercial sector to be inefficient, union-dominated, and monopolistic.[50]

The commercial liberalization of ITV

The franchise auction had been a side-issue for Peacock.[51] However, for the government it made ITV accountable to advertisers and viewers. Whilst the levy on revenues should have stemmed excessive profitability, the companies had circumvented it by reinvesting money into programming and closed shop union agreements. ITV claimed that creativity and experimentation in programming had been enhanced. Conversely, Thatcher wanted competition to remove market rigging, closed entry, monopolization and corporatism. Moreover, the Treasury contended that the levy had allowed the ITV companies to evade excessive taxation. Competitive tendering would cut costs, increase independent production and make ITV more accountable to the advertisers.

Thatcherites were influenced by the advertisers who wanted to dismantle ITV's advertising monopoly and the IBA's restrictions on the amount of advertising. These factors allowed the ITV companies to charge exorbitant rates for peak-time advertising. Further, the IBA's public service commitments had meant that ITV had indulged in unaccountable programme schedules.[52] As ITV received a third of their total expenditure, advertisers felt they had the right to intervene in the schedule.[53] They resented ITV's inability to target audiences, believing that the companies had ignored their needs. Moreover, they believed they were footing the bill for labour inefficiencies promoted by lax union agreements. They hoped that a franchise auction would produce a more responsive ITV and reduce advertising rates.

The government remained suspicious of the commercial sector's clandestine nature. In particular, it believed that the IBA had been 'captured' by the ITV companies. It concurred with market-libertarians that the 1981 franchise round had been a 'carve-up' for the major licensees. It was further annoyed by the IBA's refusal to allow Michael Green's Carlton Communications to take over Thames in 1985. Green had negotiated with Thames's owners Thorn and the IBA, yet at the eleventh hour, the Thames Chief Executive Richard Dunn lobbied IBA Director John Whitney imploring him to bury the deal. The IBA had been unaccountable and its patronage contrasted with the Thatcherites' principles of free enterprise.[54]

Therefore, the *commercialization* of ITV and the removal of the IBA was desirable. At a 1987 cabinet seminar on commercial broadcasting attended by Alan Peacock, BBC, IBA and ITV broadcasting chiefs, Margaret Thatcher criticized ITV's monopoly over advertising, lack of competitiveness and unaccountability, infamously dubbing it as 'the last bastion of restrictive practices'.[55]

Intervention, censorship and control

Conversely, Thatcher indicated an *interventionist* streak which, on one level, was situated around sex and violence on television as she feared the potential satellite invasion of foreign pornography. However, the major catalyst was Michael Ryan's 1987 Hungerford massacre. Ryan had been impressed by violent video cassettes and the government articulated populist fears over their dissemination. However, for political convenience, it mixed violent videos with terrestrial broadcast programmes. This dynamic led to the creation of the Broadcasting Standards Council (BSC).

Governmental intervention was also politically motivated. Most broadcasters believed that two agendas existed. An ostensible legislative agenda gave way to an undeclared belief that leading ministers saw the broadcasters as being too powerful and irresponsible. Consequently, as the BBC shied away from political controversy, the attention focused on ITV. The government's anger was raised by the Thames documentary *Death on the Rock* which cited eye-witness accounts of the SAS's shoot-to-kill policy against three IRA suspects in Gibraltar. This disputed the official version of events. Subsequently, a gulf appeared between the government and the IBA, which was legally responsible for airing the programme.

Before the documentary appeared, the Foreign Secretary Sir Geoffrey Howe wrote to IBA Chairman Lord Thomson asking for it to be withdrawn as it would prejudice any jury. Thomson responded that the programme would be shown in the public interest. This defence of investigative journalism, however, demonstrated the IBA's inability to perceive the sea-change in British politics. Thatcher's adversarial style meant that the IBA became the enemy. Thus, ITV was not only financially unaccountable, but was unaccountable to the politicians. This fuelled the government's desire to commercialize ITV.

This policy also highlighted the contradiction between market liberty and state repression under Thatcherism. If deregulation was taken to its logical extreme, the government would have to curb its powers over broadcasting. In contrast, it had been motivated by its desire to stem the flow of political information. A tension grew between Thatcherite arguments to liberalize the broadcast market, against the commitment to censorship. The policy made conspicuous the paradox between a free economy and strong state. This originated from the two major strands in Thatcherism; a liberal bias arguing 'for a freer, more open and more competitive economy, and a conservative tendency . . . more interested in restoring social and political authority'.[56] Samuel Brittan has provided a market-liberal definition of Thatcher's right-wing authoritarianism entitled 'New Spartanism' founded on:

1 A hawkish or super-patriotic attitude to foreign and military affairs.
2 An opposition to social permissiveness and a desire to return to 'traditional values'.
3 Hostility to government economic intervention, often partial and inconsistent, but going beyond that of previous . . . Conservative governments.[57]

Rather than the market providing political liberty, New Spartanism used market economics to direct the national effort through taxes, subsidies or bans. Through the imposition of qualified but strong state measures, the market-place could efficiently deploy resources.[58] Therefore, although Thatcher had declared that 'economics is the method . . . the aim is to change the soul',[59] her government employed market principles to enhance state power. ITV's commercialization was not only an expedient response to the report to please the advertisers and media entrepreneurs, but conformed to the pursuit:

of a nineteenth century 'contractual' model of social policy, (in which) the government would cease to provide social goods, even at an arms length, and limit itself to defining and defending individual rights *vis-a-vis* their provision. This is why the search for appropriate forms of regulation (became) so important. By playing down its role as provider in this way, government (could) present itself as *libertarian*, even though it may be acting in increasingly aggressive and even *authoritarian* ways in its supervision of the providing bodies.[60]

The 1988 Broadcasting White Paper

The 1988 White Paper *Broadcasting in the '90s: Competition, Choice and Quality* shifted attention to ITV. It recommended the auction of ITV franchises, forced Channel Four to sell its own advertising, re-regulated ITV under the Independent Television Commission (ITC), sanctioned a 25 per cent quota for independent productions on the terrestrial channels, loosened ownership controls and favoured the private expansion of the cable and satellite channels. These proposals were couched in the terminology of economic liberalization:

> The Government places the viewer and listener at the centre of broadcasting policy. Because of technological, international and other developments, change is inevitable. It is also desirable: only through change will the individual be able to exercise the much wider choice which will soon become possible. The Government's aim is to open the doors so that individuals can choose for themselves from a much wider range of programmes and types of broadcasting . . . The government believes that, with the right enabling framework, a more open and competitive broadcasting market can be attained without the detriment to programme standards and quality.[61]

However, the White Paper's proposed consumer choice carried a rider – 'In this as in other fields consumers will rightly insist on safeguards which will protect them and their families from shoddy wares and exploitation.'[62] It proposed the retention and extension of interventionist regulation within programming. It enhanced the BSC's powers, provided the ITC with sanctions over programming content, increased consumer protection obligations on taste, decency and balance and removed broadcasting's exemption from obscenity legislation. The White Paper saw broadcasting's commercialization overtake the dynamic for deregulation. It was the government's most extreme statement for economic reform. However, simultaneously through the re-regulation of broadcasting the state's controls were retained, if not extended. This may have been incoherent in terms of Thatcherism, but made perfect sense in the light of New Spartanism.

From the White Paper to the 1990 Act

With ITV's commercialization established, the final shaping of the Broadcasting Act occurred under the jurisdiction of Home Office ministers Timothy Renton and David Mellor. In particular, Mellor oversaw the legislation through from bill to act. The DTI's role diminished because of Young's reduced power within cabinet and the gradual erosion of Thatcherism. This change meant that there was less political capital in attacking the broadcasters.

Although the will for commercialization remained, this period was characterized by compromise and bargaining as controversial amendments were reduced in their impact. This was partly due to the lobbying conducted by the ITV Association, the IBA and The Campaign for Quality Television. Previously, ITV's attitude had been to dismiss competition, however, the lobby realized that it needed to be more realistic. Although their general fears about the delicate balance of the broadcasting equation were ignored, they influenced the government over parts of the franchise auction (such as reinforcing the quality hurdle and the inclusion of an exceptional circumstances clause) and regulation.

Renton and, particularly, Mellor's patrician background within the Conservative party also shaped the debate. Mellor preferred pragmatic policies shaped by consensual negotiation rather than ideological dogma. He struck the balance between deregulation, commercialization and tradition by compromising upon the key measures whilst arguing for greater general commercial reform. The act's terminology demonstrates how these imperatives were resolved. Whilst some abstract terms such as 'high quality' and 'diversity' remained, other phrases traditionally associated with broadcasting legislation were absent. The act made no reference to the public service tenet of 'educating, informing and entertaining.' This point was made by Robert MacLennan, Liberal Democratic spokesman for broadcasting, during the committee stage:

> Clause 2 is an important statement of the functions and duties of the ITC . . . The Clause is all the more remarkable, however, for what it does not say. It demonstrates no concept of public trusteeship for the dissemination of television.[63]

Mellor's response was indicative of the philosophy which underpinned the legislation:

> We could spend all the time that is available to the Committee debating this amendment, but I want to make it clear in, I hope, a reasonably sensible and disciplined time, the point is that a matter of principle is

involved. We might as well recognise it. We do not think that the services to be regulated by the ITC need, in the main, to be governed by the public service remit as it has been commonly understood.[64]

Therefore, the principal recommendations were directed at ITV to open up the market whilst maintaining a degree of intervention and protection. Consequently, the ITV companies would be protected by the quality hurdle and exceptional circumstances clause. Similarly, the ITC's power extended beyond that of a licensor. Whilst a more qualified competition would exist in ITV, the public service would be maintained by the BBC and Channel Four.

The 1990 Broadcasting Act

The franchise auction was central to the 1990 Broadcasting Act. Competitive tendering meant that the winning bids were payable directly to the Exchequer, thereby removing significant revenues from ITV. This would force the companies to streamline their programming and labour costs to maintain profitability. This commercialization extended to Channel Four which was required to be a public service broadcaster whilst competing with ITV for advertising.

Confusion surrounded broadcasting regulation. The IBA was transformed into a licensor, the Independent Television Commission (ITC). In some respects, the ITC's powers were circumscribed as it could not demand educational and informational programming in the schedule. The change from broadcasting authority to licensing commission created a *post hoc* regulator, without previewing powers, which could only defend or sanction a programme after it had been shown. This also meant that it would no longer defend the ITV companies in court over controversial programmes. Conversely, the ITC could press for the appropriate scheduling and production of 'quality' programmes. Therefore, as the ITC could sanction or revoke franchises, a degree of intervention became inevitable.

The change in the ITC's status was designed to dismantle the previous 'regulatory capture'. Yet, the act replaced one form of centralization with several others. First, the ITV Association, dominated by the major companies and advertising interests, took over scheduling and the ITV Network Centre commissioned programmes. Networking power became concentrated over regionalism. Secondly, deregulation ironically produced more regulatory bodies than before – the BBC Governors, the ITC, the BSC, the Radio Authority, and the Broadcasting Complaints Commission (BCC). Most notably, intervention was enhanced through the BSC which was created to respond to sex and violence on television. The government had appointed Lord Rees Mogg to chair the BSC in an attempt to slight the broadcasters as he had been the BBC Board of Governors' Vice-Chairman during the *Real Lives* incident.[65] Some exaggerated claims maintained that the BSC could replace the IBA. However, the White Paper reduced the council's power by removing previewing powers. Despite its impotence, this 'sex and violence' council conflicted with the Peacock report's notion of liberty.

The new media was marginalized as the act restricted its attention to the licensing of cable and satellite services.[66] As the legislation was conceived in national terms, the supra-national concerns of ownership, programme content and regulation were ignored. Implicitly, the new media was left to the market-place. This was partly reflective of the government's difficulty in legislating for channels which circumvented national borders. However, it also demonstrated an inconsistency which referred to short-termism and political reality. Primarily, the government employed the new media as a weapon to reform the traditional terrestrial broadcasting organizations.

Thus, the 1990 Act contained elements of continuity, change and contradiction. In contrast to the Peacock report's market-liberalism, where the 'public service' was defined through the relationship between the consumer and programme providers, the policy-makers focused their attention upon the reform of terrestrial broadcasters. Consequently, consumer sovereignty became a convenient political metaphor rather than being pursued. The legislation was reflective of 'laissez-faire' practices rather than market-liberalism. This, it was hoped, would satisfy those who demanded continuity, the ideologues pressing for commercial reform and the government's political interests. An incoherent act emerged in which the imperatives of accountability and liberalization became confused with normative methods of control, political will and attempts to commercialize the system.

Conclusion

Throughout this chapter we have explored the development of alternative broadcasting models. In the 1970s, the anti-statist, liberal critique underpinned the Annan report's recommendations. It was founded on Locke and Mills' democratic arguments and considered broadcasting's *social* purposes through the freedom of choice and speech. Subsequently, a cooperative trust founded on a central funding scheme, increased worker participation, and a school for research would encourage communal broadcasting and democracy. This 'open access policy' would allow freelance groups to produce alternative programmes. Therefore, the OBA provided a unique challenge to the traditional regulators and broadcasting's norms. Yet, the early 1980s policy cycle showed that political interests, industrial lobbying and tradition could curb such a reform. Ultimately, Channel Four, whilst achieving great success, resulted from a compromise between pluralism and the normative public service tenets.

By the mid-1980s, the *market-liberal* critique of British broadcasting became prevalent. This was 'pushed' by the introduction of new technologies (cable, satellite, telecommunications). It originated from the conception of society as a competitive market in which individuals are the source of wealth. As individual economic liberalization equated with societal benefit, state powers should be limited and broadcasting should satisfy individual preferences, rather than be a public service good. The Peacock Report advocated a subscription system to deliver programmes to consumers. The public and commercial broadcasting institutions would be dismantled and regulatory tiers removed. However, Peacock's analysis may be criticized on several levels.

First, in terms of policy realization, there was a drift from market-liberalism to a compromised form of legislation. Political practicalities were equally, if not more, important determinants than ideology. These included dissensions amongst competing departments of state, advisors and politicians, the Prime Minister and the Cabinet. Further, it was reflective of Thatcher's desire to commercialize sectors of the economy, whilst increasing state intervention over individual rights and civil liberties. Thus, it highlighted the contradiction between market freedoms and Thatcherite authoritarianism.

Moreover, as the government considered Peacock's market-liberalism, the controls over broadcasting manufactured through incremental understandings, self-censorship, governing ideologies and regulation were made conspicuous. Previously, clear parameters had established the degree to which broadcasters could exert independence. This was not a conscious practice, but had been developed by common assumptions about political liberty. However, through the Thatcher government's crude interventions, these normative processes came under pressure. In turn, the government found itself in a more complicated position than it had anticipated as it desired market reform but feared the political consequences of riotous pluralism. In purely political terms, the government's actions made sense as they could retain control alongside increased commercialization. In contrast to Peacock's long-term recommendations, the government was motivated by short-term gain. The process exhibited the government's preference for the expedience of commercialization over ideology.

Second, market-liberalism can be seen to restrict rather than enhance public choice. The religion of the market has led to reintroduction of the precepts of commercial enterprise and private property rights to provide free information. These do not address the medias' oligopolistic patterns of ownership. Markets often unequally distribute the wealth, allowing for a concentration of ownership through closed entry. Through the commercialization of terrestrial systems, media barons, sponsors and advertisers could achieve greater power. As we shall see, instead of a multiplication of the cultural influences and diversity of information, advertising power, cultural imperialism and media conglomeration were to be enhanced. In many respects, the widening array of delivery services has often narrowed individual choice.

John Keane has pointed out that media entrepreneurs provide choices, but these exist in the framework of *commercial viability*.[67] Corporations assume that market competition is the substructure and that citizens' choices are superstructural. Further, this reflects the truism that these policies were founded on the promise of increased consumer choice and that 'the figure of the consumer had come to dominate the imaginary landscape of late capitalism.'[68] Graham Murdock has distinguished between citizenship and consumerism suggesting that the quest for equality, fraternity and liberty has given way to individualistic, private solutions to public problems through the purchasing of commodities.[69] Consumerism urges people to spend their way out of trouble rather than demand social change and improved provision. Citizenship becomes 'less a collective, political activity than an individual, economic activity – the right to pursue one's interests, without hindrance, in the marketplace'.[70] Therefore, markets provide rival commodities but do not bestow individual participatory rights. A conflict existed between the rights of possession and expression.

The explosion of communication technologies has challenged traditional paradigms and altered notions of citizenship and mass communication. Undoubtedly, Public Service Broadcasting was flawed and needed to be reformed. However, the political responses and multimedia developments were orchestrated around an often imperfect rendition of market-liberalism. These laid broadcasting open to monopolistic exploitation rather than expanding participatory rights. For true media diversity, greater public access to communication resources was required to encourage a plurality of producers and opinions. It now remains to be seen how the imperatives of deregulation, commercialization and consumerism are impacting on mass communications towards the second millenium.

Further Reading

Annan Committee, *The Report of the Committee on the Future of Broadcasting (The Annan Report)*, Cmnd. 6573, HMSO, 1977.

Simon Blanchard and David Morely (eds), *What's this Channel Four?*, Comedia Publishing Group, 1982.

Jay Blumler (ed.), *Television and the Public Interest: Vulnerable Values in West European Broadcasting*, Sage Publications, 1992.

Jay Blumler and T. J. Nossiter (eds), *Broadcasting Finance in Transition*, Oxford University Press, 1991.

Roger Bolton, *Death on the Rock and Other Stories*, W. H. Allen, 1990.

Samuel Brittan, 'The Fight for Freedom in Broadcasting', *Political Quarterly*, vol. 58, no. 1, January–March, 1987, pp. 1–23.

Richard Collins, Nicholas Garnham and Gareth Locksley, *The Economics of Television: The UK Case*, Sage Publications, 1988.

James Curran and Jean Seaton, *Power without Responsibility: The Press and Broadcasting in Britain*, Routledge, 1991 (4th edn).

Kenneth Dyson and Peter Humphreys with Ralph Negrine and Jean-Paul Simon, *Broadcasting and New Media Policies in Western Europe*, Routledge, 1988.

Marjorie Ferguson (ed.), *New Communication Technologies and the Public Interest*, Sage Publications, 1986.

Peter Golding, Graham Murdock and Philip Schlesinger (eds), *Communicating Politics: Mass Communication and the political process*, Leicester University Press, 1986.

Home Office White Paper: *Broadcasting in the '90s: Competition, Choice and Quality, Cmnd. 517*, HMSO, 1988.

Home Office, *Broadcasting Act 1990 (Chapter 42)*, HMSO, 1990.

Jeremy Isaacs, *Storm over Four: A Personal Account*, Weidenfeld & Nicolson, 1989.

Peter Jay, *The Crisis for Western Political Economy and Other Essays*, André Deutsch, 1984 (9th edn).

Raymond Kuhn (ed.), *The Politics of Broadcasting*, Croom Helm, 1985.

——, *Politics and the Mass Media in Britain*, Harvester Wheatsheaf, 1996.

Stephen Lambert, *Channel Four: Television with a Difference*, BFI Publishing, 1982.

Michael Leapman, *The Last Days of the Beeb*, Allen & Unwin, 1986.

Tim Madge, *Beyond the BBC; Broadcasters and the Public in the 1980s*, Macmillan, 1989.

Ralph Negrine, *Politics and the Mass Media in Britain*, Routledge, 1994 (2nd edn).

Tom O'Malley, *Closedown? The BBC and Government Broadcasting Policy, 1979–92*, Pluto Press, 1994.

Peacock Committee, *The Report of the Committee on Financing the BBC (The Peacock Report)*, Cmnd. 9284, HMSO, 1986.

Wilf Stevenson and Nick Smedley (eds), *Responses to the White Paper*, The Broadcasting Debate 3, BFI Publishing, 1989.

Cento Veljanovski (ed.), *Freedom in Broadcasting*, Institute of Economic Affairs, 1989.

Notes

1   Graham Murdock, 'Citizens, consumers, and public culture', in Michael Skovmand and Kim Christian Schroder (eds), *Media Cultures: Reappraising Transnational Media*, Routledge, 1992, p. 19.

2   Throughout this period the media increasingly became an academic source of inquiry. A number of high profile centres emerged at Birmingham University, Leicester University and Glasgow University. These academics usually came from the Left and were invariably influenced by the work of Althusser and Gramsci. For further details see Martin Barker and Anne Beezer (eds) *Reading into Cultural Studies*, Routledge, 1992.

3   Nicholas Garnham, *Structures of Broadcasting*, BFI Monograph, 1973.

4   Anthony Smith, quoted from Simon Blanchard and David Morely, *What's this Channel Four?*, Comedia, 1982, p. 11.

5   *The Annan Report*, pp. 8–9.

6   Stuart Hood, *On Television*, Pluto Press, 1987 (3rd edn), p. 63.

7   David Docherty, David Morrison and Michael Tracey, *Keeping Faith?: Channel Four and its audience*, John Libbey, 1988, p. 10.

8   Jeremy Isaacs, *Storm over Four: A Personal Account*, Weidenfeld & Nicolson, 1989, pp. 19–20.

9   Ibid.

10 IBA statement quoted from Stephen Lambert, *Channel Four: Television with a Difference?*, BFI, 1982, p. 100.

11 Alan Budd, in Cento Veljanovski (ed.), *Freedom in Broadcasting*, Institute of Economic Affairs, 1989, p. 64.

12 Kenneth Dyson and Peter Humphreys with Ralph Negrine and Jean-Paul Simon, *Broadcasting and New Media Policies in Western Europe*, Routledge, p. 68.

13 Gordan Hughes and David Vines (eds), *Deregulation in Broadcasting*, The David Hume Institute, 1990, p. 83.

14 Cento Veljanovski, 'Net Improvement', *Broadcast*, 11 January 1991, p. 18.

15 R. H. Coase, *British Broadcasting; A Study in Monopoly*, Longman, 1950, p. viii.

16 See IEA Hobart Papers 15 *TV: From Monopoly to Competition – and back* and 43 *Paying for TV?*.

17 See IEA Hobart Papers 15, *TV: From Monopoly to Competition – and back*, pp. 118–19.

18 Cento Veljanovski and W. D. Bishop, *Choice by Cable*, IEA Hobart Paper, 1983.

19 The Adam Smith Institute, *Omega Report*, 1984.

20 Peter Jay, *The Crisis of Western Political Economy and other essays*, André Deutsch, 1984 (9th edn), p. 227.

21 Peter Jay, 'The Future of Broadcasting', *Television*, 1977, p. 68.

22 Ibid, p. 78.

23 Peter Jay, *The Crisis of Western Political Economy*, p. 225.

24 *The Peacock Report*, HMSO, 1986, p. 1.

25 An interview with Professor Alan Peacock by John Gray entitled 'The Economics of Competition', in Nod Miller and Rod Allen (eds), *Broadcasting after the White Paper*, Manchester Monograph, 1989, p. 127.

26 See F. A. Hayek, *The Road to Serfdom*, Routledge & Kegan Paul, 1979 (repr.).

27 Philip Schlesinger, *Putting 'Reality' Together*, Methuen, 1987, p. xviii.

28 The rest of the committee included Judith Chalmers – television personality and radio presenter; Jeremy Hardie – economist, accountant and businessman; Lord Quinton – President of Trinity College, Oxford; and Sir Peter Reynolds – Chairman of Rank, Hovis McDougall PLC.

29 Interview with Colin Shaw, April 1991. The debate primarily considered the possible effects on this market if the BBC began to sell advertising spots. Essentially, would the ITV and Independent Local Radio (ILR) companies be plunged into a crisis if the BBC began to incorporate advertising?

30 *The Peacock Report*, p. 83.
31 Ibid., p. 137.
32 Ibid., pp. 112–13.
33 Ibid., p. 133.
34 See Asa Briggs and Joanne Spicer, *The Franchise Affair*, Century, 1986 and Kenneth Dyson and Peter Humphreys, *Broadcasting and New Media Policies in Western Europe*. The franchise allocation process was criticized, as the IBA was perceived by many to have acted in the interests of the 'Big Five' ITV companies (Thames, London Weekend Television, Central, Yorkshire, Granada) and operated in a closed, clandestine manner which excluded public debate. Dyson has identified that the IBA was subject to minimalist legislation, pursued 'invisible actions', was secretive, represented 'establishment politics' and exercised patronage and self-restraint.
35 It should be noted that this recommendation was supported by only four members of the committee. These were; Alan Peacock, Samuel Brittan, Lord Quinton and Peter Reynolds. The recommendation was opposed by Judith Chalmers, Jeremy Hardie and Alastair Hethrington.
36 *The Peacock Report*, p. 112.
37 Samuel Brittan,'The Fight for Freedom in Broadcasting', *Political Quarterly*, vol. 58, no. 1, January–March 1987, pp. 9–10.
38 *The Peacock Report*, p. 146.
39 Samuel Brittan in Jay Blumler and T. J. Nossiter, *Broadcasting Finance in Transition*, Oxford University Press, 1991, p. 342.
40 Ibid., p. 126.
41 'The Peacock Debate', *Television: Journal of the Royal Television Society*, October 1986, pp. 224–33.
42 Ibid., p. 232.
43 Interview with Sue Elliott, ITC, 23 April 1991.
44 Philip Schlesinger, *Putting 'Reality' Together*, p. xviii.
45 Interview with DTI spokesman, 25 April 1993.
46 Interview with Greg Dyke, 9 November 1992.
47 See Andrew Davidson, *Under the Hammer: The ITV Franchise Battle*, Heinemann, 1992.
48 'What price more choice?: Who will benefit from the government's forthcoming white paper on television', *The Economist*, 17 September 1988.
49 Interview with Steven Barnett, 27 July 1992.
50 Thatcher's antipathy is made clear in Andrew Davidson, *Under the Hammer*, pp. 9–11.
51 *The Peacock Report*, p.143.
52 For an economic critique arguing for this scenario, see Cento Veljanovski, 'The Role of Advertising in Broadcasting policy', in Veljanovski (ed.), *Freedom in Broadcasting*, Institute of Economic Affairs, 1989.
53 John B. Thompson, *Ideology and Modern Culture*, Polity Press, 1990, p. 186.
54 Andrew Gamble, *The Free Economy and the Strong State: The Politics of Thatcherism*, Macmillan, 1988, p. 32.
55 Margaret Thatcher quoted from Andrew Davidson, *Under the Hammer*, p. 10.
56 Andrew Gamble, *The Free Economy and the Strong State*, pp. 28–9.
57 Samuel Brittan, *A Restatement of Economic Liberalism*, Macmillan, 1988.
58 Ibid., p. 145.
59 Margaret Thatcher quoted from James Donald, *Sentimental Education: Schooling, Popular Culture and the Regulation of Liberty*, Verso, 1992, p. 122.
60 Ibid., p. 128.

61   Home Office White Paper: *Broadcasting in the '90s: Competition, Choice and Quality*, Cmnd. 517, HMSO, 1988, p. 1.

62   Ibid.

63   *Hansard* (House of Commons), Broadcasting Bill, Standing Committee F., 1990, col. 158.

64   Ibid., col. 171.

65   See Sue Griffin, 'Censor Sensibility', *Broadcast*, 25 November, 1988, p. 18.

66   The provisions relating to cable and satellite services occupy only a small number of the Act's sections. Satellite services are considered in Chapter III 'Satellite Television Services' (sections 43–5), whilst cable services are considered in Part IV 'Transfer of Undertakings of IBA and Cable Authority' (Sections 129–41).

67   John Keane, *The Media and Democracy*, Polity Press, 1991, p. 91.

68   Graham Murdock, 'Citizens, consumers, and public culture', in Michael Skovmand and Kim Christian Schroder (eds), *Media Cultures: Reappraising Transnational Media*, Routledge, 1992, p. 17.

69   Ibid., p. 19.

70   M. G. Dietz, 'Context is All. Feminism and Theories of Citizenship', *Daedalus*, Fall 1987, p. 5.

6
Whither Public Service Broadcasting?
Part Two: The 1990 Broadcasting Act to the Present

Introduction

British broadcasting prior to 1990 was characterized by three major tenets – centralization, control and circumscribed competition.[1] The 1990 Broadcasting Act tried to dismantle these principles by commercializing the system. In 1988, the BBC had its licence fee pegged to the Retail Price Index (RPI) and the 1990 Act required both the BBC and ITV to incorporate a 25 per cent quota of independent productions.[2] The ITV network was subject to a franchise auction and Channel Four began to sell its advertising time in 1993.[3] The IBA was replaced by a light-touch regulator, the Independent Television Commission (ITC), whose powers over programming were reduced. Further, the expansion of cable and satellite channels was left to the market with minimal regulations over cross-ownership.[4]

The legislation forced the ITV companies to maximize audiences for greater advertising revenues in order to pay an annual levy to the Treasury calculated from the size of the tender and a percentage of their profits.[5] This trend has been exacerbated as franchisees are no longer bound by strict public service commitments, and the commissioning and scheduling of programmes has been placed under a Network Centre. Moreover, terrestrial broadcasters will be competing for viewers against subscription-based cable and satellite channels.

As a consequence of the franchise auction and the greater competition from newspapers and media conglomerates, the major ITV companies (Carlton, Granada, MAI) have lobbied for a relaxation of ownership rules. Over the last five years, they have enjoyed significant success as the Major government has acquiesced to their demands. Subsequently, there have been mergers between Carlton and Central, Granada and LWT, and United Papers and MAI.

The commercialization of ITV has affected the BBC. Although, it was not directly affected by the legislation, it has had to respond to the commercial environment due to the 1996 Charter renewal. Therefore, the BBC has aimed to retain the licence fee, although it predicted a reduced audience share by the year 2000. Director-General John Birt has pitched the corporation's future on an internal production market to promote efficiency entitled 'Producer Choice'; programming pitched on a specialized form of 'public service' broadcasting which defines itself against the market, and greater accountability to the licence fee payer. The BBC has been politically successful in retaining the fee and expanding its commercial interests in the new Charter.

In 1992, the government established a Department of National Heritage (DNH). This was initially headed by David Mellor; however, since his fall from grace Peter Brooke, Stephen Dorrell and Virginia Bottomley have been incumbents. The ministry was a response from government to the criticisms that broadcasting and the arts were not taken seriously. It has produced several policy documents. However, there are a number of qualifications; the high number of occupants would suggest that the department is a stop-gap for politicians on the way up or down and, in many areas, particularly ownership, the policies have heeded the demands of the media lobby. Throughout its tenure, the DNH has attempted to balance public service traditions with commercialism. However, as mass communications are being globalized, the usefulness of this national department is open to doubt.

Under Virginia Bottomley, it has produced its first substantive legislation – the 1996 Broadcasting Act. This addressed all areas of British broadcasting (we shall discuss media ownership elsewhere) and focused on the digitalization of terrestrial radio and television frequencies. There are seven radio frequency channels, each with a capacity of six digital stereo programme services. One of these has been given to the BBC, another set aside for an independent national service, and the other four for local services. For television, there will be six frequency channels, which each carry three television channels and potentially many more. These will be 'multiplexed' into a single digital channel before transmission. The government proposed that the Radio Authority should regulate digital radio and the ITC should licence television. Ownership rights will parallel those within analogue-based stations.[6]

This chapter will consider the current trends in British broadcasting: the commercialization of the new media and commercial terrestrial market, regulatory reform and the future of public service broadcasting. Whilst there are elements of continuity, significant changes are shaping the broadcasting landscape. Further, we will discuss whether these reforms equate with greater political liberty for the citizen or increase broadcasting's compliance to the centralizing forces of the state and the market economy. We must consider whether the reformed broadcasting environment provides greater methods of representation, democratic involvement and pluralism. Conversely, is the public sphere becoming more susceptible to greater media manipulation as elite groups negotiate for rights over and above the citizen?

The Commercialization of British Broadcasting

Communication reforms have transformed the economic, political and social worlds. Technological and corporate convergence warrant legal and constitutional changes. To this end, the free-market gospel was articulated. Economic drives would liberalize communications by circumventing the centralized and paternalistic public broadcasting structures. However, the reintroduction of market precepts such as commercial enterprise, market dynamics and private property rights has been problematic. Policy was founded on an imperfect rendition of market-liberalism, owing much to policy networks, political will, compromises and vested interests. Therefore, it is necessary to consider how the commercialization process has affected the *balance* of forces in British broadcasting.

The commercialization of the new media

The new technologies and governments' laissez-faire policies have opened up the media markets to the conglomerates across Europe (Bertelsmann, Fininvest, Hachette). In Britain, the failure of BSB and the ascendancy of Rupert Murdoch's Sky Television, later BSkyB (which merged in terms of ownership), has produced a satellite broadcasting monopoly. This contrasts with market-liberal assertions that 'electronic publishing' would create a pluralistic pattern of independent producers and consumers.

Cable

In the late 1980s, the creation of a national cable grid to facilitate a 'narrow' casting market was dismissed by the Department of Trade and Industry (DTI). Subsequently, as the cable industry was entertainment-led, its development has been subject to peaks and troughs. There were obstacles as the cable operators had to negotiate with local authorities or boroughs to lay the lines. Moreover, these installation costs have made it unfeasible to service rural areas. However, throughout the early to mid-1990s, because of the ebb and flow of investment, a significant expansion has occurred. During the last two years, there has been a massive increase in the number of lines laid. Currently, cable provides a menu of sixty channels including the Home Shopping channel (QVC), Cable News Network (CNN), the Family Channel, Discovery, Bravo and Music Television (MTV). Moreover, newspaper groups such as Associated Newspapers and The Mirror Group have backed local news services such as Channel One and entertainment channels such as Live TV respectively.

Yet, these channels rarely produce expensive original programmes, preferring a steady diet of repeats, cheap imports or small-scale productions. The newspaper groups have been careful to limit budgets to protect their interests (for instance, Channel One uses freelance cameramen/reporters). Live TV's hourly costs are as minimal as its scheduling of topless darts! The formation of Live TV also led to a spectacular fall-out between Mirror TV Chief Executive (and former *Sun* editor) Kelvin MacKenzie and the original director of programmes Janet Street-Porter. MacKenzie won the battle and commissioned a soap opera, *Canary Wharf*, about a fledgling cable station centred on a harridan programme director!

The BSB–Sky merger

The November 1990 merger of British Satellite Broadcasting (BSB) and Sky Television was a policy failure. The DTI hoped that BSB, who won a three-year monopoly on the IBA-regulated DBS frequencies in 1986, would become profitable through dish sales and subscription.[7] However, the unforeseen production of domestic equipment to receive medium-powered Astra satellite signals, the introduction of Rupert Murdoch's Sky as a competitor, a general recession, poor management and the crippling costs of the D-Mac system led to BSB becoming 'one of the great commercial disasters . . . in the history of the British media'.[8] Its financial problems meant that its shareholders, without the knowledge of the management, negotiated a merger with Murdoch.

Peter Chippindale and Suzanne Franks have compared BSB's profligate spending, eventually totalling a debt of £1 billion, against Rupert Murdoch's leanly funded Sky TV.[9] Although BSB had to cope with the expensive and untried D-Mac technology, the company was inefficient.[10] There were overpaid employees, high expense accounts, the overbidding for Hollywood films and the appointment of unsuitable managers like Chief Executive Anthony Simonds-Gooding. Further, the company was housed in the inappropriate Marco-Polo building in Battersea.

BSB fatally underestimated the resolve of the opposition. Rupert

Murdoch balanced the imperatives of finance, programming and timing. Sky's expenses were offset by employing as few staff as possible, keeping them non-unionized, locating operations in inexpensive premises at Isleworth, importing and producing cheap programmes, and using the Astra satellite technology. He appointed Australian television executives with proven track-records. Most importantly, Murdoch made Sky operational eighteen months before BSB and developed an audience as he combined with Amstrad's Alan Sugar to manufacture cheap dishes.

Whilst this managerial failure analysis is useful, it underestimates the importance of policy failures and inappropriate regulation. The inability of politicians, policy-makers, regulators and media actors to reconcile the dilemma between state intervention and the market meant that the merger not only became feasible, but was the expedient option. BSB was disadvantaged by the extraordinary costs of the high-powered D-Mac technology. These problems were exacerbated by an unforeseen recession that undermined the sales of satellite dishes and the public's resistance to buying High Definition Television (HDTV) receivers.[11] BSB was regulated by the IBA and its remit forced it to occupy a semi-public service role.[12] In such a situation, its ability to challenge the terrestrial broadcasters would have been minimal, even if it had been a monopoly.

BSB's problems were compounded by its being placed in a falsely competitive situation. Sky used the cheaper Astra PAL satellite and, as it was registered in Luxembourg, did not conform to public service norms or any particular set of technical or working practices. The government, which had been partially caught out and was already predisposed to Murdoch, argued that it could not intervene as Astra was a non-domestic satellite channel.[13] In reality, the two companies were operating under a totally different set of rules:

> As it staggered on the air, BSB campaigned hard to pressure the government to bring Sky under the regulations of the pending Broadcasting Bill. . . . As BSB pointed out, public policy was constantly challenged by new technology; legislation had to be changed to preserve the long-established principles limiting cross-media interests.[14]

Whilst the government claimed that satellite broadcasting would create competition, it had effectively allowed for the merger of BSB and Sky. This only existed at the level of ownership. Indeed, Murdoch became the majority shareholder and it was a 'take-over' at a managerial and producer level. Almost all of BSB's management were removed, the majority of the staff dismissed and operations relocated to Isleworth. The merger led to the collapse of the D-Mac satellite channels;

Murdoch's concentrated cross-media ownership; the failure of national regulations to stem the international power of News Corporation (the ITC's anger over the merger of its DBS channels was qualified, as there was little it could do to stop it); and the creation of an unregulated satellite broadcasting monopoly, British-Sky-Broadcasting (BSkyB), on the inferior Astra telecommunications satellite.

More recently, the Department of National Heritage has limited Murdoch's cross-media ambitions. The 1995 White Paper *Media Ownership*, produced by the then Secretary of State Stephen Dorrell, prevented the development of media monopolies by stopping groups from applying for a regional ITV licence if they had more than 20 per cent of the national newspaper market. They also stopped BSkyB from owning a terrestrial television station. However, it may be suggested that this was a case of too little, too late:

> But the Government's blueprint for tackling concentration of media does not make clear its stance on media corporations that already exceed the proposed thresholds. Mandy Pooler, managing director of O&M Media, said: 'The Government has legitimised Murdoch's position. They cannot require him to sell up in order to come under the threshold.'[15]

The satellite broadcasting monopoly: BSkyB

Throughout its first three years, BSkyB ran at a tremendous loss and Murdoch had to sell off parts of his media empire. Its initial financial strategy was built upon winning a critical mass of subscribers, retaining the audience's loyalty and incrementally increasing subscriptions on an annual basis. Therefore, dish owners had to pay an additional £5.99 a month for the Sports channel from September 1992 which has grown every year. Steven Barnett comments:

> The subscription market only needs a total of 15–20% of the audience and a regular monthly fee from each dish owner of £25–30. Subscription television achieves a critical mass, at which point it becomes incredibly profitable. (In this respect) revenues can be increased without increasing cost-base. People will be willing to pay for sports and movie channels, and for channels which have sole rights. Multi-channel television will only be taken up in a few households, as the general public is not all that interested in television. However, through subscription huge profits can be made and these channels can buy rights to increasingly expensive sports and movies.[16]

Between 1995 and 1996, the number of subscribers expanded from 4.16 million to 5.18 million. As BSkyB is blatantly commercial, it has increased its audience share by gaining exclusive rights to the first showing of popular American imports (such as the *X-Files*), recently released Hollywood films and sport. It has aggressively secured rights in football, rugby league and boxing. In March 1996, this intensified, with the Tyson-Bruno fight becoming the first major sporting event to be shown on a pay-per-view basis. Its acquisitiveness in sport is reflective of its growing power and, as it has been unwilling to sell highlights to the terrestrial channels, the subject of an extensive political debate.

In 1996, News Corporation announced that BSkyB had made profits of £45.2 million.[17] Further, it has invested £177.6 million in a 25 per cent stake in the German Pay TV station Premiere. Thus, in its first six years, the monopolistic satellite broadcaster has become an important player. Clearly, with audiences paying for new reception equipment and channels over the mandatory licence fee, the future will see the expansion of 'narrowcasting' rather than 'broadcasting'.

The commercialization of terrestrial broadcasting: ITV

The 1990 Act recommended significant changes to ITV. The ITC is a regulatory body and no longer previews programmes. The ITV companies have control of the schedules through the network centre which commissions programmes. As the companies need to maximize their incomes, commercial factors have determined output. Executives are keen to secure profits as this will give them an advantage in the multi-channel future.

Due to the franchise auction and the considerable sums of money which have left ITV to go directly to the Exchequer, the network has streamlined its organizational structure, constituent power blocs and labour practices. As a result, the vertically integrated broadcasting producers were replaced by carriers such as Carlton, who commission from other regional franchisees or independents. Moreover, the legislation has freed up the ITV market so that greater concentrations of ownership have become manifest. For example, Michael Green (owner of Carlton), Gerry Robinson (Chief Executive of Granada) and Lord Hollick (Chief Executive of MAI) have manoeuvred to exploit legal changes to take over other franchises. ITV has been transformed from a regulated, regional monopoly to a centralized, commercial monopoly. For instance, Green has advocated the benefits of merging:

> The fragmentation of the channel among fifteen owners was supportable under the old monopoly. But in the new world, it no longer makes sense to carry high levels of duplicated overhead – overhead that saps the channel's strength and diverts money away from the screen to unproductive activities. . . . ITV cannot . . . afford to be inefficient, or to operate

Table 6.1   The franchise winners

Area	Winner	Bid
London Weekday	Carlton TV	£43.17m p.a.
London Weekend	London Weekend	£7.585m p.a.
Breakfast TV	Sunrise	£34.61m p.a.
Midlands	Central TV	£2000 p.a.
Yorkshire	Yorkshire TV	£37.7m p.a.
North West	Granada TV	£9m p.a.
North East	Tyne Tees	£15.057m p.a.
Borders	Border	£52,000 p.a.
Scotland Central	Scottish TV	£2000 p.a.
North of Scotland	Grampian	£720,000 p.a.
Northern Ireland	Ulster TV	£1.027m p.a.
Wales and West	HTV	£20.53m p.a.
South West	Westcountry TV	£7.815m p.a.
South and South East	Meridian	£36.523m p.a.
East of England	Anglia TV	£17.804 m
Channel Islands	Channel TV	£1000 p.a

under structures designed for less demanding times. It must be allowed to evolve naturally and to consolidate.[18]

The franchise auction

In February 1991, the ITC advertised for franchisees. They were required to submit a programme and business plan, based upon projected regional advertising over the following ten years, together with a sealed bid.[19] Only after the application had passed the quality threshold, could the bid's size be considered. The ITC announced its decisions on 16 October 1991 (see table 6.1). It avoided the 'Exceptional Circumstances Clause', preferring to rule out applicants through means of the quality threshold or highest bid.[20] This meant that rivals to established companies, such as Granada's opponent North-West Television, were ruled out due to the quality of their programming and business plans rather than the size of their bid.

The tender produced several notable victims. Thames Television, who held the most-prized London weekday contract and was the largest network contributor, passed the quality threshold but was out-bid by Carlton. It had been vulnerable, as it had attracted the strongest competition and Thorn (its parent company) had been experiencing financial instability. Thus, Michael Green fulfilled his wish to own an ITV franchise. Conspiracy theorists suggested Thames lost its franchise due to its infamous television documentary *Death on the Rock* which had attracted so much governmental wrath.

Two smaller companies, Television South (TVS) and Television Southwest (TSW), lost their franchises to Meridian Television and Westcountry Television. Whilst these areas had attracted interest as they were rich in advertising revenue, TVS and TSW were ruled out for overbidding. The heaviest irony was the defeat of the Thatcherite flagship TV-AM, led by Bruce Gyngell, who had taken on the broadcasting unions in 1988, which lost out to Good Morning Television (GMTV).[21] This led to a spectacular volte-face by the ex-Prime Minister, when Gyngell famously read out a private letter to the press:

> I am only too painfully aware that *I* was responsible for the legislation. . . . When I see some of the other licences have been awarded I am *mystified* that you did not receive yours and heart-broken. You of all people have done so much for the whole of television – there seems to be no attention to that.[22]

Of the four companies, only Thames (currently owned by Pearson) continues to play a role as a production company once responsible for the popular series *Minder* and now *The Bill*.[23] Thames has also made its programme library available for the BBC-backed satellite station UK Gold.

The franchise process produced several anomolies as some companies successfully gambled upon small bids, whilst others were forced to heighten the stakes. Certain franchises were desired as they attracted advertising, whereas others were left unchallenged. Further, although the ITC had stopped excessive monies going to the Treasury, it let through too many high bidders who have been undermined by advertising recessions, the loosening of cross-media restrictions and the growth of cable and satellite subscription. Thus, the ITV companies have become more accountable to their shareholders than the public.

Takeovers, mergers and concentration of ownership

The resulting financial instability has exacerbated the trend toward greater concentration of ownership. Shortly after the tender, Yorkshire took over Tyne Tees. From 1994, all the ITV companies were open to take-over bids. Therefore, throughout 1993, the ITC and the ITV companies lobbied for an extension to the moratorium on take-over bids.[24] In the event, then National Heritage Secretary Peter Brooke did not extend the moratorium, but swayed by the arguments of the larger ITV companies succumbed to a relaxation of ownership rules.[25] Brooke recommended that each company could take over one other.[26] However, to retain the ITV network's regional flavour and stem monopolization, he decided that the London franchise would remain divided between a weekday and weekend supplier.[27]

To this end, Brooke attempted to combine two irreconcilable trends: encroaching commercialism and the networks' regional traditions. He was accused of either tinkering around to encourage greater monopolization or not being radical enough. Then Labour Heritage spokesperson Mo Mowlan commented:

> (The move is) the worst of all possible worlds. . . . We wanted the moratorium to continue for at least another year so we could conduct a proper review of cross-media ownership. . . . There will be chaos in the system with a threat to regional programmes and a huge waste of money.[28]

Alternatively, the move did not please those who wanted a greater liberalization of the ITV network. It was predicted that by stemming cross-ownership the larger ITV companies would be 'hampered by a criss-cross of regulations, of which the restriction on . . . takeovers is just one. . . . if Britain's full broadcasting potential is to be unlocked, a strategic review rather than a piecemeal approach will be needed.'[29]

Throughout the following months, a number of mergers occurred as the larger companies secured their power base. Shortly after Brooke's announcement, Carlton (which already had a 20 per cent stake in Central) bought out Central.[30] Further, after a protracted boardroom battle, Granada won its hostile take-over of LWT, resulting in the resignation of LWT's Chairman Christopher Bland and Chief Executive Greg Dyke. Subsequently, Stephen Dorrell produced the 1995 *Media Ownership* White Paper which will be seen through to Royal Assent by Virginia Bottomley. This recommended that newspaper groups with less than 20 per cent of the national newspaper circulation can apply for ITV companies constituting up to 15 per cent of the total television market (defined by audience share), whilst limiting control to two ITV or Channel 5 licences. In February 1996, the newspaper group United Papers and MAI, who own Meridian and Anglia, announced they would merge.[31] This pre-empted the legislation and also defied its spirit, as 'The merger will create one of the biggest combines in Britain and one of the top twenty press and broadcasting groups in the world. . . . The deal, which sent some media shares rocketing, has altered the strategic outlook for major media players and fuelled belief that a series of acquisitions will follow.'[32]

To exert greater control, Carlton, Granada and MAI have warehoused their shares in deadlocked companies. This has enabled them to circumvent the cross-ownership legislation. For example, Granada has built up a significantly higher stake in Yorkshire-Tyne Tees TV than allowed. This problem was addressed in the 1996 Act, as the ITC could rule that one company may control another, even if nominal control is avoided by this loophole. However, the fear remained that company lawyers would be able to exploit any specific definition. The increased corporate power of the major companies has centralized the system to extract the last drop of profit from the domestic media market. They also contend that they need to expand to be viable global players.

The ITV companies after the franchise auction

The new franchisees, in particular Carlton, differ from their predecessors. First, there has been a generational shift in the broadcasting elite. Carlton's Director of Programming Paul Jackson has argued for more popular productions and the rescheduling of current affairs programming. Similarly, the former London Weekend (LWT) Chief Executive Greg Dyke, now at Pearson, propagates the values of commercial competiveness. Thus, ITV's previous establishment, represented by the ousted Chief Executive of Granada David Plowright, has declined.

Second, there has been a significant growth of broadcasting publishers alongside programme-makers. For instance, Carlton's main concern is to commission programmes, as it has to pay out to the Treasury an estimated £67 million per annum. However, this development has caused unforeseen problems as it means that the intellectual copyright has been transferred to the independents. Therefore, major broadcasting companies could lose out over foreign sales, repeats and rental from programming libraries. Further, certain stars have established their own production companies and are able to determine the specific content of their programmes. Increasingly, the publishing model is in a state of decline.

Third, the act allowed the companies to streamline their internal hierarchies as they were no longer required to keep in-house production facilities. Subsequently, they have reduced costs by using independents and centralizing production bases.[33] Therefore, the new franchise-holders contract out to independent producers, make fewer network programmes, and have reduced staff (see table 6.2). This has gone hand-in-hand with the collapse of trade union power. In 1988, the test case TV-AM dispute resulted in the removal of a large number of technicians.[34] This has meant that there have been more short-term contracts, a large number of redundancies and a greater casualization of working practices. As Greg Dyke commented:

> The biggest change and the reason that most ITV companies have been able to survive the recession as well as they have . . . has been the collapse of the trade union movement and therefore the enormous loss of jobs and the restructuring of the industry. Now that was partly brought

Table 6.2   ITV staff numbers

October 1991		January 1993	
Thames	1400	Carlton	360
TVS	800	Meridian	322
TV-AM	399	GMTV/Visnews	190
TSW	293	Westcountry	112
Total	**2892**	**Total**	**984**

Source: *Broadcast*, 26 June 1992, p. 16

about by the auction itself. The threat of the auction meant that you had to go into the auction as efficient as anyone going against you. We (LWT) are now down 650 staff and we started off at 1400 four years ago. That has freed up television in some ways, with the end of the old union restrictive practices.[35]

ITV programming

In programming, ITV has hardened its competitive outlook and the ITV Network Centre is responsible for the commissioning and scheduling of all programmes. Formally, both independents and franchise-holders have equal access to this body. In practice, *de facto* power has been wielded by the largest companies (Granada, London Weekend, Central, Carlton).

The loosening of public service commitments has produced several changes. Previously, all the regions were required to schedule religious programmes in the 'God slot' between six and seven o'clock on a Sunday evening. This had been a constant thorn for the companies and the advertisers, who felt that they had lost potential revenue. Under the new system, ITV's religious programme, *Highway*, was removed. There has also been pressure on news and current affairs programmes. Independent Television News (ITN) has revamped the *News at Ten* to gain a wider audience and retain its position in the schedule. This presentational change has been apparent in Carlton's *London Tonight* which emphasizes human interest stories. Further, expensive current affairs programmes, which are not proven winners, have either become more populist (e.g. *World in Action*) or were replaced by consumer programmes like *The Cook Report*.

The emphasis has been on securing profits, and the Network Centre has invariably commissioned secure ratings winners. As the scheduling power has been passed on from the regulator to the companies, ITV pursued aggressive strategies to attract advertisers. Therefore, advertising power has expanded as popular dramas, situation comedies and sports coverage have proliferated. Alongside this, stands the growth of programme sponsorship. In particular, late-night programming aimed at a young audience has been reliant on sponsors. This came to light when the Dutch brewer Heineken was castigated for attempting to remove Afro-Caribbeans from *Hotel Babylon* which it sponsored.

Channel Four

The 1990 Act required Channel Four (C4) to remain innovative whilst selling its own advertising revenue. This forced the station into a balancing act between scheduling minority programmes at peak times and retaining profitability. Further, as ITV wanted to increase its audience share, it seemed C4 would lose the slots that it had previously won or find that the network would steal its most popular shows. It was predicted that the station's quality and programme diversity would decline.

In practice, however, C4 has survived remarkably well, attracting the requisite 15 per cent of the audience. This has been due to C4 Controller Michael Grade's astute scheduling and commissioning practices. Whilst commercialization has led to a more conservative menu of programmes, he has retained innovation, by defining the concept in more populist terms alongside commercial success. Grade's achievements have included *The Big Breakfast*, sustaining the success of *Brookside*, off-the-wall situation comedies such as *Father Ted*, attracting stand-up comedians from the cabaret circuit, and buying the rights to Italian football, cult shows or high quality American imports. Further, C4 developed the practice of stranding programmes into theme evenings. Indeed, C4's success has proved to be a double-edged sword. First, it faces stiffer competition from BBC2 who have employed similar scheduling practices to attract niche audiences. Second, the safety net, into which the ITV companies were required to contribute 17 per cent of their revenues to protect C4, was turned on its head. As the channel achieved high audiences it had to contribute £74 million per annum toward ITV's coffers. Paradoxically, C4 lobbied to remove a provision which was designed to protect it. In 1996, Lord Inglewood, the broadcasting minister, agreed that the funding formula would be phased out between 1998 and 1999, as C4 had accrued significant reserves to protect its status. In turn C4 pledged to reduce the number of American imports and invest in more drama.

Finally, the 1990 Act, at the behest of the advertisers, established the legislative framework for a new terrestrial station, Channel Five. Its development has been marked by several false dawns. When the ITC first advertised for the franchise the only response came from Thames, whose bid was rejected. Finally, in 1995, the franchise was won by Pearson, who had to fight off Rupert Murdoch's rather less than committed attention. As the channel will face competition from the established terrestrial, cable and satellite stations, Pearson's strategy is to fill the schedule with re-runs from video libraries in order to cut costs. There are also technological problems, as all domestic VCRs will have to be retuned and the frequency is not readily available in the key advertising areas of South-East England. Ironically, Greg Dyke, who in the meantime became Pearson's Chief Executive, has taken charge of a station he had dismissed as a charter for thieves posing as video engineers!

The BBC

Within this commercial environment, the BBC faced several problems. The licence fee became a vexed issue due to its political unpopularity, its reduction and the predicted decline in the BBC's audience share which undermined the concept of universality. Further, due to the 1996 Charter renewal, it had to please its political masters by demonstrating its competitive worth.

The policy environment

Throughout the early to mid-1990s, the government's attention returned to the BBC. Yet, in contrast to the Thatcherite 1980s, an apparently cosy relationship between the Corporation and the Major government defined the debate. The 1992 Green Paper *The Future of the BBC* established that the Corporation would remain a key actor in British broadcasting. However, it was made clear that the BBC would have to manage its resources more effectively to retain public funds.

The Corporation's response, *Extending Choice*, echoed these concerns. It provided a standard defence of the licence fee as the main source of revenue for core services. Further, despite accepting different funds for peripheral services, it suggested that advertising, subscription and sponsorship could not deliver the appropriate monies. To show that it was pursuing radical policies to promote efficiency, the BBC altered its production strategy through producer choice. To this end, Birt has centralized the managerial power base by expanding its hierarchy and reducing producer autonomy. In terms of programming, the BBC has tried to reconcile the dilemma between competing in the market, thereby being more commercial, or becoming more specialist and possibly marginalized. It has defined its mission as providing distinctiveness and quality in an increasingly commercially-led programming market.

These proposals were accepted in National Heritage's White Paper in 1994. In addition, the BBC was encouraged to expand its commercial activities and its global ambitions. Such reforms have major implications as the Corporation is inexorably tied to the public through its image, internal structure, finance and position within the British polity.

Producer choice

The three tenets of producer choice are organizational decentralization, financial transparency, and operational reform. A command economy, in which the licence fee was diverted from the centre to each resource department, has given way to an internal market, whereby centrally allocated money is directed to the main areas of the BBC's *programming* output such as BBC1, BBC2 and BBC radio. The channel controllers receive an annual budget to fund the main eleven programming areas (sport, drama, light entertainment, etc). Eighteen months before the programming year, they negotiate with the departmental heads over the programmes they require. These are commissioned with the allotted programming and departmental budgets. For instance, the Head of Drama could be given £200 million to produce a specific number of programming hours. Subsequently, the heads of department assign the budget for each programme. Previously, these were calculated by man-hours for shooting and post-production. They are now given to the producers in real cash figures. As long as the head of department approves, they can choose between in-house BBC resources or the external market (although independent producers are restricted to using outside facilities houses) both of which will compete for the tender in terms of costs and quality. Theoretically, the producer may determine the trade-off between a programme's budget and its artistic qualities. However, producer autonomy is qualified by budgetry restrictions, as the department has been constituted as a business unit which must break even.[36] Any overspend will result in cuts.

These changes have been contingent upon the privatization of BBC resources. These departments have calculated their prices in regard to the external facilities and offer to sell their resources to the individual producer. They have been set up as mini-businesses and are expected to conform to the same break-even targets. They are also subject to fixed overheads including all property and capital charges.

Producer choice was designed to justify, through an internal market, the public funding of the licence fee. However, it was also reflective of the cost-cutting and streamlining of labour which have occurred in ITV. The broadcasting unions argue that it has placed impossible responsibilities upon the resources sections by transforming them into business units. In theory, these units are required to compete with outside production houses. In practice, fixed costs, such as rent and equipment hire, undermine their competitiveness. Further, they have to prove to BBC accountants that they can continue to break even and develop a business plan that illustrates that they are conforming to market principles. There are fears that the BBC's training and craft base will be undermined as full-time workers, whose talents are only employed on particular productions (such as special effects), cannot be justified under the business criterion. It appears that the viability of the resources section is in doubt. Therefore, the work force may become casualized throughout the whole of broadcasting, creating a cheaper pool for the independent section. This could possibly spiral with independent facilities placing pressure on the already beleaguered BBC resource areas by under-cutting their costs. This development may be further exacerbated as producers have to balance their corporate loyalty against programming costs.

Producer Choice has implications for programme-making and public service broadcasting during the 1990s. John Birt comments:

> We are introducing new ways of working – and striving for a more streamlined BBC, offering increased value for money. The period up to April 1993 – and probably the year beyond – will be a challenge for us all. I am confident that we can make a success of it – that the outcome will be a leaner, more devolved BBC . . . The BBC as a whole is undergoing a transformation, carrying further processes initiated in the late 1980s.[37]

Programming

The BBC has defined its mission as providing distinctiveness and quality in an increasingly commercial market. In *Extending Choice*, Birt argued that the corporation must 'limit and define' its public service role to offer high quality programmes in several programming genres such as news and information, British-based culture and entertainment, educational output and the World Service.[38] Elsewhere, he has argued 'The BBC will need to withdraw from areas in which it is no longer able or needed to make an original contribution.'[39] Whilst Birt has suggested that the high-ground (innovative, British-made, informative programming) does not preclude the 'Himalayan' option, he risks ceding the territory to the commercial sector. As the BBC withdraws from more populist programmes, it may narrow its mass appeal and could become ghettoized like the weak public broadcasters in the United States or Australia. If the audience share declines, the legitimacy of the licence fee becomes open to question. Subsequently, scheduling and programming practices, particularly on BBC1, have been schizophrenic, ranging from high quality drama such as *Pride and Prejudice* to the popular *Noel's House Party*.

Tensions within the BBC

This phase was accompanied by a policy clash between the outgoing DG Michael Checkland and his successor John Birt due to a twenty-one month vacuum at the top from 1991 to 1993. This occurred when the BBC's Chairman Marmaduke Hussey decided that Checkland would be replaced by Birt. As Birt was appointed without an interview, Hussey, to appease board members, agreed that Checkland would remain for the following year.

Checkland's beleaguered position created several groups within the management. Although he had been dismissed as an accountant, he retained the support of the 'old guard' who had risen through the BBC. Their pre-eminence was challenged by Birt's managerial style, or 'Birtism', which had evolved at LWT. He was accused of being an outsider whose values were incompatible with the BBC. Moreover, he had been protected from criticism by Hussey and the acolytes he had appointed in the 'corporate affairs' offices. Birt's patronage was also apparent in the news and current affairs division, as allies like Glywyn Benson (Editor of *Panorama*), Peter Jay, and Samir Shah had secured a foothold. There was an irony in Checkland's position: he had initially appointed the outsider Birt, yet he was 'hoist by his own petard. . . . Checkland (found) that (his position has been undermined) as an old BBC man, as "one of the chaps", (as he was) surrounded by all these new people who have no loyalty to the organization and who were actually in the majority when it comes to circles of influence.'[40] This resulted in the Charter Renewal strategy being contested by two Director-Generals, with different views. Checkland preferred to incrementally reform the organization and retain popular programming. Birt hastened institutional reform and narrowed the BBC's mission. Eventually, Birt's plans, backed by Hussey, were accepted by the governors. Indeed, some accounts suggested that the Chairman created a vacuum so that he could become the *de facto* chief executive.[41] This interregnum left staff fearing that irreconcilable splits would undermine the Corporation's future.

The BBC governors

Marmaduke Hussey reorganized relations between the governors and the management. His appointment occurred in the aftermath of *Real Lives*. In response to Margaret Thatcher's aim that the 'BBC should put its house in order', Hussey became an interventionist chairman. After the BBC had been raided by Special Branch over the *Zircon Spy Satellite* tapes, he sacked the Director-General Alasdair Milne.

This cemented his position, as Milne was the last of the authoritarian 'Reithian' managers. Subsequently, the Board of Governors and, most especially, the chair became more powerful.

However, his steamrolling of Birt's appointment and intrusions over management signified a high-handed attitude. Accountability was the BBC's buzz word in *Extending Choice*. Yet decisions have been taken without any public debate and the BBC remains impervious to criticism from outside of the political elite. This was apparent when John Birt's tax arrangements were revealed. In its wake, Birt and Hussey faced dismissal. However, in the end, the senior members of the BBC closed ranks. During this debate the role of the governors, the official public trustees, came under investigation and it appeared the other accountable bodies, the General and Regional Advisory Councils, were impotent. Moreover, the board of governors have attracted criticisms of political compliance. Eric Barendt suggested that a new code of practice for independence should be established.[42] The government, however, did not reform the board. Instead, it suggested:

> **The Board of Governors** should keep in touch with the BBC's audiences, and should ensure that the BBC's programmes, services and other public service activities reflect the needs and interests of the public, and that its commercial strategy is soundly based. They should approve objectives for the BBC's services and programmes, the promises the BBC will make to its audience, and objectives for its commercial ventures, and they should measure how successful the BBC has been each year in fulfilling these aims. Their role is to look after the public's interest in the BBC, not to manage it.[43]

In 1996, Hussey (who had fallen out with Birt over the BBC's moral propriety and *Panorama*'s infamous interview with Princess Diana) retired to be replaced by former LWT Chairman Christopher Bland. His appointment was popular as he had worked with Birt, enjoyed an outstanding commercial record, held regulatory experience and was committed to public service broadcasting.[44] At the time of writing, it remains to be seen whether the Board will continue to manage or perform the less interventionist role defined by the 1994 White Paper.

Snatch of the Day: Sports Rights and Competition between Satellite and Terrestrial Channels

The old-style duopoly has now been dismantled and three types of broadcaster have emerged; a satellite monopoly; a more commercially dominated ITV network, and public service broadcasting (PSB) represented partly by Channel Four and mainly by the BBC. The battle for sports' rights has reflected these changes in the broadcasting ecology. BSkyB has been a determined competitor, pursuing deals in cricket, boxing, golf, rugby league and football. Initially, it secured the rights to the first Tyson–Bruno fight in 1989 and the 1991 Cricket World Cup. The major turning point occurred in 1992 when BSkyB, in league with the BBC (who received the rights to show edited highlights), negotiated with the Football Assocation (FA) to cover live FA Premier League football matches. This has meant that the authorities, clubs and top-level players have enjoyed a greater share of the spoils. It brought into question universality of coverage and led to a political debate surrounding the 1996 Act.

The FA Premier League deal

The £304 million for five years' exclusive coverage was the most expensive in the history of televised sport and secured BSkyB's future. It was controversial as BSkyB and the BBC had trumped the agreed figure of £200 million between the ITV network and the league. ITV negotiator Greg Dyke complained that he had been betrayed by the Premier League Chief Executive Rick Parry, BSkyB and the clubs' chairmen:

> the controversy over British sport's biggest television deal continued . . . with ITV demanding to know how details of its last minute bid were leaked to BSkyB, enabling the satellite broadcaster to trump it, why they were not allowed to make a counter offer, and why they were not given the opportunity to make a formal presentation.[45]

The deal reflected the convergence of football and the broadcasting industry. For instance, Alan Sugar was not only the chairman of Tottenham Hotspur, but owned the Astra satellite dish manufacturer Amstrad.[46] Consequently, when it emerged that he had spoken to BSkyB about submitting a late bid to trump ITV, he was accused of pursuing a conflict of interests.[47] The ITV companies took the FA to court claiming a breach of contract and argued that Rupert Murdoch should be taken to the 'Monopolies and Merger's Commission'. However, they failed to win an injunction to freeze the deal. Moreover, Rick Parry remained unrepentant and informed the High Court that even if ITV could submit an increased offer it would have to compensate the Premier League for the lost revenue.[48]

The football deal followed on from the controversy over the 1991 Cricket World Cup when BSkyB refused to provide the terrestrial channels with any pictures. It meant the live Premier League football matches could only be viewed through subscription.[49] The contract cemented the major changes in broadcasting's finances and demonstrated how sport had become the forum for competition.

The implications of the deal

Economic imperatives governed BSkyB's logic. Televised sport has generated large viewing figures, whilst remaining relatively cheap (£30,000 per hour) in production costs. Crews rarely have to be transported and the event's predictability means that production delays can be avoided. Sports events are clearly timetabled and generate a substantial amount of free publicity through the press. The deal demonstrated that BSkyB's principal aim was to maximize its profits. Instead of attempting to increase the number of dish sales, subscription costs would be increased for existing customers. As Harold Lind comments:

> The expenditure of hundreds of millions of pounds for the rights to show leading soccer matches for the next five years would make no economic sense for BSkyB unless matches are put out in encrypted form on a premium channel. However many dishes might be sold by a 'free' football channel, the total potential market will remain only a fraction of what ITV could offer the advertiser . . . by showing the football from the start on a subscription channel, the number of extra sales required to make massive payments economically may well be achievable.[50]

Moreover, the station became the leader in football coverage, had shown corporate prowess and had proved to be a viable competitor to ITV. This hard-nosed commercial ethos was personified by then BSkyB Chief Executive Sam Chisholm and the trade journals were replete with footballing similes:

> For Chisholm, it is a double victory. Not only will dish sales be boosted but it has dealt a blow to ITV's image as a brand leader in commercial television. This bolsters his ambition to take commercial television's throne, currently occupied by ITV centre-forward Dyke.[51]

For ITV, the failure to make a deal was a major strategic blow as the exclusive rights to Sunday afternoon football would have increased advertising revenues and enhanced ITV's position as the market-leader in national sport.

In particular, the football deal represented another example of the BBC adapting to the commercial environment. For some, the Corporation had entered into a 'Faustian' contract with Murdoch. However, it enabled the BBC to provide national coverage of the national game.

It had been starved of league football when ITV had won the contract in 1988 for £44 million, and had been left with the FA Cup and the feeling that it had been outpriced.[52] Historically, the BBC was proud of its sports coverage which had combined technical expertise, extensive resources, long-term contracts and a moral purpose.[53] The BBC had turned major events, such as the Boat Race, the Grand National, Wimbledon and the FA Cup Final, into shared national rituals.[54] Therefore, the absence of league football 'could not be shrugged off as a minor irritation. While ITV's first season of exclusive coverage (1988–89) produced the most sensational climax in the first division's history (Liverpool 0-2 Arsenal), the BBC could not even offer a few consolation pictures.'[55] The BSkyB deal re-established the BBC as the main provider of 'free' sports coverage. It gained sole rights for Premier League football on terrestrial TV at a nominal price. Moreover, it could not have justified a bid against the £200 million offered by the ITV network. This meant that it had regained a popular programme, *Match of the Day*, showing edited highlights, and could compete against ITV for viewing figures.

Finally, the deal indicated the BBC's willingness to accommodate the satellite broadcaster. The governors and management treated BSkyB as an ally rather than an enemy. Some cited the influence of Marmaduke Hussey who had worked with Murdoch as Managing Director of the *The Times*. More particularly, it demonstrated the emergence of new alliances in a more commercial environment.[56] In this flexible marketplace, the BBC sees that it will be necessary to oblige the satellite monopoly.

The political debate

The deal massively increased the football clubs' profits. Subsequently, other sports have been attracted to satellite television and BSkyB has expanded its sporting profile. Concurrently, subscription costs for Sky Sport have risen by 100 per cent from £96 per annum in 1991 to a minimum £190 in 1996. Further, the second Tyson–Bruno fight marked the first use of pay-per-view above general subscription rates. BSkyB was also unprepared to sell highlights of the fight to terrestrial television channels. With regard to these developments, Steven Barnett comments: 'With almost ruthless disregard for the television tradition of universal access, Sky are closing down the viewing options for any event for which they own exclusive rights.'[57]

However, BSkyB's actions hastened a major political debate. Throughout the second and third reading of the 1996 Broadcasting Act, a battle ensued in the House of Lords to retain the eight listed sports events (including the FA Cup Final, the Grand National, the

Derby, the Ashes, Wimbledon, and the Boat Race) on the terrestrial channels. These had been repealed in the 1990 Act. However, the government (due to John Major's populist sporting instincts, divisions within the cabinet, pressure from other media groups, and Bottomley's feeble contention that none of the listed events had yet been bought by subscription services) relented in the face of the Lords' argument that these events demanded protection.

Yet a second amendment may have more far-reaching effects. The so-called 'unbundling' provision was designed to force BSkyB to let the BBC or ITV show highlights of the events it covers exclusively live. This outlawed the deals it had made during the 1991 Cricket World Cup, the 1995 Ryder Cup or 1996 Tyson–Bruno fight, whereby the vast majority of viewers were excluded. Sensing the tide had turned, BSkyB had already allowed the BBC to show highlights of the 1996 Cricket World Cup. In turn, this controversy draws our attention to a wider debate about the future of Public Service Broadcasting (PSB).

Public Service Broadcasting towards the Second Millenium

The changes occurring within broadcasting are complex and on-going. Both BSkyB and ITV have a commercial agenda. The BBC is still facing up to difficult questions about its role in the new environment. The future of PSBs has been complicated by the financial pressures, niche markets, audience fragmentation, ideology and political incorporation. These changes question the role of a national broadcaster producing programming as a public good.

Financial pressures

The internationalization of the new media, hastened by deregulatory policies, has encouraged the development of global media conglomerates. Subsequently, public service assumptions, notions and structures have become difficult to sustain. PSBs are being transformed from publicly regulated bodies into increasingly *commercial* organizations forced to incorporate public and private funding. This has taken several forms. In Italy, RAI included spot ads between programming. In Britain, the broadcasting institutions remain committed to the public service ideal. Yet both the BBC and Channel Four have had to become more commercial in a national and global market as they are faced with increasing programming costs, capped incomes and the competitors. William H. Melody comments: 'This is a privatization of purpose, if not ownership.'[58]

Programme consumption

Throughout the development of British broadcasting, Reithian cultural homogeneity was challenged by ITV, and changes within the BBC response and Channel Four which reflected the cosmopolitan nature of British society. Yet, despite these changes, the broadcasting institutions have been accused of promoting a white, male ethno-centrism. In the 1980s, this viewpoint was expressed by the New Right, as public choice theories provided an alternative discourse about relations between the state, broadcasters and the audience. The viewer was seen as a consumer of private goods rather than a citizen enjoying a public good and freedom of information. As Kuhn and Wheeler comment: 'The Reithian legacy was challenged across a wide front, as a radical libertarian alternative to the established public service paradigm claimed the high ground.'[59]

In a multi-channel future, delivered through the subscription, there could be greater access for women, ethnic or minority groups. The new technology provides generic channels catering for specific needs which fragment the audiences into niche markets. Consequently, viewing patterns may alter as people are drawn away from the terrestrial channels. This brings into question whether broadcasting institutions, providing a public service and concept of national culture, are still required.

However, this trend may be offset as the proliferation of new media channels has failed to increase the availability of political information to citizens. Multiplicity does not necessarily secure diversity. More has often meant the same cultural forms being packaged to a variety of markets. Invariably, the widening array of choices has narrowed individual choice. Indeed, the major expansion in the audio-visual industries has been in distribution channels, not original production. Alternatively, with the dominance of major media moguls, a bland international cultural dominance may be constructed with programming becoming dominated by imports and cheap productions.

Political liberty

These developments demonstrate the recurring political pressures on the public service institutions. The deregulatory agenda has made conspicuous the dichotomy between liberalization and political control in state–broadcasting relations. Although the BBC is formally independent, its position has been complicated as it has been incorporated into the state through regulation, financial intervention and covert political controls. British broadcasting's success has been conditional upon the ideological, if not overt, support of the political elite.

The BBC's willingness to conform to its political masters raises questions about its liberty in a market-dominated environment. It has become more commercial, but remains susceptible to state intervention through the volatility of broadcasting finance, commissioning, self-censorship, reformed regulatory practices and the omnipresent threat of constant legislative changes. In the light of this, several commentators have proposed reformed public service models.

Alternative models for public service broadcasting

James Curran argues that the elite control of the media may be reformed as alternative goals will be established. Subordinated classes should enjoy a greater access to ideas and more empowerment to define a normative vision of the world. Through diverse public debate, the media may provide a plurality of views. Simultaneously, it should create social consent by mobilizing collective and individual consciousness. Through the staging of a more equitable public dialogue between conflicting groups, common objectives, collective aims and problems can be resolved.[60] John Keane concurs with this vision:

> A fundamentally revised public service model would aim to facilitate a genuine commonwealth of forms of life, tastes and opinions, to empower a plurality of citizens who are governed neither by despotic states nor by market forces.[61]

Keane proposes a mixed public service system comprising state funded and protected outlets, alongside a plurality of non-market, non-state communications institutions. There will be a need to regulate the market which should become open, accountable and positively enabling. In practice, the non-state media outlets will restrain the political elite's power (undermining censorship) and, with constraints over private media markets, act as the principal means to circulate views amongst the citizenry. The model recognizes that, in a cosmopolitan society, traditional public service assumptions of cultural, social and political homogeneity are undesirable. Further, he suggests that a written constitution, legal protections for freedom of information and state regulations will force governments to justify their intrusions over the free circulation of opinions.[62]

Curran presents a more radical vision. He advocates a core public service sector surrounded by different media outlets. As the core reaches a mass audience, it addresses general concerns, provides a forum for debate and enables public discourse across all social areas. It allows different communities, constituencies, interest groups, sub-cultures and social strata to engage in dialogue with one another to achieve shared public conceptions. In this manner, the media satisfies its representative role, alongside the democratic need to achieve social consensus:

> By mediating public events to a large undifferentiated audience, by providing a common stock of shared experience and by offering up common symbols of identification to be shared and also exchanged, core public service institutions serve as a focal point of collective unity and reinforce ties of social association in society.[63]

However, Curran is aware that centrifugal forces may stem debate, therefore peripheral sectors are required. First, there will be a civic media sector to establish diversity of representation between political organizations and the public. Second, a professional media sector may remove journalists from market pressures within the commercially-driven organizations and political constraints in public ones. Third, a limited private market could be established, under strict guidelines related to advertising and subscription, in the new media sector. Finally, a publicly funded social market should be created to incubate new forms of competition which cannot be delivered by the market. These diverse media will invigorate the core system, provide checks and balances for pluralism, access a more differentiated audience and strengthen democratic institutions within civil society. Thus, this proposed model is a reworking of Habermas's idyll of the public sphere.[64]

Conclusion

Several significant trends have occurred in British broadcasting. First, new media technologies (cable, satellite, telecommunications, personal computers) have have become domestically available. Moreover, there has been a convergence of different media services promoted through the technology. For example, media groups such as Pearson, the Mirror group and Associated Newsapapers seek to exploit cable and satellite technologies in order to enter the broadcasting market.

The concentration of media ownership belies the myth of greater access and representation in a free market. In particular, the merger between Sky and BSB allowed Rupert Murdoch to enjoy a monopolistic position in satellite broadcasting. This resulted from the government's failure, through accident and design, to place effective cross-ownership regulations on his media interests. BSkyB enjoys a monopoly and, as its power in sport coverage indicates, has become a stronger competitor. Consequently, the ITV network and the BBC have responded to the new environment. The major ITV companies successfully lobbied the government to reform ownership rules.

Subsequently, there have been mergers between the main players to secure their national and international future. Concurrently, they have commercialized their operations, centralized their organizational structure, streamlined the labour force and become advertising-led in scheduling and programming. The desire for ensuring profitability has meant that the ITV companies have produced more populist, entertainment-led programmes. Pressure has been placed on the scheduling of the news and the commissioning of current affairs documentaries. ITV has demonstrated a shift from a regulated private monopolistic system into a commercially driven monopoly. Steven Barnett is pessimistic about its future:

> this commercialization will restrict choice instead of increase diversity. Moreover the amount of money will not increase, instead there will be the same amount of money being used to fund more hours as multi-channels lasting for longer hours increase. The equation means that the money will be more thinly spread and the equation will not allow for quality. . . . There has been a substitution of commercial power for state power. State power has been displaced by the big corporations.[65]

The concentration of ownership in terrestrial, cable and satellite channels has been the source of public debate, with advocates such as the Campaign for Press and Broadcasting Freedom arguing that it should be divested. In response, recent British media policy has evidenced limited and belated attempts at cross-media legislation. This has been problematic due to the political will of governments, the lobbying power of the companies and the supranational nature of satellite and telecommunications links that allow media conglomerates to circumvent national regulations. Concurrently, British broadcasting is experiencing a shift from the norms of the public service tradition into market provision. Within political circles, consumerism has been equated with citizenship. Subsequently, the growth of niche markets and fragmented audiences has been deemed desirable. PSBs have also had to demonstrate that they are more commercial in their practices.

The 1990 Act did not affect the BBC, however its measures have indirectly altered its development. Subsequently, the Corporation attempted to show that it will use the licence fee in an efficient manner. It has also defined itself as a 'specialized' public service broadcaster. These internal policy-making processes have arisen from the Corporation's need to respond to the market, the renewal of the Charter and the management's interpretation of its future role.

This leads to a central question; has the market reform of British broadcasting promoted greater political *autonomy* or hastened increased political *complicitness*? The ITV companies, due to financial necessity, have concentrated on providing entertainment-led programmes. They are wary of involving themselves in political controversies due to potentially expensive legal costs, as they will no longer be cushioned by the ITC. As Colin Shaw comments:

> To make controversial programmes you need two things – brass and courage. Thames had a large amount of money and spent over three-quarters of a million pounds setting up the *Windlesham–Rampton* report to justify [*Death on the Rock*]. The new system puts both finances and courage in some jeopardy. Whether boardrooms will be as courageous remains to be seen, but the prospects are not as hopeful as they were ten years ago.[66]

Alternatively, the BBC has attempted to out-think government by proving that it is more efficient and accountable to the political elite. In effect, these strategies and the thinking that has guided them, have generated a greater amount of political compliance. The BBC has often referred to public accountability, yet there has been little public debate about its future.

Consequently, several reformed public service models have been proposed. These are designed to make the PSB more accountable to the public, stem market controls and assure political independence. However, at the time of writing, they only exist in the abstract, as governments of all political hues remain reluctant to cede their power over the national broadcasting institutions. The digitalization of terrestrial services may also expand the number of channels and reform the nature of broadcasting services. Further, as we shall discuss in chapter 7, such reforms will have to take into account the increasingly global flow of communications. Therefore, the changes in British broadcasting are complicated and on-going. There will be a constant need for research to determine how these developments are being realized.

Further Reading

Steven Barnett (ed.), *Funding the BBC's Future*, The BBC Charter Review Series 2, BFI, 1993.

Jay Blumler (ed.), *Television and the Public Interest: Vulnerable Values in West European Broadcasting*, Sage Publications, 1992.

Jay Blumler & T. J. Nossiter (eds), *Broadcasting Finance in Transition*, Oxford University Press, 1991.

British Broadcasting Corporation, *Extending Choice: The BBC's role in the New Broadcasting Age*, BBC Publications, 1992.

Peter Chippindale and Suzanne Franks, *Dished! The Rise and Fall of British Satellite Broadcasting*, Simon & Schuster, 1991.

Richard Collins, *Television: Policy and Culture*, Routledge, 1990.

Tim Congdon, Brian Sturgess, National Economic Research Associates

(N.E.R.A.), William B. Shew, Andrew Graham and Gavyn Davies, *Paying for Broadcasting: The Handbook*, Routledge, 1992.

Andrew Davidson, *Under the Hammer: The ITV Franchise Battle*, Heinemann, 1992.

Department of National Heritage, *The Future of the BBC: Serving the Nation, Competing World-wide*, HMSO, 1994.

Department of National Heritage, *Media Ownership: The Government's Proposals*, HMSO, 1995.

Department of National Heritage, *Digital Terrestrial Broadcasting: The Government's Proposals*, HMSO, 1995.

Department of National Heritage, *Broadcasting Bill (H.L.)*, HL Bill 19, 1995.

Independent Television Commission, *Invitation to apply for Regional Channel 3 Licences*, ITC, 1991.

Independent Television Commission, *Channel 3 Networking Arrangements*, ITC, 1992.

Stuart Hood (ed.), *Behind the Screens: The Structure of British Television in the Nineties*, Lawrence & Wishart, 1994.

Stuart Hood and Garret O'Leary, *Questions of Broadcasting*, Methuen, 1990.

Chris Horrie and Steve Clarke, *Fuzzy Monsters: Fear and Loathing at the BBC*, Heinemann, 1994.

Raymond Kuhn, *Politics and the Mass Media in Britain*, Harvester Wheatsheaf, 1996.

Nod Miller and Rod Allen (eds), *Broadcasting Enters the Marketplace*, University of Manchester Broadcasting Symposium, John Libbey, 1993.

Geoff Mulgan and Richard Patterson (eds), *Reinventing the Organization*, The BBC Charter Review Series, BFI, 1993.

Tom O'Malley, *Closedown? The BBC and Government Broadcasting Policy, 1979–92*, Pluto Press, 1994.

Jeremy Tunstall, *Television Producers*, Routledge, 1993.

Notes

1　Jay Blumler and T. J. Nossiter (eds), *Broadcasting Finance in Transition*, Oxford University Press, 1991, p. 98.

2　See Home Office, *Broadcasting in the '90s: Competition, Choice and Quality*, HMSO, November 1988 and *Broadcasting Act 1990* (Chapter 42), HMSO, November 1990.

3　See *Broadcasting Act 1990*.

4　Ibid.

5　Ibid.

6　Department of National Heritage, *Digital Terrestrial Broadcasting: The Government's Proposals*, Cm2946, HMSO, August 1995, pp. 1–2.

7　Interview with DTI spokesman, 25 March 1993.

8　See Debbie Kruger 'Simonds-Gooding's Brief Orbit', *Management Week*, 4 December 1991, no. 20, p. 34.

9　Peter Chippindale and Suzanne Franks, *Dished! The Rise and Fall of British Satellite Broadcasting*, Simon & Schuster, 1991, p. xi.

10　Debbie Kruger 'Simonds-Gooding's Brief Orbit', p. 35.

11   The Dutch manufacturer Philips had invested large amounts of resources in the development of High-Definition Television by the early 1990s.

12   The contract between BSB and the IBA contained provisions over technology and the content of programming. For instance Part II, Section 2, p. 54:

> The programmes provided by the Contractor shall at all times be such as in the opinion of the Authority: –
> (1)   are of high general standard in all respects and in particular in respect of their content and quality;
> (2)   are capable of high quality transmission by the Authority.

13   For the variations on this argument see (House of Commons) *Hansard*, HMSO, 18 December 1990 col. 53:

> **Mr Hattersley**: . . . Once upon a time the Government pretended that it was impossible to limit the connections between newspapers and owner-ship of Sky because that company is registered in Luxembourg . . .
> **Mr Gale**: . . . Does he (Hattersley) not appreciate the difference between BSB, which is a domestic satellite licensed by the United Kingdom, and Astra which is a non-domestic satellite? Is he seriously suggesting that this control should not only be exercised over Mr Murdoch, who happens to uplink from the United Kingdom but could just as easily uplink from any-where else in Europe, but should be extended to every newspaper proprietor throughout Europe who uses a foreign satellite?

14   William Shawcross, *Rupert Murdoch: Ringmaster of the Information Circus*, Chatto & Windus, 1992, p. 501.

15   'Government leaves room for Murdoch', *Media Week*, 26 May 1995.

16   Interview with Steven Barnett, 27 July 1992.

17   Tony May, 'News International Climbs', *Guardian*, 9 February 1996, p. 16.

18   Michael Green, 'Green Politics: RTS Fleming Memorial Lecture', *Television: The Journal of the Royal Television Society*, April–May 1994, pp. 9–10.

19   Ibid., pp. 23–55.

20   For general criticisms of the legal process see for instance, 'ITV Auction Fiasco', *The Times*, 17 October 1991, p. 19 or 'Television's dog's dinner', *Evening Stand-ard*, 16 October 1991, p. 7.

21   Joanna Coles, 'Champagne and tears breakfast', *Guardian*, 17 October 1991, p. 4. Also see Jamie Dettmer, 'Anger and Tears as losers hear news', *The Times*, 17 October 1991, p. 5 when David Frost, TV-AM founder and presenter com-mented: 'When I was at school I was told the important thing was not the winning but taking part. I did not believe that then and certainly do not believe that now.'

22   Georgina Henry, 'Thatcher Repudiates TV auction', *Guardian*, 18 October 1991, p. 1.

23   Melinda Wittstock, 'Thames, a wounded phoenix, take flight into production', *The Times*, 17 October 1992, p. 5.

24   Alexandra Frean, 'ITV rule changes herald takeovers', *The Times*, 25 November 1993, p. 25.

25   Ibid.

26   Raymond Snoddy, 'Battle begins for future of ITV', *Financial Times*, 25 Novem-ber 1993, p. 1.

27   Ibid.

28   Mo Mowlan quoted from Nicholas Hellen and David Shaw, 'Stampede to buy as ITV network faces big carve-up', *Evening Standard*, 24 November 1993, p. 1.

29   Editorial, *Financial Times*, 25 November 1993, p. 21.

30   Ibid., p. 25.

31   MAI provide an interesting case of how a pressure group, The Campaign for Quality Television, became an important media actor.

32   Lisa Buckingham, 'Media shares soar as deal fuels speculation', *Guardian*, 9 February 1996, p. 1.

33   For a detailed examination of potential changes to broadcasting's labour, see Colin Sparks, 'The Impact of Technological and Political change on the Labour force in British Television', *Screen*, Winter/Spring, vol. 30, 1989, nos 1 and 2, pp. 24–39.

34   The TV-AM dispute occurred in 1988. It led to the mass redundancy of many of the companies' technicians. For further details see William Leith, 'Bruce Gyngell: Maggie's heart breaker', *Independent on Sunday*, 20 October 1991, p. 25.

35   Interview with Greg Dyke, 9 November 1992.

36   *Producer Choice Documentation*, BBC Internal Publications, May 1992, Section 2.1.

37   John Birt, introduction to ibid., p. 1.

38   See British Broadcasting Corporation *Extending Choice: The BBC's role in the New Broadcasting Age*, BBC Publications, 1992.

39   Ibid., p. 2.

40   Interview with Tony Lennon, 7 October 1992.

41   Henry Porter and Georgina Henry, 'Second Front: Blunders of the Iron Dukie', *Guardian*, Section 2, 17 March 1993, pp. 2–3.

42   See Eric Barendt, 'Legal Aspects of Charter Renewal', *Political Quarterly*, vol. 65, no. 1, January–March, 1994.

43   Department of National Heritage, *The Future of the BBC: Serving the nation, Competing world-wide*, Cm2621, HMSO, July 1994, p. 2.

44   Marianne MacDonald, 'Winning player in the world of franchise deals', *Independent*, 10 January 1996, p. 2.

45   Georgina Henry, 'Soccer Chief says no to ITV rematch', *Guardian*, 22 May 1992, p. 3.

46   Alan Sugar built up his company Amstrad through a mixture of corporate endeavour and the ability to manufacturer imitation products with cheap components.

47   Martin Thorpe, David Sharrock and Georgina Henry, 'ITV goes to court in soccer row', *The Guardian*, 23 May 1992, p. 1.

48   Lisa O'Carroll, 'Pay-TV key to ITV challenge', *Broadcast*, 29 May 1992, p. 3.

49   Steven Barnett, *Games and Sets*, British Film Institute, 1990, p. 23.

50   Harold Lind, 'No such thing as a free channel', *Guardian*, 27 July 1992, p. 29.

51   Lisa O'Carroll, 'Chisholm's gamble nets the big prize', *Broadcast*, 29 May 1992, p. 13.

52   Mick Dennis, 'BBC in £304 million TV soccer deal', *Evening Standard*, 18 May 1992, p. 1.

53   See for instance Garry Whannel, *Fields in Vision: Television Sport and Cultural Transformation*, Routledge, 1992.

54   Ibid., p. 15.

55   Steven Barnett, 'Controlling the Ball', *Broadcast*, 29 May 1992, p. 16.

56   Interview with Jonathan Rooper, 5 August 1992.

57   Steven Barnett, 'Cash in the Box', *Guardian*, Section 2, 11 March 1996, p. 13.

58   William H. Melody, 'Communication Policy in the Global Information Economy; Whither the Public Interest', in Marjorie Ferguson (ed.), *Public Communications: The New Imperatives: Future Directions for Media Research*, Sage, 1990, p. 29.

59   Raymond Kuhn and Mark Wheeler, 'The Future of the BBC revisited', *Political Quarterly*, October–December 1994, vol. 65, no. 4, p. 434.

60 James Curran, 'Mass Media and Democracy: A Reappraisal', in James Curran and Michael Gurevitch (eds), *Mass Media and Society*, Edward Arnold, 1991, pp. 102–3.

61 John Keane, 'Democracy and the Media – Without Foundations', *Political Quarterly* vol. 60, Special Issue, 1992, pp. 116–29.

62 For further details, see ibid., and John Keane, *The Media and Democracy*, Polity Press, 1991, pp. 164–5.

63 James Curran, 'Mass Media and Democracy', p. 107.

64 Ibid., p. 111.

65 Interview with Steven Barnett, 27 July 1992.

66 Interview with Colin Shaw, 25 April 1991.

7
A Changing Landscape –
The Globalization of the Media:
Liberalization or Constraint?

In the previous chapter, we considered how several changes (technological, political and economic) are affecting British broadcasting. First,
the new media services (cable, satellite, telecommunications, personal
computers) have had a greater influence as they have become domestically available. Moreover, the technology has promoted a convergence
of different media services allowing for commercial exploitation. Second, the government's media policy attempted a complex balancing
act between protecting public service broadcasting, encouraging competition and serving the media companies. Monopolization has occurred
as entry costs have risen, governments have turned a blind eye and 'infotainment' has become the order of the day. Therefore, recent media
policy has evidenced limited and belated bids at cross-media legislation.

This is problematic due to the political will of governments (who need
the support of the media during elections) and the lobbying power of
the companies. Further, supranational satellite and international telecommunications links allow media conglomerates to circumvent national
regulations. Currently, the British media and, in particular, broadcasting is experiencing a shift from the norms of the public service tradition
into market provision. Consumerism has been equated with citizenship. In many respects, Britain stands as a microcosm for a larger set
of phenomena.

Similar imperatives have faced communications and media systems
in advanced and developing nations. These comprise technological convergence, policy reforms, the concentration of media ownership and
alternate notions between citizenship and consumerism. In each nation,
depending on local needs, political cultures, respective wealth, status of
the broadcasting systems and the variants on policies – usually asserting
forms of deregulation – the outcomes have been different and unique.

LIVERPOOL JOHN MOORES UNIVERSITY
LEARNING SERVICES

However, underpinning all these changes is the realization that media systems are becoming *internationalized*. They are bypassing the traditional boundaries of nation states as fibre-optic cable, telecommunication and satellite links become available. The globalization of media services is increasingly apparent, alongside the globalization of other businesses and the distribution of knowledge. As a consequence, several pertinent issues have become conspicuous.

For example, there have been concerns about cultural imperialism. In many ways, the current desire to exploit the Third World's airwaves parallels the colonial imperialism of the nineteenth century. The media organizations see the developing nations as a lucrative market to be exploited. Therefore, Asian countries have expressed doubts about the infiltration of media services which invoke Western values and political ideals. They fear that their national characteristics will be replaced by a homogeneous, supranational identity. Moreover, in totalitarian states, such as China, governments have been able to control information through centralized media structures and continue to police the boundaries with zeal. Such political restraint has led to media conglomerates equating their rapid evolution with greater freedom of speech. In 1993 Rupert Murdoch commented:

> Advances in technology of telecommunications have proved an unambiguous threat to totalitarian regimes everywhere. Satellite broadcasting makes it possible for information hungry residents of many closed societies to by-pass state controlled television channels.[1]

Although he was later to regret his statement, as the Beijing mandarins closed the Chinese satellite market, Murdoch's comments raise a fundamental point. Should we understand the unfettered growth of the media market as being progressive or retrogressive in allowing the citizen to exercise his/her full democratic rights? The optimistic case would maintain that a free market encourages plurality of access, diversity of ownership and participation. The old media systems may be circumvented, and their reliance on professionalism and closed institutional power will decline. As broadcasting is no longer a limited resource, the sources of information are dramatically increased and liberalization will be achieved through economic deregulation. In turn, state control will be ameliorated as the media is decentralized. Moreover, with the widening array of information sources Marshall McLuhan's conception of a 'global village' may be realized.

Further, in spite of the criticisms of monopolization, moguls argue that the media has become too large and diverse for one person or small group to control and direct it. As they are part of the fourth estate, their role is to promote a diversity of ideas but not to shape the political discourse. They suggest that they are not political actors as the media can only reflect the established public consensus. Thus, their influence is limited and confined to the publication of criticisms of governments. However, others would suggest that this view is misleading. The media moguls promote a specific perspective of society and they do not allow their outlets to be used as platforms for opposing opinions. The pessimistic case would stress concentration of ownership, political clientelism and restriction. As media conglomerates provide the sources of news and entertainment that we consume both locally and globally, they centralize information and set the agenda. As they construct meaning, they may influence our attitudes and define issues for their own advantage:

> The worriers fear that, in the hands of fewer and fewer people, these powerful conduits will be manipulated by equally powerful interests, interests that may wish us to view the world from a particular perspective, to form or reform our opinions in a particular way, to encourage us to use our votes for a particular party, or to gain our support for the wars and military interventions that we are told are necessary to sustain world peace and world trade.[2]

For instance, many have suggested the involvement of Ted Turner's Cable News Network (CNN) in the Gulf War proved to be regressive. Moreover, Italy witnessed the short-term take-over by Fininvest media mogul Silvio Berlusconi of its political system. Through his proprietorial control, Berlusconi filled the vacuum which had emerged due to the old order's corruption and demonstrated how media power could usurp representative responsibility. According to this view, the free media market has restricted consumer choice, enforced greater centralization, concentrated the power of elites, and undermined the citizen's democratic rights.

In this chapter, we will be concerned about how these changes are altering the composition of the international media economy. Therefore, we will analyse, assess and explain the major economic trends of media globalization and conglomeration. Further, there will be a discussion of how these reforms should be interpreted and whether they enhance or undermine free speech and liberty of expression.

The Globalization of the Media

When, in the 1960s, Marshall McLuhan, the Canadian philosopher on the mass media, commented that television could establish a global village, his vision was impeded by bi-polarism, national identity, public service broadcasting, economic boundaries and the limits of transmission technologies. However, contemporary rhetoric suggests that there has been a globalization of the unitary world in which time, space and geography have all imploded. The world market is expanding to exclude localism, nationalism, the culturally specific, political dictatorships and heterogeneous social relations. As Annabelle Sreberny-Mohammadi comments:

> The antagonistic blocs of East and West are giving way to international markets, moneys and media. Germany is unified. A new and expanding 'Europe' looms. The centrifugal force of 'globalization' is the catchphrase of the 1990s.[3]

Technology and media globalization

The globalization of mass communications has been determined by the international supply of money, transport innovations and the dissemination of information through electronic and photographic forms. More recently, the re-combination of domestic, communications hardware – the telephone, VCRs, radio, television and personal computers – have all impacted on the mass media. Several trends may be identified:

First, there has been a miniaturization of the technology. This has affected the transmission of information. For instance, news crews are able to report from around the world with the establishment of 'backpack' satellite links. It has also meant that cheaper domestic hardware has become increasingly available. In particular, the Japanese company Sony miniaturized an American invention, the transistor, to build portable radios. This idea was similarly applied to television, telephones, hi-fi, compact discs and home computers.

Second, this has allowed audiences to enjoy greater access to sources of information due to the declining costs of hardware equipment, increased satellite links and the introduction of fibre optics. Theoretically, every citizen can receive material from around the world (although, the inequitable distribution of incomes clearly stems this development). This leads to two accompanying factors – the *personalization* and *autonomization* of the audience. The former refers to the fragmentation of the audience, as mass entertainment can be consumed in the private rather than the public sphere. Previously, large audiences had to be located in one venue to receive entertainment (e.g. the cinema), yet with the development of television, personal hi-fi and home computers, access to such material has become domestically orientated. As people overcome their technophobia, their autonomy increases as they can consume a greater amount of material, engage in interactivity through telephones and computer networks, use home video-cameras and schedule programming through video cassette recorders (VCRs).

Third, there has been a greater integration of media services at a technological and economic level. From the 1970s onwards, the new media technologies (cable, satellite and telecommunication) were established to distribute low-cost, world-wide communication. The limitations of a few terrestrial television transmitters would be overcome through multi-channel systems. For instance, the digitalization of television has allowed for the compression of over 500 terrestrial and cable channels. Commercial, educational and entertainment information could all be sent on the same highways. This has led to the convergence or 'synergy' of different technologies. The evolution of 'Information Superhighways' and the Internet also has global implications. This is expressed in terminology such as the 'World-Wide-Web' and the 'Global Network Navigator'. At an economic level, there has been a vertical integration of hardware and software companies. This is best exemplified by Sony, who not only manufacture the machinery, but also own music corporations such as Columbia and CBS records.

Therefore, due to these imperatives, the globalization of the media appears to be well underway. Between 1965 and 1986, the world total of television receivers increased from 192 million to 710 million.[4] Consequently, the number of televisions rose from fifty-seven per 1000 inhabitants to 145 per 1000 inhabitants.[5] However, from 1965 to 1986, the number of television sets was unevenly distributed between the developed and developing countries. Whereas, there were 783 television receivers per 1000 inhabitants in North America, the figure stood at only thirteen per 1000 in the non-Arab states of Africa.[6] In the subsequent decade, there has been an expansion in the allocation of technology in Third World societies. Asia has been perceived as a lucrative market for Western media organizations. Yet we should remember that the globalization of the media still remains within the purview of the Northern rather than poorer Southern countries due to the distribution of wealth, income and the investment of capital from the Western media companies. Moreover, this expansion has not only led to a synergy of technologies, but of corporations to create media conglomerates (led by moguls) who have close ties with governments and political institutions. John Keane comments on the double-edged nature of technological reforms:

> Such developments in global communications media, in theory at least, make the world smaller and more open. The media operate to an extent as a global fourth estate – as during the recent 'Velvet Revolution' in Central-Eastern Europe. Telephones, fax machines, photocopiers, electronic bulletin boards, video and audio recordings, especially when linked to global telecommunications networks, are now used worldwide to subvert repressive governments. Developments in global communications theoretically ensure that events anywhere can be reported anywhere else on radio within minutes; on television within hours. But theory and practice are often far apart. Government regulation, combined with the

high costs of installing telecommunications equipment and providing publicly accessible terminals, prevents citizens of most countries from accessing such global telecommunications networks as teleconferencing and electronic mail systems. Meanwhile, private broadcast news has become a global business . . . streamlining . . . opinions and tastes. A few major news organizations control the newsflow. Syndicators guarantee that wider and wider audiences get to read, see or hear the same stories.[7]

Further, the forces of localism, nationalism, ethnicity, race and xenophobia have also accompanied the integration of the global media economy. News reports demonstrate how tensions have grown in Northern Ireland, Bosnia and the former Soviet Union. Instead of world unity:

> the centripetal forces of old and new tribalisms and nationalisms are at work amd ethnic struggles are breaking out all over. Armenians confront Azarbaijanis, Serbs fight Croats, Mowhawk Indians confront Quebecois, there is violence between Umkatha and the ANC. Race-related violence increases in New York City, with a new Black-Asian dimension. The Soviet Union acts violently against (the republics) putting perestroika in peril. Iraq invades and annexes Kuwait. . . . Far from the 'loss of subject', identity seems to lie at the heart of politics in the late twentieth century.[8]

Theories of Media Globalization

Despite the problems described above, there has been a steady theorization of the globalization of the media. Some commentators suggest that a distinctively 'new' or post-modern type of economic-cultural-structure has emerged, whilst others maintain that these changes indicate the extent to which global capitalism has been established, typifying it as 'late capitalism' or 'high modernity'. Roland Robertson has shown how globalization has altered people's consciousness. Throughout these debates, the media has been seen as a crucial actor in the 'new world order'.

Throughout the 1980s, Robertson directed the emphasis away from the paradigm of nation–state–society towards globalization. He defined two major features. First, there has been the global compression of the world as the imperatives of international trade, military alliances and cultural imperialism have created greater degrees of interdependence amongst national systems. This predates modernity (the modern era) and the growth of capitalism, and can be divided into several stages:

- The *germinal phase* (Europe 1400–1750) which was marked by Christendom's dissolution; the emergence of state communities; universal (Catholic) religion; general concepts of humanity; individualism; early maps of the planet; a sun-centred universe; a universal Western calendar; global exploration; and colonialism.

- The *incipient phase* (Europe, 1750–1875) which included the development of the nation state; formal diplomacy amongst states; citizenship and passports; international exhibitions and communication agreement; international legal conventions; the first non-European states; and the first constructs of internationalism and universalism.
- The *take-off phase* (1875–1925) which was distinguished by the conceptualization of the world with regard to four globalizing factors – the nation state, the individual, a single international society and a single (masculine) humanity; international communications; sports and cultures; a global calender; the First World War; mass migration and restricted immigration; and more non-Europeans in the international club of nation states.
- The *struggle for hegemony phase* (1925–69) comprising the League of Nations and the UN; World War Two; the Cold War; war crimes against humanity; the universal threat of nuclear weapons; the development of the Third World.
- The *uncertainty phase* (1969–onwards) noted for the exploration of space; post-materialist values and rights discourses; world communities located around sexuality, gender, ethnicity and race; complex and fluid international relations; global environmental issues and the globalization of the mass media through space technology (satellite television, telecommunications, internet, fax etc).[9]

Second, Robertson has commented upon the growing global consciousness. He suggests that it is now reaching maturity as the world is becoming more united, but not more integrated, as cleavages exist and there is no clear direction toward a single system. Crucially, constructs of individual self and nationality are being defined by the wider reference points of an international system of societies and a general concept of humanity.

In several ways, our consciousness has been globalized. In the economic sphere, considerable attention has been paid to the internationalization of finance. There is a World Bank and organizations such as the International Monetary Fund (IMF). Further, business communication links have been established between major trading centres to bypass time zones and national economies. In the diplomatic environment, bi-polarism has given way to a 'new world order' and the United States continues to consider itself as a 'world policeman'. Moreover, religion is perceived in terms of ecumenism, citizenship with regard to human rights and the environment in relation to 'saving the planet'.

In many respects, globalization is a cultural phenomenon. For instance, consumerism has become a key unifying force with the industrialization of commodities and leisure. The use of global brand names, such as MacDonalds or Disney, now identifies both a product and an underlying ideology. For post-modernists, such as Jean Baudrillard, the distinction between the product and its symbolic worth has imploded, whereby the real and the virtual cannot be distinguished. Thus, reality has been turned into hyper-reality. In many respects, the global dissemination of information, advertising and entertainment through mass communications systems has advanced this 'hypersimulation' or simulacrum (the implosion of real and virtual). Therefore, the mass media is a centrifugal feature of the new world order and may be defined in economic, political and cultural terms.

Media globalization theories: 1 Marshall McLuhan

Some commentators argue that the globalization of the media will lead to the decentralization of power and allow for more control from below. With regard to this position, Marshall McLuhan provided two crucial terms; 'the medium is the message' and 'the global village'. He was concerned about technologies' ability to reconceive social relations rather than its content. As modern technologies alter perceptions, they extend the human body or nervous system. Previously, the print medium was a continuation of eye and had stemmed the oral dissemination of information. Moreover, print had regimented space and time into calculable units. Since the Enlightenment, writing has been conditioned by rational concepts such as linear logic to reflect the uniformity of clock time. For example, the printing press has allowed for maps, transport timetables, and perspectives within art. As the sense of sight was developed over others, a particular form of human rationality emphasizing national forms of uniformity and individuality emerged.[10]

However, this was to change when print was replaced by electric forms of communication. Accordingly, McLuhan developed the concept of hot and cool medias. For instance, a conversation may be considered to be cool as there are gaps, repetitions and delays, in which the participants must interpret the information. Conversely, a lecture, in which the material has been concentrated into a steady flow and can be easily absorbed, would be seen as being hot. Thus, traditional, hot media (print) limit participation as they are high on informational content, thereby setting the agenda and filtering arguments. Alternatively, cool media (telecommunications, television) provide more spaces for audience participation as they provide a lower intensity of information. Consequently, people must fill in the gaps and become active.

McLuhan suggested that cool media have replaced hot media. The new media challenge the one-way flow of information by enhancing interactivity. Thus, the production of knowledge is decentralized and democratized. Through such decentralization, technologies prevent dominant authorities from managing the flow of information. In turn, the new technologies allow for the globalization of the media economy, compress time, make spatial relations horizontal, relocate information and undermine the role of nation states. As the co-ordinates of time and space have evaporated, communication systems become constant and immediate, providing a diversity of opinions. Individualistic print cultures have been disrupted as many-to-many communications become possible. Thus, the globe's citizens may engage in a shared culture, a global village, which undermines the previously hierarchical, uniform or individualizing methods of ideological control.

Media globalization theories: 2 Anthony Giddens

Anthony Giddens has built on McLuhan's construct of 'time–space distanciation' by demonstrating how the media transcend the constraints of clock time and geographical location. Thus, as international media organizations can convey images and representations to the global citizenry, they may convert distant issues into major events. However, in Giddens's view the role of the global media is far more equivocal. This is because he perceives modernity as a runaway juggernaut, in which each bid to order its development produces a series of unintended consequences causing it to spin even further out of control. Modernity alters at a much faster pace than any previous social formation as it has extended its global reach and significantly transforms social practices.

Thus, in contrast to McLuhan, who argued that the globe had imploded, thereby removing the constraints of time and space, Giddens suggests 'time–space distanciation' establishes a complicated relationship between *local involvements* (circumstances of co-presence) and *interaction across distance* (connections of presence and absence). There has been 'a relocation of information from localized contexts, evident within modern communication networks, (that has been) . . . made possible via the uncoupling of time and space, and disembedding mechanisms such as technical media. These devices involve the separation of social relations "from local contexts of interaction and their restructuring across indefinite spans of time-space".'[11] He delineates globalization as 'the intensification of world-wide social relations which link distant localities in such a way that local happenings are shaped by events occurring many miles away and vice versa.'[12]

The presentation of world events on television has become part of everyday life. This 'window on the world' not only provides us with information, but also means, at a local level, our thinking and actions are dictated by the presentation we receive of the world's major events. For Giddens, this process is becoming more and more prevalent as there is a global linkage of localities through the mass media. For instance, during the 1989 Tiananmen Square massacre, the 1991 conflagration in the Gulf, the 1995 O. J. Simpson trial or President Yeltsin's bombing of the Chechen rebels, most viewers were not directly involved yet became immersed through television. Others such as the post-modernist Jean Baudrillard have taken this linkage between real events and their representation even further, suggesting the event and its image are indistinguishable in most people's minds. The media shape our views and discourse on the world.

However, Giddens also suggests that tensions exist between the processes of globalization and localization. As we become more aware of the global imperatives, people are becoming increasingly conscious of both shared opportunities and problems. For instance, in the news, representations of world events are contextualized for the needs of the local environment. This became apparent when Galtlung and Ruge analysed foreign crises in Norwegian newspapers. They discovered that the dissemination of such information was shaped by, amongst others, the criterion of cultural relevance or proximity.[13]

Invariably, the more elite a nation or set of people, the more likely it will be to appear in the advanced nations' media outlets. Third World nations may often only appear on the news if events directly touch on the interests of the British State or there has been an outstanding catastrophe. The recent example of Rwanda would be an example of this, where a civil war and long-term crisis only came to light once a genocidal campaign had been conducted. Further, the explanations often reinforce particular Western conceptions of the world's events. Through this selective process, human diversity and fragmentation, rather than a unification of cultures may be established. Therefore, for Giddens, in the analogous yet conflicting imperatives of globalization and localization, the central role of the media makes conspicuous the pressures between the macro and micro socio-economic-politics processes.

Implications of Media Globalization

There is a considerable debate about the role and shape of a global media. In this respect, several perspectives have been used; economic dependency and cultural imperialism; global pluralism; and variants on Giddens's analysis of the interplay between global and local.

Economic dependency and cultural imperialism

For some, media globalization represents the economic, political and cultural domination of advanced nations over developing ones. This development thesis has been subject to several interpretations, including an analysis of the obstacles stemming the growth of post-colonial states and the paradigm of 'dependency theory'. Thus, the flow of information and entertainment programming will be drawn from central to peripheral states.

The emergence of independent post-colonial states such as India, Algeria and Ghana produced an academic debate about the nature of the Third World's development. Some analyses focused on the obstacles which precluded any major reforms; the lack of capital investment, and the developing countries' reliance on the World Bank's international loans. Others stressed the lack of entrepreneurship and training infrastructures. For instance, Daniel Lerner and Wilbur Schramm demonstrated the cultural obstructions to political participation and economic reform.[14] As Annabelle Sreberny-Mohammadi comments:

> The 'solution' for their analysis was the promotion of the use of communications media to alter attitudes and values, embodied in 'media indicator' (minimum numbers of cinema seats, radio and television receivers and copies of daily newspapers as a ratio of population necessary for development) which were adapted by UNESCO and widely touted in the developing world. This perspective has been roundly criticized for its ethnocentrism, its ahistority, its linearity, for conceiving of development in an evolutionary, endogenist fashion and for solutions which actually reinforced dependency rather than helping overcome it.[15]

An alternative critique was drawn from Leninist notions of imperialism. This argued that the global flow of capital was shaped by the economic dependence of peripheral states on metropolitan nations. This could take several forms; the exploitation of cheap raw materials to create surplus profits for investing multi-nationals, or strategic control of local or international markets to restrict entry and retain price controls. To this end, Gunder-Frank's dependency thesis contended that developing nations were constrained by the post-colonial interests of metropolitan nations, the United States's 'Empire without Frontiers' and the internationalization of capitalism. For instance, in many Asian, African and Latin American states, client regimes received economic and political support from Western governments. Thus, these political elites felt greater loyalty to their benefactors and willingly allowed them to exploit raw materials and cheap labour. Invariably, this led to political dictators securing Western backing, as they were seen as bulwarks against incipient Communism, and the abuse of human rights. If a developing state attempted to rebel against this predominant order it found itself, as in the case of Allende's Chile, subject to economic blockades and US-backed military coups.

This perspective has the advantage of placing international media systems into the context of foreign policy interests and capitalist expansion. For instance, due to the new technologies' costs, only a few wealthy countries can afford to own and operate satellite communications. Moreover, Herbert Schiller argues that the media conform to the needs of the world-wide capitalist system and supply material which fulfils the interests of multi-national corporations.[16] The unfettered expansion of media conglomerates has also hastened this process in the dissemination of the news and all 'departments of culture'. As they contribute to an unequal global flow of information, they exacerbate the gulf between a media-rich North and media-poor South. According to Edward Said:

> This has a number of consequences. For one, the international media system has in actuality done what idealistic or ideologically inspired notions of collectivity – imagined communities – aspire to do. . . . (For instance) the way the four major Western news agencies operate, the mode by which international English-language television journalists select, gather, and rebroadcast pictorial images from all over the world, or the way Hollywood programmes like *Bonanza* and *I Love Lucy* work their way through even the Lebanese civil war . . . (mean that) the media are not only a fully integrated practical network, but a very efficient *mode of articulation* knitting the world together.[17]

Concurrently, indigenous media companies are constrained by the international flows of media hardware. Further, political economists have shown how uneven the flow of cultural or software products between advanced and developing nations remains. Consequently, rather than retaining any autonomy, Third World media systems are forced to mimic Western structures. For example, Northern (predominantly American) news values, films, television programmes, organizational structures, professional values and advertising have all been exported to the Southern nations. Peter Golding and Graham Murdock suggest that such an economic domination will have inevitable consequences for the output and ideologies of world-wide programming.[18]

This has led to the charge that the global media economy encourages *cultural imperialism*. Schiller extends his criticisms of corporate power, commenting that the 'apparent saturation through every medium of the advertising message has been to create audiences whose loyalties are tied to brand named products and whose understanding of social reality is mediated through a scale of commodity satisfaction'.[19] Anthony Smith concurs:

> The threat to independence in the late twentieth century from the new electronics could be greater than colonialism itself. We are beginning to learn that de-colonialization and the growth of supra-nationalism were

not the termination of imperial relationships but merely the extending of the geo-political web which has been spinning since the Renaissance. The new media have the power to penetrate more deeply into a 'receiving' culture than any previous manifestation of Western technology. The results could be immense havoc, an intensification of the social contradictions within developing societies today.[20]

In turn, criticisms have emerged that hegemonic values such as entrepreneurship, individualism and consumerism, drawn from Western nations, have supplanted traditional Third World cultures. With regard to this critique, a notable contribution was made by the Chilean writers Ariel Dorfman and Armand Matterlart in their 1975 study *How to Read Donald Duck: Imperialist Ideology in the Disney Comic*. Through a close textual analysis, they aimed to reveal the values underpinning Walt Disney's apparently innocent cartoons. Instead of viewing Disney's comics as harmless fun, they maintained that specific ideological assumptions shaped their output. These naturalize and normalize the social relations of Western capitalism. For instance, the Disney comics were replete with 'imperial themes'; consumerism and an obsession with money; references to 'exotic' (Third World) countries which could be plundered by Western adventurers; racial, sexual and cultural stereotypes; the justification of bourgeois class relations and direct anti-revolutionary propaganda. In such a manner, Disney became another weapon in American imperialism's ideological arsenal.[21]

Another set of criticisms have referred to the manner in which Third World nations have been represented in Western, principally American, news and current affairs programmes. Edward Herman and Noam Chomsky have provided a detailed statistical analysis to demonstrate how client Latin American countries have been under- or misrepresented. Through an examination of American newspaper articles, column inches and editorials, they compared and contrasted the coverage of Jerzy Popieluszko, a Polish priest murdered by the then Communist leaders in 1984, against 100 murdered religious victims (including El Salvadorian Archbishop Oscar Romero) in Latin and Central America. They discovered that Popieluszko's worth as a victim stood between 137 to 179 times the worth of victims in US-backed regimes. Effectively, 'a priest murdered in Latin America is worth less than a hundredth of a priest murdered in Poland.'[22]

More recently, commentators such as Edward Said have critically analysed the American media's presentation of the 1991 Gulf War.[23] Said contended that Ted Turner's Cable News Network (CNN) had dominated the international flow of information during the dispute. This presentation was highly selective as it demonized 'Islamic fundamentalism' and the Iraqi dictator Saddam Hussein as 'Hitler'. This creation of Arab 'others' was reliant on specific, stereotypical views of the Middle East. Indeed, Said explicitly compares the news representation of the war with a decade's worth of films pitting American commandos, such as Sylvester Stallone in *Rambo* or Chuck Norris in *Delta Force*, against Arab/Muslim terrorist-desperadoes.[24]

Whilst most criticisms have been aimed at the exploitation of developing countries, many have argued that the Americanization of advanced nations has occurred as the US media predominates in the distribution of popular music, television programming and film production.[25] This is exemplified by the phenomenal growth of the American-owned Music Television (MTV), with its sisters MTV Europe, Australia, Brazil and Asia. MTV was launched in August 1981 to 1.5 million American subscribers; by 1991 it was available to 201 million households across seventy-seven countries. This has meant that bands can be quickly introduced to a world market:

> Nirvana, a Seattle band, was completely unknown, except for a few 1991 summer festivals and a screening on *120 Minutes*, when the video of *Smells Like Teen Spirit* was put on the *Buzz Bin* in November 1991. It soon charted all over Europe.[26]

Presently, the Hollywood film majors enjoy an 80 per cent domination of the European market. This may explain why Quentin Tarantino's *Reservoir Dogs* and *Pulp Fiction* struck such a chord in Britain amongst younger generations brought up on a steady diet of American sit-coms, cop shows, music shows and films. More seriously, it led to a dispute between the Hollywood film companies and the French government in 1993. The history of British film may also be seen as a fruitless attempt at rebuffing America's domination, as cinema owners have always preferred to exhibit major Hollywood vehicles rather than support an indigenous film industry.

Global pluralism

For others, these critiques are too simplistic, invariably dated by the demise of bi-polarism, and are often polemic rather than analytical. For instance, Dorfman and Matterlart can be accused of underestimating the intelligence of the audience and assuming a straightforward relationship between the text and passive readers.[27] Similarly, Schiller has been criticized for being functionalist by exaggerating the materialistic domination of media and directly equating ownership with output. Subsequently, he describes abstract media flows, rather than the cultural meaning of these flows to the public.[28] Further, the cultural imperialism argument may be seen to be founded on a false situation of comparative global scarcity. Yet the speeding-up of modernity has meant that there has been a rapidly evolving spread of global communications systems and providers over the last fifteen years. Consequently, a more pluralistic environment will be created in which a diversity of cultures, ideologies and opinions will be exchanged.

As we have seen, McLuhan foresaw an implosion of time and space, allowing for a world-wide communications system to encourage global citizenship. Whilst McLuhan suggested this would lead to a homogeneous world culture, other accounts anticipate a 'de-massification' of the mass media. Globalization may foster a change from the standardized (or 'Fordist') mass-produced commodities to flexible, differentiated products directed at niche markets. Therefore, 'global pluralism' will encourage a diversity of producers and two-way flows of cultural and informational programming.

The statistics would appear to bear this out. The Southern states have increasingly exported home-made productions to the rest of the world. The Egyptian and Indian film industries regularly sell their products to a world market. For example, the 'Bombay Movies' (or 'Bollywood') are the largest film-producing system outside the United States. Moreover, the popularity of these films has allowed the Indian film industry to maintain investment in high art films. Ancient Hindu epics have also been translated into mainstream television series which have been sold to other countries.

In Brazil, *TV Globo* has enjoyed spectacular foreign sales of its *telenovelas* (soap operas) in over 128 countries. Its income from foreign markets grew from $300,000 per annum in 1977 to $14 million in 1985. In particular, there has been a form of 'reverse cultural imperialism' in the exportation of Latin-American *telenovelas* to Spanish-language American channels, whilst the flow of television product from Brazil to Portugal demonstrates a role reversal in the historic roles of imperialism. As Roberto Mader comments: 'This success took Rio's accent to Portugal, where it began to affect the former coloniser's speech patterns: a sweet historical revenge.'[29]

Consequently, the 'global pluralism' model suggests that a diversity of producers will challenge the hegemony of advanced over developing nations. An 'active audience' may bring their own interpretative frameworks of meaning which resist the apparently dominant views. Therefore, writers such as John Fiske, have maintained that viewers can interpret information which is 'polysemic' or can engender a multiplicity of meanings.[30] Moreover, within Europe, some commentators have argued that the mediatization of cultural products will produce a 'third culture' in which new allegiances and identites can be forged. According to Barrie Axford and Richard Huggins:

What we may be seeing is the creation of a European media ecumene, consisting of increasingly widespread and diverse networks of businesses, exchange students, users of the Internet, subscribers to satellite pay channels, or avid video-conferencers, in other words 'a "Europe of more-or-less specialist discourses or tastes, and in some cases, a virtual Europe. This is . . . because perspective and identity result from the meaning an actor brings to and extracts from the networks and the different realities with which he or she is in contact, rather than taking place behind the backs of participants. The result may be a process of unity which is altogether more 'pluralistic, decentralized and mutable', than is often assumed.[31]

Global pluralism also suggests a decline in state control over the media. The significantly differentiated nature of global media systems means that state power becomes more diffuse. In turn, this may make it 'more susceptible to the initiatives of social movements and citizens' groups, backed by countervailing networks of communication'.[32] To this end, civil society may be transformed as dominant elites are checked from below.

Globalization and localism

Annabelle Sreberny-Mohammadi has suggested a third variant which builds on the work of Anthony Giddens. Giddens has shown that a dialectic exists between the global and the local, in which our local environs are informed by our access to international information, yet simultaneously the local culture shapes our interpretation of the world's events. To this extent, the global pluralists' view of an active audience is borne out. However, the pluralist model tends to ignore issues of dominance, cultural appropriation and media effect. An alternative perspective is required to recognize the dynamic tension by the global and the local.[33] As Tony Dowmunt comments:

The evidence . . . challenges the picture of a single all-inclusive 'global village', suggesting instead a diversity of smaller 'villages'. Some are certainly more powerful and dominant, others are in some ways dominated; but they all contain distinct communities which relate to each other, and to the television available to them, in varied ways. There is no single, homogenised, global audience. A Polish teenager marvels overs a Sinead O'Connor video on MTV Europe; 25,000 fans of a Brazilian *tele-novela* (soap opera) gather in a Rio stadium to salute the stars of the show; an ANC supporter in South Africa sees previously jailed representatives of her party on national TV for the first time; and in the Australian outback an Aboriginal community watches *Miami Vice*, then switches over to a locally made video of traditional songs and dance. World television is a site of complex cultural mixing – sometimes harmonious, often conflicting – at global, national and local levels.[34]

In terms of media flow, this means there are contradictions between global and local imperatives. For instance, the Brazilian *TV Globo* stands as the fourth largest television network (behind the United States's CBS, NBC and ABC). This was reliant on two major developments; the transformation of scattered regional stations into a satellite-based network and the Brazilian government's insistence that the channel be subject to quotas of home-grown product. This qualifies the belief that all the world media empires are drawn from Northern (in particular, the American) states. However, in many other ways, *TV Globo*'s growth exemplifies American media imperialism, due to the backing of American advertising agencies, technical support, administrative expertise, and capital investment. Thus, whilst Globo is indigenously owned and targeted at a Brazilian audience, its growth is still determined by North American media power.[35]

Another manifestation of this contradiction refers to the development of regional, city and community media players in America and Western European states. The explosion of fibre-optic cable delivery systems has meant that a more fragmented and heterogeneous audience can be reached. For instance, in 1994, a London-based news service, Channel One, was established on cable explicitly to report on local issues. However, Associated Newspaper's ownership of this channel may be seen to demonstrate the extent to which major media companies are now diversifying their interests.

These examples lead us on to a major trend of globalization which we have only elliptically referred to: media conglomeration. Ultimately, globalization may be seen to allow for the dissolution of the nation state as the principal focus of political, economic and cultural identity. In its wake, we will see the irresistible expansion of multi-national conglomerates. The media has been no exception, as the global flow of communications has become increasingly dominated by media conglomerates either led by individual moguls or corporate boards. John Keane has suggested that this means that there will have to be a major reconceptualization of the press liberty. Previously, it had been conceived in a framework of the system of single nation states.[36] However, the conglomeration of media companies focuses our attention on supernational legal and political arrangements, and demonstrates new forms of centralization which may or may not undermine media freedoms. The conglomeration of the media has major economic, cultural and political implications for citizenship toward the second millenium.

The Conglomeration of the Global Media Economy

The growth of media conglomerates has gone hand-in-hand with the evolution of new technologies, neo-liberal ideologies and deregulatory policies directed at broadcasting. According to market-liberal theory, broadcasting has been unchained from its shackles through consumer sovereignty, and multiple forms of ownership. For free marketeers, communications are most efficiently produced and distributed through the market. Globally, this has led to the reformulation of public service broadcasting as deregulation has been augmented by the new media technologies.

The deregulation of mass communications

Deregulation within communications and broadcasting was exported from the United States to the advanced and developing economies. Two factors may be perceived as contributing to this movement. First, a general consensus between politicians, policymakers and the media industry that deregulation would benefit both the national and international economy.[37] Second, the technological revolution meant that major transformations within the distribution of communications were available for business and domestic use. While the previous technological limitations had produced normative forms of regulation, reforms made these regulatory structures increasingly anachronistic, irrelevant, bureaucratic and inefficient. Moreover, the opening of the market-place to cable and satellite, enabled hardware manufacturers to invest in research and increase their profitability.

Throughout Western Europe, most of the national broadcasting regimes were subjected to a partial or full implementation of these policies. Kenneth Dyson and Peter Humphreys have defined several imperatives for deregulation. First, new technologies including cable, satellite and video cassette recordings have changed policymakers's attitudes toward broadcasting. Therefore, their receptiveness to regulatory reforms was not only a response to the 'shock-wave' engendered by these new technologies, but also referred to the motivation of 'demand-pull' of new ideologies and altered social habits.[38]

Second, technology has produced a convergence within the communications industries in which broadcasting can no longer be understood as being divorced from telecommunications, publishing and consumer electronics. This development radically altered the media market-place and enabled new or different entrants to seek access to broadcasting services. Throughout Europe new groups have sought entry, for instance, Bertelsmann, Hachette, and News International from book/newspaper publishing; Havas from advertising; Fininvest from building and W. H. Smith from retailing.[39] These economic pressures have led governments to look for lighter regulation at a national and Pan-European level (for example, the European Commission's 1984 Green Paper *Télévision sans Frontières* (*Television Without Frontiers*)).

Third, this combination of technological and market flexibility has provoked an internationalization of the broadcasting market. Satellite signals can bypass national territories thereby allowing new entrants to operate multinational broadcasting operations. In addition, this has opened up the possibilities of international investment. For example, Compagnie Luxembourgeoise de Teledefusion or CTL, a Luxembourg-based company, is predominantly funded by French and Belgian capital.[40]

Fourth, such internationalization has resulted in the creation of a highly integrated, international broadcasting environment and has consequently provided the context for the *de facto* exportation of deregulation as being once 'one environment (the United States) . . . (had changed) . . . (it) forced change in another'.[41]

Finally, the combination of these factors had produced a complicated broadcasting environment in which the traditional regulatory rules and agencies were inadequate. Essentially, national sovereignty could be undermined. In 1982 the West German company Bertelsmann lined up with CTL to broadcast the German language station RTL from the media 'haven' of Luxembourg.[42] This meant that a national German television station could broadcast from outside of the country's borders and consequently circumvent regulatory, business and scheduling procedures. As Dyson and Humphreys comment:

> Over twenty satellite channels were available in 1987. Their development raised the spectre of circumvention of national regulation and a breakdown of state sovereignty in broadcasting regulation. The proposal of 'offshore' operators had major implications for broadcast regulation. These new actors have exposed the 'Achilles heel' of regulation in the age of transfrontier broadcasting.[43]

The implications of deregulation

Whilst deregulation, or, more correctly, regulatory reform, has been introduced to right the perceived ills of regulation, it has produced its own anomalies, inconsistencies and unforeseen consequences. This is partly due to the fact that deregulatory policies are conditioned by political will, ideological support, national culture and an industry's readiness to adapt. Moreover, as Trevor Hayward comments:

> Deregulation is the hoped-for key to the emancipation of all radio waves, fibre-optic cables and even old-fashioned telephone wires, wherever they exist or are planned to exist. But the pace of change is making it more and more difficult to define what should be regulated. Should it be non-discriminatory access to the rush-hour on the electronic superhighway;

should it be a regulation of ownership, using limitations such as nationality and residence; should we try to regulate content; should it be limiting the number of hours that suppliers can broadcast; or a maximum percentage of revenue from, say, the total advertising income available?[44]

Further, the removal of regulators may produce its own dynamic as different rules and principles apply. In the mass media, rather than a total removal of rules, there has been a change in overall rationales. This may be characterized as a shift from the defence of the public service broadcasting to the encouragement of a free broadcasting market.

This has been justified by the belief that the market will decentralize power and encourage a plurality of providers. According to Cento Veljanovski, this will allow for a flourishing of ideas and opinions from below.[45] Previously, market-liberals have been criticial of public service broadcasting, accusing it of institutional ossification and political clientelism. Conversely, it has been argued that the widening array of choices has often narrowed individual choice. Multiplicity does not necessarily secure diversity. Instead of the relatively differentiated product drawn from a regulated public service system, we may be subjected to the same cultural forms which are packaged to a variety of international markets.[46] Further, PSBs, faced with increasing programming costs, capped incomes and commercial competitors are confronted with commercialization of practices or marginalization. As Peter Humphreys comments:

> There is little sign indeed that audience fragmentation (due to channel multiplication) has induced many broadcasters to become less concerned about audience maximation. An international trend identified nearly a decade ago, towards intensified competition for large audiences and an increased bias towards mass-appeal programming (that is, 'more of the same'), would seem to stand for the most part confirmed.[47]

More fundamentally, the new technologies and governments' laissez-faire policies have opened up the media markets to the conglomerates across Europe (Bertelsmann, Fininvest) and the world (News International, Time Warner). First, multinationals have benefited from the reduction of labour rules and, more profoundly, they have gained from the relaxation of ownership rules. Second, the major expansion in the audio-visual industries has been in the distribution of channels, not original production. Thus, there has been a multiplicity of transmission services, but as programming expenditure remains high, a decline in diversity. Significant amounts of capital are required to run major, international broadcast channels. This means that there is no greater access for smaller, local broadcasters as conglomerates are allowed to fix entry costs.

Major media players

Therefore, there has been a steady conglomeration of the global media economy. Presently, the world's largest media player is Time Warner. In 1989, Time, owners of Time Magazine and other major publishing titles, resisted a hostile bid from Paramount Communications. Subsequently, it merged with Warner Communications Inc., owners of Warner Film Studies and Lorimar, to accrue joint assets of $14 billion. Warner also supplied 14 per cent of American prime-time networked programming, had movie packages, ran a television distribution arm and was the main supplier of the American cable market. The conglomerate is currently diversifying its interests in film and television production, amusement parks, magazines, publishing, information holding and other related leisure industries.

Thus, its policy has been one of expansion. In September 1995, Ted Turner announced that he would merge Turner Broadcasting into the Time Warner stable. It has also moved into the lucrative Asian market by backing a joint venture to create an Indian television channel. Time Warner demonstrates how global corporations are becoming vertically integrated. For instance, it controls the film production process from the conception of the idea to the cinema in which it will be shown. For media corporations, vertical integration has several benefits, including 'creative synergies' and economies of scope and scale.

In Britain, Rupert Murdoch's News Corporation owns News International which controls four national newspapers and a satellite broadcasting monopoly. In 1995, the company made half-yearly profits of £76 million from increased newspaper circulation and advertising.[48] Recently, Murdoch's power has become the subject of political debate and the National Heritage Department's recommendations of cross-ownership were seen as a method to stem his overweening control.

However, Murdoch's international growth appears to be unstoppable. News Corporation owns newspapers in America, Australia, Hong Kong, Fiji and Papua New Guinea. In Europe, he has made strategic alliances with Bertelsmann, Canal Plus and Havas to develop digital pay-TV across Europe. In America, Murdoch owns the movie studios 'Twentieth Century Fox' and has established a fourth TV network, the Fox Broadcasting Company. Murdoch has been quick to seize his opportunities in the Pacific Rim and South East Asia. In 1993, he acquired the loss-making Star Television service, for which he paid $525 million (or £338.7 million). Star TV has a satellite footprint running from Turkey to Japan, and professes to broadcast to 53.7 million households across Asia reaching an estimated audience of 220 million. It claims to reach more than 30 million homes in China alone.[49] Murdoch has also involved News Corporation in new telecommunication deals, publishers such as HarperCollins, and pay-TV. In early 1996, it announced a revenue of £3.3 billion for the preceeding six months.[50] Murdoch has commented:

> The great move now is globalization. Because it is electronic, it is so easy to do now in one country that which you can do in another country, barring the problems of local regulations.[51]

Other major players include: the American Walt Disney Corporation which owns film studios, theme parks and satellite channels; the British media giant Pearson which holds publishing houses such as Penguin and Longman, the *Financial Times*, the former ITV London weekday contractor Thames and has moved into the Asian market by taking a 10 per cent stake in Hong Kong's Television Broadcasts (TVB); the Japanese manufacturer Sony which has diversified its interests into CBS and Columbia Studios, whilst investing into High Definition Television (HDTV) research technology; the merged Reed Elsevier which holds £6.8 billion worth of publishing interests; the German magazine publisher Bertelsmann which owns *Der Stern*, RCA, Ariola records and Bantam books; and Silvio Berlusconi's Fininvest which benefited from the 1976 Constitutional Court decision to free the Italian airwaves and has subsequently controlled Italy's three private television channels, accounting for 90 per cent of the audience.

The dynamics of media conglomeration

Some media conglomerates are controlled by external companies and financial institutions, whilst others reflect older patterns of personal ownership, in which moguls, families or founding groups retain control. Edward Herman and Noam Chomsky have demonstrated that sixteen out of the top twenty-four American media corporations are closely held or still controlled by originating family.[52]

Graham Murdock has also shown that there are three basic types of media conglomerate; industrial, service and communication.[53] The first two reflect general forms of commercial diversification. For instance, an industrial conglomerate would be a company that owns media facilities but whose main operations are located in manufacturing. A classic example would be the Italian car company Fiat, owned by the Agnelli family, which is a major shareholder in the publisher of two daily newspapers. Similarly, service conglomerates hold real estate, building companies, financial agencies and retailing outlets, alongside their media interests. Thus, Silvio Berlusconi's Fininvest owns three major TV networks, a major housing development outside Milan, AC

Milan football club, cinema chains, a leading property company and a national newspaper. For Berlusconi, some of these investments have been highly compatible. For example, the television coverage of his football team has brought about the revenues to attract top players whose success has increased viewing figures of his channels. These interests enabled him to launch a campaign to become Italian Prime Minister in 1994.

In contrast to this diversification, communication conglomerates, such as News Corporation and Bertelsmann, have expanded their core industries and shed unrelated services. There has been a greater interdependency or synergy between the old and new media markets as established actors enter the emerging areas. For example, newspaper groups have been moving into on-line data, amalgamating with broadcasting groups (as in the case of United Newspapers and MAI) and investing into cable operations. Therefore, synergy does not promote significant differences, as the same commodity may be differently packaged to a variety of alternative markets.

This dynamic has enhanced the trend of conglomerate mergers. The marriage of Time Warner instigated take-over battles such as QVC and Viacoms' fight for Paramount and the merging of the telephone companies Bell-Atlantic and Telecommunications Inc. The key players are continually examining the media business to see who may correspond to their needs. As Trevor Hayward comments:

> (They) want marriage, particularly to that part of the marriage vow that emphasizes 'to the exclusion of all others'. Telephone companies, publishers, movie studios, cable operators, computer manufacturers and television companies are all now jostling to see who fits, who is available and, just as importantly, who might be denied to another suitor. They are seeking to secure control of all components of creating, owning, distributing and recycling information: they want ownership of every genre and every medium. They want them exclusively and they are willing to pay way over the market price to get them.[54]

The Concentration of Media Ownership and Democratic Rights

As the world's population requires more information, it is increasingly being orchestrated by media combines who exercise greater power over people's disposable time. For many, this has been a regressive development. Deregulation has allowed for unrestricted forms of ownership and control. Instead of a diversity in production, which should provide a variety of outlets for information, this means that power has been placed in the hands of fewer and fewer moguls or corporations. They are not only concerned about their profit margins, but can set the political agenda. This has led to a growing controversy about the concentration of media ownership and citizens' democratic rights to free information.

Media ownership and media freedom

Despite such a concentration of ownership, the conglomerates argue that the media has become too big for one person or small group to direct it. This position contends that a free market encourages plurality of access and participation. The closed media systems will decline, as technology has provided a diversity of channels and outlets through which alternative views can be disseminated. Consequently, media moguls cannot shape the political discourse. Their influence is limited to the traditional role of 'public watchdog' and means that the media can now truly mirror the general consensus. Rupert Murdoch commented that technology:

> (has) . . . liberated people from the once powerful media barons. The days when a few newspaper publishers could agree to keep an entire nation ignorant of an important event are long gone. Technology is racing ahead so rapidly, news and entertainment sources are proliferating at such a rate, that the media mogul has been replaced by a bevy of harassed and sometimes confused media executives, trying to guess what the public wants. The consumer is in the saddle, driving the telecommunications industry. The technology is galloping over the old regulatory machinery. . . . (Some) of the world's biggest industries – computing, consumer electronics, publishing and entertainment – are converging into one dynamic whole.[55]

Further, post-modern theory has conceived capitalist society in terms of the proliferation of images. The media is viewed 'as a black hole that absorbs all content, social reality, politics, and so on, into a vortex of noise, meaninglessness and implosion'.[56] Within this new form of culture, reality is obliterated as the distinction between reality and irreality disappears. In turn, advocates of hyper-reality claim that it is futile to delineate between institutional structures, their historical trajectories or political effects. As it is impossible to construct meaning, the owner's power cannot be measured and is incomprehensible.

Critiques of media conglomeration

Conversely, media conglomerates have been subject to a number of major criticisms. Their unfettered growth means they can determine

entry to the media market, thereby protecting their interests by excluding the opposition, cross-promoting their services or engaging in the
takeovers of smaller competitors. This constant manoeuvring has led
to some spectacular bids and counter-bids. For instance, in the summer of 1995, Rupert Murdoch announced his intention of buying Ted
Turner's CNN; simultaneously Turner was bidding for CBS:

> The heart of Mr Murdoch's plan is a 'domino theory' centred on the
> latest manoeuvrings for ownership of the CBS TV network. Ted Turner
> is desperate to buy the network, which would be his first move into the
> non-cablebroadcast market. He failed to land CBS in 1987 and is cur-
> rently seeking to outflank the Westinghouse corporation's $5.4 billion
> agreement with the network. But if Mr Turner's effort fails there is in-
> tense speculation that he might quit the industry altogether and sell out.
> That would leave the door open to a Murdoch bid for his company.[57]

The cut and thrust of these battles may grab the imagination of business editors. However, they are reflective of an erosion in the diversity
of ownership which, alongside the decline of public service broadcasting, has curtailed countervailing power centres and qualified the variety of information available to the public. As conglomerates enjoy global
jurisdiction over the proliferating sources of information and entertainment, they can become 'gatekeepers' for these services. In such a
manner, they will have unprecedented control over the public's cultural life.

This leads on to another major criticism: as the conglomerates regulate the output of their companies, they may employ their media outlets as a megaphone for their own social or political ambitions. Where
personal forms of ownership are prevalent, media moguls may directly
intervene in day-to-day operations by undermining editorial autonomy
(although they cannot supervise all areas of output). Alternatively, as
media corporations have grown larger and are supervised by boards
general goals have been established. In turn, through the allocation of
resources and the appointment of compliant managerial or editorial
staff, overarching rules may be implemented.

As the privately owned media becomes increasingly concentrated,
the presentation of issues has become more homogenous with the gap
between the number of voices in society and those heard in the media
growing. The media conglomerates propagate a narrow perspective and
do not allow their outlets to be used to promote dissent. As they centralize the sources of news and entertainment that the public consume,
they set the agenda and construct meaning. This has meant that there
are 'no-go' areas for critical reporting.

This has been evident in Rupert Murdoch's attempt to introduce

Star TV into Asian states, often built on feudalistic or totalitarian political principles. The Malaysian government was assured by News Corporation that Star's services would be friendly and useful. In his trip
to India in February 1994, Murdoch offered to drop the BBC's World
Service Television (WSTV) from the Star networks. In China, he went
further, and eliminated WSTV from the Asiasat Northern beam –
the footprint covering China – and replaced it with a movie channel.
Murdoch admitted that he did this to please the Chinese government
and help establish the satellite service there. Previously, China had
clamped down on Star TV dishes and it had expressed its displeasure
toward the BBC over a documentary on Mao Zedong and references
in programmes to the 1989 Tiananmen Square massacre:

> Despite his insistence that satellite technology is 'an unambigous threat
> to totalitarian regimes everywhere', enabling the information hungry res-
> idents of such regimes to by-pass censorious state controls, Murdoch
> has come to learn that even such satellite beams can be searched out
> at the border. The People's Republic of China has shown itself to re-
> quire sweetening by some pretty robust self-censorship if it is to return
> favours later. . . . Although Murdoch could not be expected to hold any
> kind of brief to protect the BBC, an interesting twist of info-geopolitics
> has seen the free market, bucaneer of the airwaves, joining with a total-
> itarian regime to suppress certain forms of information in order to secure
> future licence agreements.[58]

John Tusa has noted 'if you are friendly to the government, you are
unlikely to be useful to its citizens who are also your audience.'[59] This
returns our attention to Jürgen Habermas's analysis of the decline of
the public sphere. Effectively, rational public discourse has been overridden by power politics as major organizations have negotiated with
one another and states, thereby excluding the public. Murdoch's con-
summate deal-making demonstrates the extent to which he has been
incorporated into the political elite, as politicians and media barons perceive the mutuality of their interests. As the media manipulates publicity, the political discourse has become state controlled, sensationalist
and market-led. Politics has been defined as a predigested spectacle.

Moreover, critical political analysis has declined as the media moguls
have become political actors in their own right. Previously, we have
seen how press barons, such as Beaverbrook and Rothermere, used
their newspapers to channel their political ideas directly to the public.
This historical example was recently paralled by Silvio Berlusconi's
successful campaign (though ultimately unsuccessful tenure) to use his
television channels to support his candidacy for Italian Prime Minister. Although Berlusconi had benefited from the void that had been
left in Italian politics by the 'Tangentopioli' (Bribesgate) scandal, his

electoral success raised a debate about the safety of the democratic process. News programmes, on Berlusconi-owned channels, advocated his views, his leadership ability, endorsed his candidacy and encouraged people to join local 'Forza Italia' organizations. Some suggested that Italy was becoming a videocracy, in which its political system had been appropriated by the media and Berlusconi had become a new 'Big Brother.' Stanley Baldwin's criticisms of a media which enjoyed power without responsibility appeared to be unerringly apt:

> It is the media (as a whole) who are thought to *decide* who should be the actors, what the rules, what the messages, what the issues at stake, who the winners and the losers in elections and in the common political domain. In a similar scenario there is little or no room left for the traditional functions of the political party, unlike the parties, the media are *not accountable* to their 'voters', and with this go all the worrying implications for the survival of the traditional Montesquieuian separation of power (the media an actual 'fourth estate'?). As can be easily inferred, it is a trend – and a risk – that affects most western democracies, not only Italy.[60]

Further, during Berlusconi's eight-month period as premier, the conflict of interest between his continued ownership of a large media business and his position as prime minister was the subject of heated debate. In Italy, there are no laws to force politicians to divorce themselves from their corporate interests once they reach public office. Therefore, when he was in office, there was no separation between public and private interests.

The power of the leading corporations illustrates the dilemma that faces liberal democracies between freedom of ownership and regulated pluralism. If key communications facilities continue to be placed in the private hands of a few media conglomerates consumer choice diminishes, expression is restricted to being a property right and the concept of fourth estate is undermined. Ultimately, such a concentration undermines democratic pluralism:

> Centralized . . . conglomerization of media and communications seriously threatens democracy and gives the major transnational corporations massive political, economic and cultural power. The entertainment and information industries in particular have rationalized cultural production and produced new forms of cultural hegemony through the new electronic media. Television stands at the centre of the new media in that cable and satellite delivery systems, video-recorders, disk systems, and computer/information systems also operate through television, providing it with even more power than it had during the era of over-the-air broadcasting.[61]

Conclusion

The globalization of mass communications has emerged through the new media technologies. The distribution of information has proliferated as world-wide satellite, telecommunication and broadcasting links have been established. Therefore, the process of transmission cannot be solely conceptualized by the boundaries and interests of the nation-state. Moreover, the domestic hardware revolution – the telephone, VCRs, radio, television and personal computers – has meant that news and entertainment facilities are available in the private sphere.

These reforms have been accompanied by several different theories of media globalization. For some, a global village will encourage universal citizenship and allow national cultures to interact. There are new opportunities for independent producers to create and distribute programmes. For others, the flow of media from the rich Northern states to the poorer Southern countries will exacerbate the gap between information rich and poor. The media has been alternatively perceived as a means to propagate cultural imperialism, encourage global pluralism or act as a site for the interaction between global and local.

The globalization of mass communications has also allowed for the growth of media conglomerates. In the light of greater internationalization, national governments have either loosened ownership restrictions or turned a blind eye to the expansion of these corporations. This has been justified by the theories of market-liberalism and deregulatory policies which are designed to encourage the free flow of investment. Further, as media companies can aid politicians during elections they have been perceived as valuable allies. Therefore, the new media's development may parallel the concentration of ownership within the newspaper and publishing industries, as the new outlets are controlled by fewer and fewer media moguls or conglomerates. This has a significant impact on the media's role as a public watchdog. Many critics contend that global corporations either uncritically propagate political elites or have so many controls within the political mainstream that they are serving their own, rather than the public's, interest. Jürgen Habermas's argument that the media have become the site for ideological manipulation, appears to be increasingly sustainable. Thus, due to the dynamics of globalization and conglomeration, the citizen's democratic rights are being undermined by the needs of the state and the media companies.

This leads us to ask whether a new type of media system, placing the citizen's needs first, could be organized in a global enviroment. This would have to be independent from both the state and market controls. John B. Thompson has suggested:

Since the deployment of new communication technologies is rendering mass communication increasingly global in character, the principle of regulated pluralism must itself be placed within a trans-national context. . . . Given the trans-national character of the new media of transmission, the regulation necessary to avert this outcome will have to be both national and international. Particular states, as well as states in association with one another, will have to take steps to ensure that the new channels of transmission which are being opened up by the deployment of new technologies will not be controlled in such a way that pluralism and responsiveness will be sacrificed on the altar of free enterprise. (This) . . . responsibility must be openly and directly faced; to fail to do so would be to lose, or significantly and perhaps irreversibly to diminish, an unprecedented opportunity for the enrichment of social and political life in modern societies.[62]

Alternatively, multi-media technologies have been seen to challenge the problems of political clientelism and media incorporation. The Information Superhighway made up of telecommunication, broadcasting and computer links has been commonly perceived as creating a digital revolution. This will encourage citizenship by undermining state control, diminishing the power of corporations, reformulating political activity and changing social habits. It now remains to be seen how the multi-media is being developed and whether it provides a realistic response to the problems identified in this chapter.

Further Reading

James Curran and Michael Gurevitch (eds), *Mass Media and Society*, Edward Arnold, 1991.

Peter Dahlgren and Colin Sparks (eds), *Communication and Citizenship: Journalism and the Public Sphere*, Routledge, 1991.

Tony Dowmunt (ed.), *Channels of Resistance: Global Television and Local Empowerment*, BFI, 1993.

Marjorie Ferguson (ed.), *Public Communication: The New Imperatives: Future Directions for Media Research*, Sage Publications, 1990.

Anthony Giddens, *The Consequences of Modernity*, Polity Press, 1990.

——, *Modernity and Self-Identity: Self and Society in the Late Modern Age*, Polity Press, 1991.

Trevor Hayward, *Information Rich and Information Poor: Access and Exchange in the Global Information Society*, Bowker-Saur, 1995.

Edward Herman and Noam Chomsky, *Manufacturing Consent: The Political Economy of the Mass Media*, Pantheon Books, 1988.

Douglas Kellner, *Television and the Crisis of Democracy*, Interventions: Theory and Contemporary Politics, Westview Press, 1990.

Marshall McLuhan, *Understanding the Media: The Extensions of Man*, Routledge, 1994 (repr.).

Marc Raboy and Bernard Dagenais (eds), *Media, Crisis and Democracy: Mass Communication and the Disruption of Social Order*, Sage Publications, 1992.

Edward W. Said, *Culture and Imperialism*, Vintage, 1994.

Michael Skovmand and Kim Christian Schroder (eds), *Media Cultures: Reappraising Transnational Media*, Routledge, 1992.

Anthony Smith, *The Age of Behemoths: The Globalization of Mass Media Firms*, Priority Press, 1991.

——, *Books to Bytes: Knowledge and Information in the Postmodern Era*, British Film Institute, 1993.

Nick Stevenson, *Understanding Media Cultures: Social Theory and Mass Communication*, Sage, 1995.

John B. Thompson, *Ideology and Modern Culture: Critical Social Theory in the Era of Mass Communications*, Polity Press, 1990.

John Tomlinson, *Cultural Imperialism*, Pinter, 1991.

Jeremy Tunstall and Michael Palmer, *Media Moguls*, Routledge, 1991.

Malcolm Waters, *Globalization: Key Ideas*, Routledge, 1995.

Notes

1   Rupert Murdoch in John Tusa, 'Pollution of the global village', *British Journalism Review*, vol. 5, no. 4, 1994, p. 43.

2   Trevor Hayward, *Information Rich and Information Poor: Access and Exchange in the Global Information Society*, Bowker-Saur, 1995, p. 211.

3   Annabelle Sreberny-Mohammadi, 'The Global and Local in International Communications', in James Curran and Michael Gurevitch (eds), *Mass Media and Society*, Edward Arnold, 1991, p. 118.

4   Figures quoted from ibid., pp. 122–3.

5   Ibid., p. 122.

6   Ibid., pp. 122–3.

7   John Keane, 'The Crisis of the Sovereign State', in Marc Raboy and Bernard Dagenais (eds), *Media, Crisis and Democracy: Mass Communication and the Disruption of Social Order*, Sage Publications, 1992, p. 27.

8   Annabelle Sreberny-Mohammadi, 'The Global and Local in International Communications', p. 118.

9   Malcolm Waters, *Globalization: Key Ideas*, Routledge, 1995, pp. 43–5.

10 Nick Stevenson, *Understanding Media Cultures: Social Theory and Mass Communication*, Sage Publications, 1995, p. 119.

11 Ibid., p. 130.

12 Anthony Giddens, *The Consequences of Modernity*, Polity Press, 1990, p. 64.

13 J. Galtlung and M. Ruge, 'The structure of foreign news', in Jeremy Tunstall, *Media Sociology*, Constable, 1969, pp. 262–4.

14 Annabelle Sreberny-Mohammadi, 'The Global and Local in International Communications', pp. 119–20.

15 Ibid., p. 120.

16 Herbert Schiller, 'Transnational Media and National Development', in K. Nordenstreng and H. I. Schiller (eds), *National Sovereignty and International Communication*, Ablex, 1979, p. 21.

17 Edward W. Said, *Culture and Imperialism*, Vintage, 1994, p. 374.

18 Peter Golding and Graham Murdock, 'Ideology and the Mass Media: the Question of Determination', in M. Barrett (ed.), *Ideology and Cultural Production*,

Croom Helm, 1979. For further details see Peter Golding, 'Media Professionalism in the Third World: the Transfer of an Ideology', in James Curran, Michael Gurevitch and Janet Woollacott (eds), *Mass Communication and Society*, Arnold/Open University Press, 1977.

19 Ibid., p. 23.
20 Anthony Smith, *The Geopolitics of Information: How Western Culture Dominates the World*, Oxford University Press, 1980, p. 176.
21 Ariel Dorfman and Armand Matterlart, *How to Read Donald Duck: Imperialist Ideology in the Disney Comic*, New York, International General Editions, 1975.
22 Edward Herman and Noam Chomsky, *Manufacturing Consent: The Political Economy of the Mass Media*, Pantheon Books, 1988. In a similar vein, Chomsky has shown how the relative coverage of genocidal atrocities in East Timor and Cambodia differed due to the United States's strategic interests in Indonesia and Pol Pot's communism in South East Asia.
23 Edward W. Said, *Culture and Imperialism*, pp. 353–4.
24 Ibid., p. 356.
25 See for instance, Jeremy Tunstall, *The Media are American*, Constable, 1977.
26 Corinna Sturmer, 'MTV's Europe: An Imaginary Continent' in Tony Dowmunt (ed.), *Channels of Resistance: Global Television and Local Empowerment*, BFI Publishing, 1993, p. 54.
27 For further details see John Tomlinson, *Cultural Imperialism*, Pinter Publishers, 1994 (2nd edn), pp. 43–4.
28 Michael Tracey, 'The Poisoned Chalice? International Television and the Idea of Dominance', *Daedalus*, vol. 114 (4), p. 45.
29 Roberto Mader, 'Globo Village: Television in Brazil', in Tony Dowmunt (ed.), *Channels of Resistance*, p. 83.
30 See John Fiske, *Television Culture*, Methuen, 1987.
31 Barrie Axford and Richard Huggins, 'Media Without Boundaries: fear and loathing on the road to Eurotrash, or transformation in the European cultural economy?', in Joni Lovenduski and Jeffrey Stanyer (eds), *Contemporary Political Studies 1995*, Volume 3, PSA, 1995, p. 1420.
32 John Keane, 'The Crisis of the Sovereign State', p. 30.
33 Annabelle Sreberny-Mohammadi, 'The Global and Local in International Communications', p. 122.
34 Tony Dowmunt, introduction to Dowmunt (ed.), *Channels of Resistance*, pp. 1–2.
35 Ibid., pp. 4–5.
36 John Keane, 'The Crisis of the Sovereign State', p. 30.
37 Jeremy Tunstall, *Communications Deregulation*, Basil Blackwell, 1986, p. 26.
38 Kenneth Dyson and Peter Humphreys, 'Deregulating Broadcasting: The West European Experience', *European Journal of Political Research*, Kluwer Academic Publishers, vol. 17, no. 2, March 1989, p. 141. For further details see Kenneth Dyson and Peter Humphreys, with Ralph Negrine and Jean-Paul Simon, *Broadcasting and New Media Policies in Western Europe*, Routledge, 1989.
39 Kenneth Dyson and Peter Humphreys, 'Deregulating Broadcasting', p. 143.
40 Ibid., p. 142.
41 Ibid., p. 143.
42 Ibid., p. 142.
43 Ibid.
44 Trevor Hayward, *Information Rich and Information Poor: Access and Exchange in the Global Information Society*, Bowker-Saur, 1995, p. 204.
45 See, for instance, Cento Veljanovski, introduction in Veljanovski (ed.), *Freedom in Broadcasting*, Institute of Economic Affairs, 1988.

46 Peter Humphreys, 'Nature of the Broadcast Media in Europe: Some Key Policy Issues', in Joni Lovenduski and Jeffrey Stanyer (eds), *Contemporary Political Studies 1995*, pp. 1403–11.

47 Ibid., p. 1407.

48 Tony May, 'News International Climbs', *Guardian*, 9 February 1996, p. 16.

49 Tony Walker and Simon Holberton, 'Murdoch cultivates his Asian contacts: Media chief prepares to chaperon Deng Rong – News Corporation', *Financial Times*, 13 February 1995, p. 3.

50 Tony May, 'News International Climbs', p. 16.

51 Andrew Culf, 'Murdoch claims his technology will conquer national media laws', *Guardian*, 13 October 1993, p. 24.

52 Edward Herman and Noam Chomsky, *Manufacturing Consent*, pp. 8–10.

53 Graham Murdock, 'Redrawing the Map of the Communications Industries: Concentration and Ownership in the Era of Privatization', in Marjorie Ferguson (ed.), *Public Communication: The New Imperatives: Future Directions for Media Research*, Sage Publications, 1990, pp. 4–6.

54 Trevor Hayward, *Information Rich and Information Poor*, p. 182.

55 Rupert Murdoch in ibid., p. 193.

56 Douglas Kellner, *Television and the Crisis of Democracy*, Interventions: Theory and Contemporary Politics, Westview Press, 1990, p. 13.

57 Jonathan Freedland, 'Murdoch eyes the big Turner prize on way to becoming world's leading media magnate', *Guardian*, 25 August 1995, p. 18.

58 Trevor Hayward, *Information Rich and Information Poor*, p. 199.

59 John Tusa, 'Pollution of the Global Village', *British Journalism Review*, vol. 5, no. 4, p. 43.

60 Gianpietro Mazzoleni, 'Towards a "Videocracy"?': Italian Political Communication at a Turning Point', *European Journal of Communication*, vol. 10 (3), 1995, p. 314.

61 Douglas Kellner, *Television and the Crisis of Democracy*, p. 13.

62 John B. Thompson, *Ideology and Modern Culture: Critical Social Theory in the Era of Mass Communications*, Polity Press, 1990, pp. 263–4.

8
Democracy and the Information Superhighways

Introduction

The globalization of mass communications has produced a varied picture of Western media imperialism, conglomeration and a degree of local resistance. In many cases, governments have been happy to deal with the competing media conglomerates to attract investment. This has implications for the media's role as a public watchdog as it has been steadily incorporated into the political mainstream. Many critics concur with Habermas that the mass media have become the site for ideological manipulation and the distortion of information. Consequently, citizens' democratic rights are excluded from decision-making.

Alternatively, advocates of new multi-media technologies argue that such problems can be challenged through the emerging Information and Communication Technologies (ICTs). In particular, the Internet (the global web of computers on international telecommunications networks), has been popularized as a means to increase the citizen's participation. As millions go on-line, a digital revolution will reform monolithic state edifices, corporations, political parties, schools, workplaces, orthodox economics and popular entertainment. For instance, the traditional and new media actors can no longer determine the dissemination of information, instead television receivers will be *broadcatchers* whereby citizens can choose their data from an array of multimedia sources.

Internet devotees claim that electronic 'billboards' will circumvent the centralized, conglomerate and outmoded media structures. In turn, they will provide new and different services, more responsive to the users' requirements. Moreover, the Internet reforms the flow of communication distribution. Rather than being a top-down process in which media organizations disseminate information to the public, many-to-many interactivity is achievable. Jon Katz has commented (my italics):

> Digital media could make it possible for people to interact – maybe even changing each other's minds in the process – something traditional media inhibit through their addiction to objectivity, spokespeople, and sensationalism. Every on-line user knows that this kind of communication often breaks down barriers, forcing senders and receivers to deal with *each other* as individuals rather than group members.[1]

The current attention being paid to the ICTs has been overwhelmingly positive. State control and market closure will be ameliorated to allow citizens to participate in their civil, political and social rights. The Information Superhighway will provide the electronic landscape for a reinvented civil society. The unregulated cyberspace of the ICTs allows information to bypass state interventions and produce greater citizen empowerment. Top-heavy, concentrated media monopolies will be displaced by a responsive, multiple source model of communications. Governments, regulators and owners will be impotent against a system in which millions can adopt the interconnecting technology and engage in political discourse. Moreover, some believe such interactivity can increase democratic participation through a constant series of referenda. Thus, the technological revolution will enhance freedom of belief, conscience, speech, movement, association and enfranchisement. Marshall McLuhan's arguments have been resurrected:

> The medium or process of our time – electronic technology – is reshaping and restructuring patterns of social interdependence and every aspect of our personal life. It's forcing us to reconsider and reevaluate practically every thought, every action and every institution formerly taken for granted.[2]

In particular, the Internet offers instant global communication, in which all citizens can access the same informational and cultural resources. In turn, global citizenship presupposes a supranational identity.

For some, the prospect of realizing a true Athenian democracy appears to be achievable. However, Athens was built on the back of slavery and its democratic principles applied to a few. Therefore, will the proliferation of communications networks increase the availability of political information? In the main, these multi-media developments have been orchestrated around market precepts such as private enterprise and individualism. American Vice-President, Al Gore, has warned that a gap between the information rich and information poor could develop. Pessimists suggest an information underclass may be created which would intensify social tensions in advanced and Third World countries:

> (the Internet will) not be a data superhighway accessible to everyone equally. Use of the Internet will remain the purview of the educated and the affluent. No matter how ubiquitous online access becomes, no matter how easy software is to use, no matter how many gigabits of data can flow down cable television connections, the uneducated and the poor will not be active participants in the electronic environment. Information flows stratify societies and erode large-scale structures. A 'market of one' is possible in an Internet environment.[3]

In this chapter we will address the development of ICTs, consider the possibilities for users, define the arguments for liberalization and those which maintain electronic democracy which will be narrowed through the imposition of state controls or market closure. To what extent can the new information environment increase participation and activate citizenship? Can a free trade of ideas and information be achieved? Alternatively, will this stem the public's access to information as the hardware is being distributed according to income? Further, will the public sphere become susceptible to greater manipulation as political and media elites use the Internet to promote their own interests above the citizen's? Ultimately, will the information superhighways activate electronic democracy or retard it?

The Technological Revolution

The technological revolution has meant that major transformations within the distribution of communications have become available for business and domestic use. Effectively, several decades of new technology have been unleashed in the last fifteen years. The changes comprise: a computer revolution hastened by cryptography, the modem, domestic personal computers and more sophisticated software to be down-loaded; microwave technology drawn from radar and rockets, for launching satellites; high-definition television reception; terrestrial broadcast reforms such as digital compression; the domestic video-recorder; and telecommunication advances including the long-running (now reaching fruition) introduction of narrow-band fibre-optic cable.

Currently, the technology to support direct communication is becoming widely available. For example, interactive cable systems and cheap fibre-optic connections are developing alongside the widespread use of computer and videoconferencing. A new generation of networks have been or are currently being constructed to advance low-cost broad-band communication. These developments provide access to a greater number of communications links, permit the distribution of commercial and entertainment material, and advance telephony along the same highways. Moreover, new electronic services located around telecoms, computers and satellites have meant that a global electronic mail service has come on-line. The creation of integrated computer networks from universities, companies and other organizations, generically entitled the Internet, have grown at a staggering rate: 'In 1990 it connected 200,000 computers and 3000 networks, and by early 1993 this had grown to around 1.3 million computers, 8000 networks and perhaps 10 million users all over the world.'[4]

The application of information and communication technologies

K. Laudon argues that ICTs are applicable in three ways. First, they provide data transformation technologies. Computers, therefore, allow for the collection, storage, manipulation and retrieval of information. Second they can be used to enhance mass participation technologies, such as broadcasting, which transmit information from a central source to millions. Finally, and most dramatically, they provide interactive communications flows among individuals and organized groups to correspond with each other.[5] Thus, ICTs may have the following effects:

- They explode all the previous limits on the volume of information that can be exchanged.
- They make it possible to exchange information without regard, for all practical purposes, to real time and space.
- They increase the control consumers have over what messages are received and when.
- They increase the control senders have over specific audiences who receive the messages.
- They decentralize control over mass communication.
- They bring two-way or interactive capacities to television.[6]

Consequently, with a personal computer and a modem, on-line information is only a telephone line and a mouse click away. The Internet covers a wide array of material. It is predominantly used for electronic mail (e-mail) and information is swapped by approximately 25 to 30 million people. This figure has risen by between 5 to 10 per cent a month. However, there are other on-line sources of information including thousands of Bulletin Board Systems (BBS) largely run by computer enthusiasts, news groups and a wide range of commercial on-line information services.

Telematics, the integration of computing with communications technologies, may also transform the democratic process. Whilst the capacity of different interactive services to enhance participation varies, they are distinguished from the previous mass media as the information recipients are no longer passive. Interactivity enables citizens to actively participate in, and control, the flow of communications. Thus, teledemocracy becomes a realistic possibility.

Push-button technology allows for widespread access to databases and telecommunciations. It may make for a better informed and participatory citizenry who can by-pass normative political structures such as parties and parliaments. Further, the media's ability to 'manufacture consent' (Walter Lippman) is significantly challenged. The political economist Noam Chomsky has commented:

> The new electronic technology, in fact, has given opportunities for lots of spreading alternatives. . . . Things are going in both directions. Institutionally, the major tendency is centralization. The other tendency in the opposite direction, which is the only hopeful one, in my opinion, is much more diffuse and nothing much in the way of organized institutional forms. . . . There are tens of thousands of people hooked into various networks on all kinds of topics and lots of discussion goes on and lots of information comes through. It's of varying quality, but a lot of it is alternative to the mainstream.[7]

A Changing Political Climate

The ICTs challenge political orthodoxies on several levels. Industrial policies have to be developed to effectively utilize the technology. A debate about technological reform, citizenship and democracy is also underway. This questions the current political structures and whether they remain applicable. Thus, there has been some discussion of how ICTs can alter liberal democratic institutions such as representational assemblies. Further, direct or communitarian forms of democratic behaviour have been propagated, alongside anarchistic libertarian views to advance citizenship. Finally, there is the fear that electronic democracy is far from inevitable. The whole idea is a cruel illusion and state or capitalist power will ultimately prevail.

Policy responses from Western governments:
information superhighways

Since American President Bill Clinton and Vice-President Al Gore were elected in 1992, the metaphor of an 'Information Superhighway' has become the centrepiece of an emerging American industrial policy. This will advance information and communications networks to change the way people live, work and govern. It has already influenced policy formulation in many countries and transnational institutions. In 1993 the American government announced the development of a national information infrastructure which would create: 'A seamless web of communication networks, computers, databases and consumer electronics that will put vast amounts of information at users' finger-tips.'[8]

The British Labour Party has similarly provided an optimistic account of the new ICTs. Labour leader Tony Blair maintains that they will become the key dividing line in British politics. Graham Allen, a former Labour spokesman on the Media, has argued that the Internet, alongside a Bill of Rights and a Freedom of Information Act, will decentralize power and rebuild democratic infrastructures. He also suggests that local cable television will be another vital component in regenerating politics by opening direct dialogue between political representatives and the people. Thus, local television and the Internet may allow the citizenry to control their own lives.[9] Chris Smith, the former National Heritage spokesman, was so enthusiatic about the imminent communications revolution that he claimed increases in wealth and health provision would occur:

> Soon the UK will be provided with a whole range of electronic communications services made possible by advances in telecommunications and computing. Technical advances . . . allow vast amounts of information to be carried at great speeds and over long distances by fibre-optic cables. Advances in the way information is transmitted using digital technology can enhance delivery on even established transmission systems such as the radio spectrum. Add to all of this advances in satellite communications and the growth of mobile telephony in the 1980s and 1990s and the potential for a much more sophisticated national communications infrastructure is clear.[10]

Politically, the metaphorical vision of the Information Superhighway has proved attractive. However, others have suggested that such policy-making has been a matter of good public relations. For instance, there is still much uncertainty about what the Information Superhighway means both conceptually and as a set of concrete policies. Essentially, the term refers to telecommunications infrastructures which are capable of delivering all kinds of electronic information and communication services. Yet, a multitude of possible approaches exist:

> The motorway imagery could be thought of as implying a traditional telecommunications model of a network. In this, traffic goes from a to b using fixed links between locations with switching 'roundabouts'

to choose the right roads. Yet the US government's view of the Information Superhighway . . . is clearly anchored in the Internet model, which employs a network of networks through which information packets are routed more flexibly using sophisticated computer-based controls. Other valid models are also competing to be the basis from which the information superhighway will evolve.[11]

This confusion spreads to the debate on the best methods to implement policies. Some believe governments should force a particular model of technology, such as optical fibre or cable, and create a futurist welfare state. Others believe this decision should be market-led. Invariably, a compromise between state provision and a free market has been reached. For instance, an initiative from the G7 countries contends that a global market will exist through the provision of communications technology. Thus, governments should provide minimal legislation to ensure fair competition, private investment, light regulation, open access to networks, universal provision of core services, equality of opportunity, content diversity and the involvement of developing nations. The Labour Party has proposed policies to establish a competitive framework so that the private sector can develop the communications market in exchange for societal provision of hardware.[12] Tony Blair, in his leadership speech at the 1995 Labour Party conference, announced that Labour had struck a deal with British Telecom to furnish every college, school, hospital and library in Britain with free high-band networks in return for full access to the cable market.

In the United States, however, the dichotomy between limited state intervention and total deregulation produced a political battle between the Vice-President Al Gore and the Congressional Speaker Newt Gingritch during the debates surrounding the 1995 Telecommunications Act. In the event, the bill permitted local telephone and cable companies to offer different forms of telecommunications services and removed many existing price controls. However, the dispute was illustrative of two different approaches to the policy. Gore has constructed a 'third way' between the bureaucratic state and the libertarian anti-state. He believes that governments should establish the appropriate regulatory environment for the private expansion of the net:

> His (Gore's) superhighway imagery was meant to convey . . . that, just as the concrete highway system had linked the nation and spurred its unprecedented economic growth in the post-World War II years, so . . . the infobahn (would) be socially binding and economically essential in the information age.[13]

Whilst favouring a market, the Vice-President is concerned about market failures. He wants steady deregulation which ensures core goals

Table 8.1 Attempted links between telecommunications and media or related companies – some of the bigger deals

Date	Telecoms Company	Media/Related Company	Deal
May 1995	MCI	News Corp.	MCI planned to invest $2 billion for 13.5% of the Murdoch-owned group
January 1995	US West Time	Warner/Toshiba etc.	A five-company joint venture in Japanese cable TV costing $400 million
December 1994	Telefonos de Mexico	Televisa	Telemex paid $211 million for a 49% stake in a cable TV arm
December 1994	TCI of US	Sumitomo of Japan	A Japanese cable TV joint venture
November 1994	Deutsche Telekom	Bertelsmann/Leo Kirch	A proposed pay-TV venture which was blocked by the European Commission
October 1994	Sprint Telecommunications of the US Inc.	Comcast and Cox Cable	Telephones and multi-media deal
August 1994	Ameritech, Bell South and South-western Bell	Disney	An agreement was announced to develop and deliver interactive video programmes
April 1994	Bell Atlantic Inc.	Tele-Communcations Inc.	A proposed $20 billion deal which was abandoned when the US changed cable tariff regulations
April 1994	South Western Bell	Cox Enterprises	A proposed $4.9 billion cable TV partnership which was abandoned
May 1993	US West	Time Warner	US West invested $2.5 billion for 25% of Time Warner Entertainment

Source: Alan Cane, 'An entertaining alliance: Alan Cane on this week's multimedia tie-up between Rupert Murdoch and a US telecoms company', *Financial Times*, 12 May 1995, p. 15

such as open access, competition and private investment. Gore fears that 'deregulation sauvage' will encourage monopolization, limit consumer choice and undermine the public interest.[14]

Conversely, Gingritch, a self-styled 'conservative futurist', contends that the private sector knows no bounds. He is against 'big government' and treats Washington with contempt. The Speaker helped inspire a White Paper 'The Telecom Revolution – An American Opportunity' which argued for rapid, radical deregulation. The Federal Communications Commission (FCC) would be replaced with a small office in the Executive. Further, cross-ownership restrictions, cable-rate regulation, and universal provision of service should be abolished. Gingritch believes that telecommunication companies should be free to buy cable providers and that the computer industry, freed from Federal restrictions, provides a model for the development of the info-bahn. The market will redistribute resources most effectively and commodification will be the principle means for expanding choice.[15] The Gore–Gingritch dispute is a contest between government as a referee and government as a spectator.

The other principal actors have been the media organizations who are investing in multi-media delivery systems (with varying degrees of success, see table 8.1). They employ traditional libertarian arguments to suggest that a free communications market will expand horizons. Rupert Murdoch commented that technology has undermined the power of media barons as news and entertainment sources are proliferating. Instead of media moguls, media executives are responding to the public's needs. Therefore, the telecommunications industry is consumer driven and as there is a convergence between computing, domestic electronics, publishing and entertainment the traditional regulators are irrelevant.[16]

Subsequently, Murdoch has been involved in several deals to tap the ICTs' potential power. In 1993, Murdoch announced that News Corporation (NC) would, alongside British Telecom (BT) and Cellnet, invest in the Information Superhighway. BT's expertise in telecommunicatons could combine with NC's knowledge of satellite, allowing for a multitude of different services. More recently, NC (whose media resources comprise print, television and video) has collaborated with MCI Communications, America's second biggest long-distance telecommunications operator, to distribute electronic information across the United States and, due to its partnership with BT, the world. On announcing the deal, Murdoch claimed that previously, 'no one has put together the right building blocks – programming, network intelligence, distribution and merchandising – to offer new media services on a global scale.'[17] At the time of writing, however, the deal was looking precarious with MCI planning to reduce its stake from 50 to 20 per cent. In turn, NC announced that it would sharply curtail its online interest by cutting back the number of employees from 500 to 300 and shift its focus to the Internet. The service has stalled, although no one is counting Murdoch out. As one competitor commented, 'We've seen him bounce back too many times.'[18]

Alternatively, Murdoch and others' alliances may be seen as being indicative of greater centralization and ideological domination. For instance, BT is restricted by OFTEL from showing live broadcasts on its telephone network until 2001. However, it claimed in its proposed deal with Murdoch that it would be a 'narrow' rather than 'broad' caster and, therefore, should not contravene the regulations. This liberal intepretation of the rules demonstrates how powerful telecommunications companies are seeking to exploit the market. In June 1993, Bill Gates's Microsoft established a joint venture with Tele-Communications Inc., the cable television giant, and Time-Warner, the biggest media conglomerate in the world. This combined computing and television to determine the delivery of a considerable amount of popular culture. James F. Moore, an expert consultant, commented:

> This has tremendous economic and social importance; it is the gateway for popular culture. . . . This is the substitute for newspapers and magazines and catalogues and movies, and that gives it enormous economic potential for those who control the gateway.[19]

In the pursuit of such a strategy, Gates has also formed partnerships with telephone companies such as BT and France Telecom, publishers, Hollywood producers and Visa, the credit card company, so that goods and services may be bought online.

Such a usage of a free communications market has a number of implications. First, it shows how communications remain subject to the brokering of power between political, social and economic elites. ICTs have been perceived as a largely anarchic, dirt-cheap, uncensored forum, dominated by amateurs and enthusiasts. However, the reality is different as governments have allowed media monopolies, computer and cable companies to structure the market. In turn, this may mean that ICTs replicate the strengths and flaws which have appeared in traditional media systems. The Information Superhighway favoured by governments may restrict participation and allow media monopolies to orchestrate 'Infotainment'. Media monopolies appreciate that the new communication outlets can broadcast more of the same to more people, with interactivity limited to channel selection. For instance, Robert W. McChesney compares the evolution of the Internet with the development of the marginal American public service broadcasting system:

It was the educational broadcasters who played an enormous role in developing AM broadcasting in the 1920s, and then FM radio and even UHF television in the 1940s and the 1950s. In each case, once it became clear that money could be made, the educators were displaced and the capitalists seized the reins. Arguably, too, this looks like the fate of the Internet, which has been pioneered as a public service by the non-profit sector, with government subsidies, until the point when capital decides to take over and relegate the pioneers to the margins.[20]

If informational rights are the purview of the market rather than the citizen, an information rich and poor may be created as universality of service is no longer guaranteed. The distribution of information will be centralized and access commodified. In these circumstances, Tony Blair's proposals to employ the technologies for social provision have a downside, as they allow a private monopoly, British Telecom, to shape the evolution of cable services. BT's profits will easily dwarf any costs in linking up public institutions and, to access services, public bodies will still be required to pay.[21] Exclusion and manipulation could become the order of the day. This draws our attention to the potential reforms to liberal democratic political structures and the wider issues surrounding electronic democracy.

Electronic Democracy

Citizen participation in the political process has been undermined by time, size, knowledge and access. These have made direct participation impractical and led to elitist or representative models of democracy. Alternatively, a wired world would stem the difficulties of time because communication and participation become instantaneous. Similarly, problems of size are solved because physical space becomes irrelevant as people do not have to be gathered in a single place. Concurrently, the distribution of knowledge is now widely available through networks, which in turn removes the difficulty of access. Whether representational, direct or communitarian forms of democracy are preferred, electronic technologies appear to guarantee success.[22] For some, such as Howard Rheingold, it is more than a matter of changing the democratic models:

> Access to alternate forms of information and, most important, the power to reach others with your own alternatives to the official view of events, are, by their nature, political phenomena. Changes in forms and degrees of access to information are indicators of changes in forms and degrees of power among different groups. The reach of the net, like the reach of television, extends to the urbanized parts of the entire world

(and, increasingly, to far-flung but telecom linked rural outposts). Not only can each node rebroadcast or originate content to the rest of the net, but even the puniest computers can process that content in a variety of ways after it comes in to the home node from net and before it goes out again. Inexpensive computers can copy and process and communicate information, and when you make PCs independent processing nodes in the already existing telecommunications network, a new kind of system emerges.[23]

There are several critiques of electronic democracy. First, democratic decisions are not just based on citizen choice. They are often characterized by the electoral system as no natural majority exists and democracy is no more than a device for registering preferences. Second, information does not necessarily enhance a democracy as many decisions are matters of judgement. A distinction between information and knowledge has to be made. Graham Murdock has commented that cultural rights comprise entitlements in four main areas: information, knowledge, representation and communication. Information rights enable people effectively to determine personal and political judgements, and analyse the actions of public and private agencies with significant power over their lives. However, as information is of only limited use in its raw state 'it needs to be placed in context, and its implications teased out and debated. Knowledge rights promote these processes by underwriting the public's access to the widest possible range of interpretation, debate and explanation.'[24]

As information is not an agency but conditional on those who govern it, our attention returns to a fundamental problem – that the electronic technologies promote the interests of the powerful. This belief partly draws on the gap between promise and practice in the operation of actual systems of electronic participation. It also suggests that the problems of access that beset previous forms of democracy will be reproduced, with similar imbalances and inequality of resources continuing to distort participation. John Street comments:

> It is, furthermore, possible to read into the rhetoric and practice of electronic democracy the interests and ambitions of dominant groups, to see it as part of a larger project to depoliticize politics, transforming the citizen into the consumer.[25]

The critiques of teledemocracy tend to fall into the utopian/dystopian paradigm. ICTs may establish 'direct democracy' or an Orwellian society in which citizens are controlled by a new class of technocrats. However, the implementation of electronic democracy is dependent on the context of the political environment and conditional on a democratic ideal that is being attained. Interactive technologies can be employed to reform representative democracies, extend our ability to exchange information in direct democracy or be employed to develop communitarian forms of democratic behaviour. As Street further comments:

> Equally, it may be that electronic democracy is heralded as a last desperate life-line for a vision of democracy that is sinking in the face of all-enveloping complexity that makes it almost unviable.[26]

Changes to Liberal-Democratic political structures

Advocates of information technologies maintain that the problem of political clientelism which exists between governments, media organizations and other capitalist institutions will be overcome as ICTs make the representative process increasingly transparent. This may be seen to occur in two ways. First, it may enhance the normative, vertical top-down political communication between the parties and the electorate; and second, through the creation of horizontal networks between different interest groups, new communities and forums may emerge.

The British political parties have started to respond both internally and externally. The major parties have engaged in office automation with word processing and database management through networked PCs and shared office resources. Electronic communication and e-mail are more widespread with Labour in the lead. Labour has also established a new media headquarters at Millbank which is funded by millionaire and former *New Statesman* benefactor Philip Jeffrey.

The Liberal-Democrats have a speech database on their political opponents to highlight contradictions and inconsistencies over issues. The Labour Party has invested in the American 'Excalibur' database system which, loaded with speeches, policy comments, figures and reports, allows facts to be checked instantaneously. It was effectively used by Clinton and Gore in the 1992 American Presidential Election. For instance, the Democrat team was able to produce a fourteen page rebuttal of Dan Quayle's allegations during a head-to-head with Gore. Similarly, Labour hope to maximize the political mileage of their opponents' errors and also rebut counter-productive accusations.[27] Further, they are using databases for fund-raising, canvassing, direct-mailing, local newsletters and membership drives. Main-frame and mini-computers have been employed to target supporters and to keep track of elected representatives.

The three main British parties have established 'bulletin boards' on the Internet containing information available for public access. For instance, the Labour Party publishes conference speeches and members are encouraged to subscribe to an e-mail service on Poptel network. Further, through databases, faxes, press releases and campaign news, MPs' voting records can be accessed. Leading political figures such as Paddy Ashdown and Tony Blair have published their e-mail addresses to encourage direct communication with the public. Ashdown has even conducted MP surgeries on the Internet. They are hoping that as a result, casual voters 'surfing the Internet' will be wooed by their on-line campaigning during future general elections.

Whilst mainstream political parties have used ICTs to streamline their communication processes, American pluralists argue that they can make representative democracy more responsive by creating a level playing field for a diverse range of interest groups. For instance, cable television allows for a multiplicity of responses as it provides a varied menu to a more fractured and heterogeneous audience. Similarly, there will be greater access to information for alternative interest groups through freenets (local network-hooking onto national networks) to encourage discourse within the norms of the representative system.

In the 1992 American Presidential Election, the independent candidate, Ross Perot, promised on-line debates and votes through the model of an Electronic Town Hall. This would circumvent a corrupt and aloof Congress, and establish a direct link between government and electorate. After his electoral victory, President Clinton built on Perot's theme by establishing a series of Electronic Town Hall events to produce a closer relationship with the public (and bypass a critical press corps). Subsequently, Clinton has publicized his e-mail address and placed White House information on-line.[28]

In Britain, on the Internet's open government page, there have been calls for an on-line *Hansard* so that the public will have direct access to Parliamentary debates.[29] In turn, if political decision-making goes on-line, it will no longer remain the bastion of the civil servants, politicians and vested interests. Due to their capacity to store data and disseminate information, ICTs appear to be an appropriate mechanism to decentralize political power. Moreover they could reform state secrecy and establish campaigns for open government. As Mike Holderness commented, two of the favourite topics of discussion on the Internet refer to freedom of information, and whether information should be provided free.[30] The Internet may also be a productive agent for British single-issue pressure groups. Charter 88 has provided on-line details of its 'Parliament for our Times', and has established a competition to examine solutions for the future of democracy. ICTs have also carried opinion polls to enhance interactivity. However, problems surround these reforms as ICTs may compound biases in distribution of information to societal groups. Thus they will augment asymmetries of information and power could be limited to a technocratic elite. Moreover, many users of ICTs, particularly the Internet, suggest that technological changes will go far beyond reforms to old liberal-democratic structures. These will be subsumed, as Athenian forms of direct democracy or communitarian models reach fruition.

Athenian/direct electronic democracy

In Athens plebiscites, or citizens' forums, provided the mechanisms through which democracy was achieved. For many, the plebiscite remains the symbol for true democracy, empowering citizens to actively make political choices. However, due to the limitations of time and physical space it proved to be impractical for registering political preferences. Consequently, representative democratic institutions such as parliament have been given this power. ICTs can remove these time/space requirements and *direct democracy* can become a reality as information is processed to unlimited numbers to enable them to participate simultaneously in debate. Through digital means, voting and public preferences could be directly registered. Constant referendums may become a reality. Problems, however, exist.

A danger in an electronic, plebiscitary democracy is the focus on speed and numbers. This may undermine discussion and deliberation. Political participation may become a private act of registering one's own preconceived bias. The interactive discourse which is a key feature of a developed democracy will be replaced by push-button voting. Consequently, as the citizens' knowledge and awareness are subsumed, their ability to make informed and rational decisions are undermined:

> Continuous computerized referendums on all matters of public importance may appear to be a logical extension of Western democracy, but if attempted, would almost certainly be its ultimate downfall! Could any political system survive the volatility of ill-educated public opinion?[31]

Communitarian electronic democracy

ICTs may also promote communitarian democracy in which public discourse will encourage the common good. Howard Rheingold develops this communitarian model by claiming that many-to-many communication can provide the framework for collective goods. The package of cable television, networked computers and telephones enables two-way debate over issues before beliefs are polled. Therefore, more direct forms of voting and opinion-giving become available. ICTs also provide new mediums to form communities which previously, due to distance or geographical barriers, had been restricted. To this end, people can use the technology to address social problems. Non profit-making organizations on neighbourhood, city, and regional levels, and

Non-Governmental Organizations (NGOs) on the global level, may become modern manifestations of 'civil society'.[32] Thus, the new technologies can be used for humanitarian purposes:

> Nonprofits and NGOs are organizationally well-suited to benefit from the leverage offered by . . . technology and the people power inherent in virtual communities. These groups feed people, find them medical care, cure blindness, free political prisoners, organize disaster relief, find shelter for the homeless – tasks as deep into human non-virtual reality as you can get. The people who accomplish this work suffer from underfunding, overwork, and poor communications. Any leverage they gain, especially if it is affordable, will pay off in human lives saved, human suffering alleviated.[33]

Changing the Goal-posts in a Modern Political Society: the Philosophy of the Internet

Proponents of certain ICTs, in particular the Internet, claim that the technologies' democratic potential goes far beyond simply reforming political structures or inaugurating alternative democratic models. The technological revolution is upon us and the Internet model (a network of computer networks and telecommunication links) can redefine concepts of political culture, globalize citizenship, challenge normative ideas of objectivity and change identities.

Technological utopias and Marshall McLuhan

A number of Internet technocrats, including George Gilder and Alvin Toffler, have outlined a utopian view of computers. Nicholas Negroponte, a founding director of the Massachusetts Institute of Technology's Media Lab and the magazine *Wired*, exemplifies this form of liberation technologist. He argues that the hardware is already available to effect significant change – almost every home has copper phone lines which are capable of delivering 6 million bps, modems may be easily obtained and fibre-optic cable can handle 1,000 billion bps. Therefore, letters and printed forms ought to be digitalized, virtual reality conferencing must replace business travel, and television should be transmitted by a digital signal (over cable, not the ether). There will be no choice but to switch from dealing with atoms to dealing with 'the DNA of information': binary digits or bits.[34] Digitalization will lead to decentralization, globalization, harmonization and empowerment. Technology is an agency for change which cannot be denied or ignored.[35]

These beliefs are drawn from the arguments of Marshall McLuhan. As we have noted in chapter 7, McLuhan considered how technologies are an extension of the human body and restructure social relations. In the past, the press was a continuation of the eye, thereby stemming the oral flow of information and advancing individualism over communal effort. As Nick Stevenson comments:

> Print supplies the cultural resource for national forms of uniformity, while simultaneously giving birth to notions of individuality. In achieving this, the Gutenberg press converted space and time into the calculable, the rational and the predictable. The linear and logical emphasis of writing was mirrored in the uniform regimentation of clock time. The rationalising impact of the printing press paved the way for geographical maps, railway timetables, and notions of perspectives in painting. According to McLuhan, the advent of print culture had both developed certain human senses (sight) rather than others, and shaped a particular form of human rationality. This, however, was all to change with the arrival of electric forms of communication.[36]

To this end, McLuhan developed the concept of hot and cool medias. Traditional, hot media (print) stem participation as they are high on informational content, thereby setting the agenda and filtering arguments. Alternatively, cool media (telecommunications, television) provide more spaces for audience participation as they provide a lower intensity of information. Consequently, people must fill in the gaps and become active. Thus, the new media decentralize the production of knowledge and democratize opinion formation through interactivity. Through such decentralization, technologies check dominant authorities from managing the flow of information.

In turn, the new technologies allow for the globalization of the media economy, compress time, make spatial relations horizontal, relocate information and undermine the role of nation states. As the co-ordinates of time and space have evaporated, communication systems become constant and immediate providing a diversity of opinions. Individualistic print cultures have been disrupted as many-to-many communications become possible. Thus, the globe's citizens may engage in a shared culture, a global village, which undermines the previously hierarchical, uniform or individualizing methods of ideological control. McLuhan's words remain the gospel of the Internet and the popular net-user's magazine *Wired* quoted him in their original editorial:

> The medium or process of our time – electronic technology – is reshaping and restructuring patterns of social interdependence and every aspect of our personal life. It's forcing us to reconsider and re-evaluate practically every thought, every action and every institution formerly taken for granted.[37]

The public sphere, global citizenship and the Internet

Many net users suggest that the outmoded media structures have failed the public and the Internet provides the forum for public debate. In effect, it has replaced the Greek *agora* and the coffee shops of the eighteenth century. It is the public sphere in which issues are debated and politics framed. Moreover, the Internet offers instant global communication so that all citizens can enjoy access to the same informational and cultural resources. Therefore, global citizenship presupposes a supranational, global identity. In particular, *Wired*'s media correspondent, Jon Katz, argues that the Internet offers a vast, diverse, passionate, global means for transmitting ideas and opening minds. Net culture provides a medium for individual expression akin to the eighteenth century pamphleteers in colonial America. Through bulletin boards, conferencing systems, mailing structures and web sites political organizations, academics, and ordinary citizens can post messages, raise questions, share information, offer arguments and change minds.[38] Moreover, Katz has suggested that the traditional democratic structures have failed the citizenry. Instead of the normative imperative of objectivity, he argues that diversity, argument and debate mark out the Internet and ensure the health of the democracy. An electronic *agora* will exist and the emancipatory potential of the new technologies will mean, in Thomas Paine's words: 'We have it in our power to begin the world over again.'[39]

Thus, thousands of news groups and giant bulletin boards will enhance Thomas Paine's arguments for a 'universal society'. Citizens can transcend narrow interests and consider humankind as one entity.[40] As the Internet is the first world-wide medium, people can communicate directly, quickly, personally, and reliably. They can form distant but diverse and cohesive communities to send, receive, and store vast amounts of information.

Latterly, revolutionary groups have been attracted to the Internet. British anarchist groups, such as Class War, have several sites on the Web. The Trotskyist Socialist Workers Party (SWP) went on the World-Wide-Web with a selection of articles taken from its print edition and an archive of material dating back to January 1995. Its content allows users to view the main Marxism page, from where they can download several pamphlets and order audiotapes from the SWP's annual conference.

One of the most advanced uses of the Internet occurred in Mexico. The left-wing Zapatistas, led by the mysterious Marcos, disseminated their declarations across the world and gained extensive international sympathy. Their messages reached Santiago, Berlin, Barcelona, Paris and London. This usage of multi-media technology appeared to sustain the arguments of those who believe that ICTs could transform the public sphere and advance global communications. Marshall McLuhan's concept of a 'global village' has been resurrected. Instant global communication will create a global community. Communication is not only changed but the nature of citizenship, with all citizens able to access the same informational and cultural resources. Moreover, with the plentiful supply of computers, digital communciations are nearly uncensorable:

> This reality gives our moral and media guardians fits; they still tend to portray the computer culture as an out-of-control menace harbouring perverts, hackers, pornographers and thieves. . . . The political, economic, and social implications of an interconnected global medium are enormous, making plausible Paine's belief in the 'universal citizen.'[41]

The net as public sphere?

Mark Poster provides a critical account of Jon Katz's arguments. He suggests that throughout Western civilization the Greek *agora*, the town hall, local church, coffee shop, village square and street corner have been the forums for public debate. These spaces remain, but do not continue to be arenas of such interactivity, as they have been replaced by television and other media forms which isolate citizens rather than unify them. Currently, Internet newsgroups and other virtual communities are seen as nascent public spheres that will renew democracy in the twenty-first century.[42]

However these claims are misguided as they dismiss the profound differences between Internet 'cafés' and the *agoras* of the past. Disembodied video text cannot replace face-to-face interchange. The net has its own logic and ways of forming opinion. In the digital era, it should be understood that the net diverges from historical public spheres and its effect on politics differs.[43] Poster suggests that the public sphere was an arena in which people could talk as equals. However, this is not the case in the on-line world. Although the net allows people to talk as equals, rational argument rarely prevails and consensus is widely seen as impossible. These are symptoms of the fundamentally different ways identity is defined in the public sphere and on the net:

> Traditionally, a person's identity is defined by contact. Identity is rooted in the physical body. The stability forces individuals to be accountable for their positions and allows trust to be built up between people. . . . The Internet, however, allows individuals to define their own identities and change them at will. . . . This kind of protean identity is not consonant with forming a stable political community as we have known it.[44]

Clifford Stoll argues that being on-line is anti-social as it replaces face-to-face communication with a mere interactivity between on-line users.[45] The mass of undigested data misleads the public into thinking that they are accessing a great library. However, data is not information or knowledge. Information has content but has to be placed in context, so that its implications can be analysed, assessed and explained. Human understanding, knowledge and wisdom lead to empowerment. The best ideas still go to the journals and important news stories are sold to media corporations. Therefore, access to apparently limitless data does not enhance participation. It's a very different social 'space' from that of the public sphere:

> We must remember that the net is something entirely new, and its ef-
> fects on democratic politics can't be predicted using historical precedent.
> The Internet threatens the government (unmonitorable conversations),
> mocks private property (the infinite reproducibility of information) and
> flaunts moral propriety (the dissemination of pornography). The tech-
> nology of the Internet shouldn't be viewed as a new form of public
> sphere. The challenge is to understand how the networked future might
> be different from what we have known.[46]

Moreover, dissent on the net does not lead to consensus. Instead a profusion of different views exist without any embodied public co-presence. Therefore, individual charisma has no force and the conditions to encourage compromise, the hallmark of the democratic political process, disappear. Since identities are fluid, dissent is encouraged and 'normal' status markers are absent. User groups tend to polarize political opinions.

Net culture: extremist politics and the Internet

Whilst we have seen that mainstream and revolutionary parties have started to employ ICTs, the Internet has been often been the domain of extremist political organizations. This has occurred across nation states and the international environment.

In the United States, the Internet's ideology has been a combination of techno-utopian futurism and libertarian anarchism with deep roots in a culture which mistrusts central government. In particular, American anti-governmental groups have used the net. This became apparent after the Oklahoma City bombing, when the alleged perpetrators used the Internet to communicate with each other. On some sites, extremists claimed that the Bureau of Alcohol, Tobacco and Firearms bombed itself to discredit self-proclaimed 'patriots'. Other right-wing pressure groups such as the National Rifleman's Association (NRA) have used net sites to mobilize support for the Second Amendment to the US Constitution – the right to bear arms. An 'anarcho-capitalism' is emerging in which individual rights override traditional collectivist principles and state structures:

> The political sub-culture that has grown up on the Internet enjoys watching such senior government officers squirm as they realise how little they understand the future. The oxymoron *'anarcho-capitalist'* used to refer to a few on the wacko fringe of US politics. In the 90s, it's the norm in Usenet news: the position you don't need to explain. And its assumptions – minimal government interference in everything, from sex to income to the Internet itself – are spreading.[47]

In the United States and Western Europe, the net has also provided an outlet for fringe groups, from Evangelical Christians to more reprehensible extremist organizations. For instance, white supremacists and fascist groups have realized that the net can circumvent legislation which outlaws reprehensible material denying the Holocaust.[48] These developments, alongside the wider dissemination of hard-core pornography, have led to calls for governments to renew their attempts to regulate the net. Currently, a debate exists between those who demand total freedom of expression against those who feel that certain societal precepts should be retained. These arguments draw our attention to the variety of criticisms which have been directed at electronic democracy.

Criticisms of Electronic Democracy

ICTs have been seen to retard citizenship as much as aid it. John Gray has argued that the utopian view of technology is misplaced. Historically, technological reforms have not created new societies, solved intractable difficulties or redistributed wealth. Instead, they alter the terms for societal or political conflicts as the uses 'to which new technologies are put depend on the distribution of power and access to resources, and on the level of cultural and moral development in society'.[49] Gray's criticisms suggest that a quick, technological fix will not empower citizens. Instead, the public's attention is falsely distracted from state and capitalist power. To this end, a number of major arguments have been advanced.

A virtual class

It is suggested that the utopian view of information technology ignores cultural differences, political antagonisms, and immense economic inequalities. Information and knowledge resources are not being equally distributed due to centralized political control, concentration of production and limited consumer access. Steven Barnett has commented that three major forces restrict expansion: (1) *Cost* – as a third of British households have an income of less than £200 a week, hardware costs will preclude involvement; (2) *Confidence* – the ability of people to use the new technology will be undermined by technophobia; and (3) *Convenience* – newspapers still remain the easiest forms to buy, read and carry around.[50] The failure of ICTs to redistribute societal resources may create a divide between information 'haves' and 'have nots'. Thus, global citizenship (pitched on free speech, total access, the ability to comprehend relevant information, having a stake in the global flow of information, and being fairly represented) is undermined. In effect, a technocratic elite or *virtual class* will determine the dissemination of communications.

Research suggests that those on the lowest incomes are being excluded from the communications revolution. As the telecommunications market has been liberalized and universal services have declined, access has been determined by people's earnings. Thus, British Oftel's 1994 national connection figures indicated that only 80 to 90 per cent of households had a telephone. This meant that more than 2 million homes are 'unphoned'. Previously, the government believed that non-connection was a rural problem, but this phenomenon has become a major problem in the marginalized, poor urban areas.

Inner city inhabitants, who would benefit most from a basic telephone service, are the least likely to have a domestic telephone. They have major difficulties paying their bills and do not use sophisticated telecommunication services. These problems are compounded because poor areas do not attract other suppliers and connection costs spiral as the existing operators remove their subsidies to retrieve the full cost of services. Therefore, customers have to pay more for their connection or drop off the network. The constant threat of disconnection, alongside higher bills in the other utilities, discourages many from having a phone.

The level of phone connection in deprived inner city areas is significantly lower than the national average of 91 per cent.[51] For example, in Cruddas Park, a Newcastle upon Tyne council estate, the connection rate is just 26 per cent.[52] Therefore, those on lower incomes are becoming the information poor. As more public and private phone services develop, including welfare and emergency provisions, the unphoned will be disenfranchised. Further, the hardware of the digital superhighway – fibre-optic cable – will not arrive in many poorer areas for many years.[53]

The distinction between information rich and poor is further ad-

vanced by the economics of ICTs. These services have been predominantly used by businesses and are dominated by the profit motive. Their
commercial significance refers to the direct contact they allow between
buyers and sellers. The growth areas in networked computing are col-
laborative working and electronic commerce. Transactional rather than
publishing applications are fuelling the ICTs' progress. In this respect,
Arthur Kroker and Michael Weinstein maintain that a virtual class
has seized the new communication channels for its own interests. The
Information Superhighway provides the veneer of empowerment, but
in reality:

> The virtual class has driven to global power along the digital super-
> highway. Representing perfectly the expansionary interests of the recom-
> binant commodity-form, the virtual class has seized the imagination of
> contemporary culture by conceiving a techno-utopian high-speed cyber-
> netic grid for travelling across the electronic frontier. In this mythology
> of the new technological frontier contemporary society is either equipped
> for fast travel down the main arterial lanes of the information highway,
> or it simply ceases to exist as a functioning member of technotopia. As
> . . . the specialist consultants of the virtual class triumphantly proclaim:
> 'Adapt or you're toast.'[54]

The erosion of the public sphere and ICTs

From a political economist perspective, it is asked whether the new
mediums will be any less corruptible than previous media. Should contemporary, democratic claims for ICTs be taken any more seriously
than those made for the press and television? The commercialization
of Information Technology is well under way as 'infotainment' deals
(e.g. Microsoft, Time Warner etc.) have emerged and ICTs have been
largely used for business transactions. As the mass media has been
overwhelmed and monopolized by large corporations, becoming inac-
cessible to individuals and motivated primarily by profit, can ICTs be
any different?

Mass communications have been the central focus for mediating the
power between state and society. Thus, the media has occupied the public sphere, the arena for free information which exists between the state
and civil society. Similarly, ICTs may provide the conduits for informal
conversations in communities or virtual communities. A web of free,
informal, personal communications will establish the foundations for
democracy, enabling people to govern themselves.

The golden age of the public sphere occurred during the period of
bourgeois democracy in the eighteenth century. However, as the public sphere eroded, either through totalitarianism or market forces in liberal democracies, a fake discourse emerged to manipulate the citizenry.

The development of the press in the nineteenth century meant that advertising became the principle means of finance and a nascent public relations industry emerged. These forces undermined the public sphere by commodifying a phony rather than genuine discourse. Further, French philosophers Guy Debord, the situtationist who wrote *Society of the Spectacle* and Jean Baudrillard, the post-modernist who conceived hyper-reality, have argued that the political arena has been commodified. Politicians are sold to citizens, who become consumers. Issues are framed through sound-bites and political demonstrations are staged for the benefit of television. According to Jürgen Habermas and others, the mass media's commodification has led to the deterioration of the public sphere. Discourse degenerated into publicity, and publicity used the increasing power of electronic media to alter perceptions and shape beliefs. These are all manifestations of the consumer society which has become the accepted model for individual behaviour and political decision-making, thereby dismantling rational discourse.

Similarly, ICTs contribute to the erosion of the public sphere. One myth of technological progress is that citizens will be enlightened as the new communications media decentralize power and dismantle the concentration of ownership. However, this may be a misnomer, as media monopolies, computer giants and telecommunication corporations combine to shape the flow of information. Therefore, ICTs may merely be a more effective way to commercialize the public discourse. In effect, the Internet becomes an invisible yet inescapable cage which is falsely legitimized by users' unwarranted beliefs that they are being empowered. As Howard Rheingold comments:

> When people who have become fascinated by BBS or networks start spreading the idea that such networks are inherently democratic in some magical way, without specifying the hard work that must be done ... They run the danger of becoming unwitting agents of commodification. First, it pays to understand how old the idea really is. Next, it is important to realize that the hopes of technophiles have often been used to sell technology for commercial gain. In this sense, ... enthusiasts run the risk of becoming unpaid, unwitting advertisers for those who stand to gain financially from the adoption of new technology.[55]

The hyper-realist school and society as a spectacle

Hyper-realistic critiques build on the arguments surrounding the erosion of the public sphere. They suggest that information technologies have replaced what used to pass for reality into a slicked-up electronic simulation. The world is one of hyper-reality in which the real world is mimicked and money is extracted from the consumers.

As illusion and reality become entwined, ICTs become another form of disinfotainment. The public has been manipulated as surface level freedoms have falsely convinced citizens of their democratic rights. John Gray has argued that new communications technologies do not provide political freedoms. The vision of a globalized culture is impatient with the civic and political duties incurred in sustaining local environments and communities. This world view is inhospitable to the idea that insuperable limits are imposed on human freedom by living in a fragile physical environment. It is even more resistant to the thought that we are defined by our histories and local attachments. The new virtual freedom is, in effect, freedom from these immemorial conditions of human life.[56]

Thus, human perceptions have been shaped so that the wonders of communications technology provide the façade of true democracy. All authenticity, from nature to human relationships, has been replaced with a simulated, commercial version. Utopian illusions simply distract our attention from the real power behind the scenes. Democracy has been subsumed by a global mercantile state and assisted by the media (and multi-media's) manipulation of desire.

Debord claimed that the media are part of the hegemony of power in which the rich and powerful rule through *consent*. Everything is turned into a media event. The stage management of politics, society and environments (for example, shopping malls) allows falsehoods to abound and stifles independent, rational thought. Baudrillard has discussed the increasingly synthetic nature of technological civilization. There is a degeneration of meaning as reality has been commodified. Consequently, the fluidity of identity on the Internet realizes this fear. In a hyper-real situation people may forget that information technologies only convey the illusion of direct communication. For instance, a computer conference only imparts the illusion of a town hall meeting. Previously, it has been possible to manipulate images, but new technology makes it practical on a large scale. Sixty years ago, Stalin's retouchers took a day or so to remove Trotsky from every photograph. Now changes may occur in a matter of seconds. In the near future, video may be manipulated in real time. Characters may be added, removed or altered in live footage. As Howard Rheingold comments:

> It's when we forget about the illusion that the trouble begins. When the technology itself grows powerful enough to make the illusions increasingly realistic, as the net promises to do within the next ten to twenty years.[57]

There is no model of democracy that does not depend on an accurately-informed people. Thus, if strict codes between the virtual and the real are removed, democracy is in trouble. Such manipulation of information suggests that state or central power may be enhanced and leads to the final major criticism of the new technologies.

The surveillance society

Most straightforwardly, the utopian vision has been replaced by a dystopian vision in which the powerful control communications technology. In particular, an Orwellian use of information technology for surveillance and disinformation through propaganda has emerged. This critique suggests that the citizen's privacy, a necessary condition for both participatory or liberal democracies, will be subsumed.

This school of criticism is known as *panoptic*, in reference to Jeremy Bentham's eighteenth-century proposal for a perfect prison. The panopticon or inspection house has been used for schools, prisons and factories. Individual cells are placed in a circular wall around a central well with an inspection tower on top. The cells are lit and the tower dark so one person could inspect many. There are also inspectors of the inspectors. This social control mechanism suggests a mental state of being seen without seeing your watcher.

This theoretical model fits the capabilites of new technologies. Future tyrants may be able to use surveillance technologies to invade privacy. As some commentators suggest, 'sooner or later debates about the social impacts of ICT come round to the question of "Big Brother".'[58] The storage of personal information for governmental purposes provides a major test for privacy or data protection. These may also exacerbate the underhand power of a secretive 'state-within-state' rather than openness.

With regard to the Internet, founded by the US Defense Department to link research centres, military computers can be used by totalitarian regimes to control political discourse and public tastes. A future dictatorship could be sustained by private police forces constantly surveying the populace. Citizens would be coerced, confused and controlled.

In the United States, a variant of these arguments was rehearsed during the debate which surrounded Senator James Exon's, the Nebraskan Democrat, proposed decency amendment to the 1995 Telecommunications Bill. It promised to penalize anyone who 'makes, transmits, or otherwise makes available any comment, request, suggestion, proposal, image or other communication which is obscene, lewd, lascivious, filthy, or indecent'. It was designed to control the flow of pornography on the Internet, particularly to children. However, its fall-out had a variety of implications. Originally, Exon's amendment would have forced bulletin board operators to monitor all data passing through their systems.

Thus, they were required to expand their staffing and undermine their potential profitability. On 23 March 1995, a modified version recommended that bulletin board and Internet access providers would only be liable for traffic they relayed 'knowingly'. Commentators suggested that this system could only be effective if they read nothing at all. For instance, if they took action against a Nazi user they rendered themselves liable for pornographic stories. Further, a *New York Times* editorial (28 March) contended that computer surfers invariably had to seek out such sex-related material. In response Exon argued that he wanted to ensure that the Information Superhighway would be safe for children and families. He concluded that whilst pornography could be regulated through adult bookstores, anyone, including children, could easily access it within private spaces on home computers.

An electronic petition mobilized 107,983 signatures against Exon's amendment and the list of organizations opposing it included the American Civil Liberties Union, the Electronic Frontier Foundation and the Internet Business Association. Opponents argued that controls were required for the Internet, when they did not apply to the press. Others suggested that pornographic material be considered as a matter of 'private speech' rather than 'publication'. Underpinning their concerns stood the concept of freedom of speech.

Therefore, American legislators were presented with the dilemma of doing something about pornography existing in a technology they did not understand, against maintaining the liberal traditions of free speech. In the event, Exon's amendment was approved by an 84:16 majority and made the transmission of obscene material a crime. However, Newt Gingritch, the House Speaker, bluntly opposed legislation and criticized it as 'a violation of free speech . . . and it's a violation of the right of adults to communicate with each other. . . . I don't think it's a serious way to discuss a serious issue.'[59] One sponsor of the amendment thought the Speaker's opposition could kill the whole measure. An opponent of the Senate bill applauded Gingritch's 'opposition to an unconstitutional, unworkable solution to the problem of protecting children'.[60]

This debate made conspicuous the issues surrounding government intervention and implied that such state control was deleterious to the individual's privacy rights. However, rather than as an Orwellian model or a state attempt to centralize the dissemination of information through legislation, the most insidious attack on privacy may come from the market. Panopticons can be established as people let supermarkets sell information about their transactions. Instead of telephone taps or a secret police, covert totalitarian weapons will include computer programmes that link bar codes, credit cards, social security numbers, and the digital trails we leave throughout the information society. Through these electronic tell-tale signs our liberties are being commodified (for example, the blacking of credit).

Digital trails, emerging through credit information, transaction processing and health information, can undermine personal liberties. Thus, the channels providing many-to-many communication may also allow governmental and private interests to gather information for use against the public. One possible remedy would be citizen encryption of information. A unbreakable, public-key encryption code (which the technology allows for) might act as safeguard. However, the most potent issue will refer to the laws, or absence of laws, that enable improper uses of information technology to erode what is left of citizens' rights to privacy.

Conclusion

The new information and communications technologies are becoming increasingly available. They allow for infinite data storage, a wider distribution of information and, most importantly, interactivity so that many-to-many communications become a reality. They have policy and political implications. With regard to industrial policy, the metaphor of the Information Superhighway has been proffered as the future source of wealth and societal benefit.

ICTs may determine appropriate democratic models in the near future. They can be used to reform traditional liberal-democratic structures such as representational assemblies and political parties and break down official secrets systems. Alternatively, they overcome the problems of time and space which have previously constrained Athenian or communitarian democratic models. Citizens may enjoy greater access to information and consequently attain the knowledge to develop empowerment.

Internet users suggest that the information technologies have the potential to change working habits, decentralize power structures, limit state or capitalist organizations, and reform the public sphere. Interactivity provides a two-way flow of information and means that the traditional media's power to set the agenda is undermined. The concept of objectivity can be replaced by diversity, so that political issues can be framed and debated. From this perspective, the multi-media will succeed the mass media which has been perceived to fail due to its incorporation within the political elite and the global concentration of ownership. Conversely, it has been suggested that a growing divide between an information rich and poor is emerging. Governments, to varying degrees, have decided to let markets orchestrate the development of ICTs. This creates problems in distribution and usage. In particular, it means that rights of access will be determined by incomes. Those on low incomes will be excluded and omitted. Further, consumerism may replace citizenship, as media moguls make deals with telecommunications/cable organizations and computer entrepreneurs.

Thus, a number of potent criticisms of electronic democracy exist. A political economist critique suggests that ICTs will add to a general erosion of the public sphere as corporations frame the agenda and a consumer society subsumes previous versions of political behaviour. This links into a hyper-realistic argument that the fluidity of identity and commodification of objective realities will result in disinfotainment. As the distinction between virtual and real evaporates, democratic choices will be stemmed. Finally, a panopticon model suggests that the information channels provide the appropriate surveillance technologies for totalitarian regimes. More insiduously, it has been argued that the public sell their privacy rights away through credit cards and telephone banking. Therefore, despite the technophile's arguments, the new information technologies do not necessarily enhance democracy. Technology is not an agency, for it may be employed positively or negatively. Consequently, multi-media futurists must ensure that ICTs are governed through appropriate legislation and regulation to realize their democratic potential.

Further Reading

F. Christopher Arterton, *Teledemocracy: can technology protect democracy?*, Sage Publications, 1987.

Noam Chomsky, (interviews with David Barsamian), *Keeping the Rabble in Line*, AK Press, 1994.

William Dutton, Jay Blumler, Nicholas Garnham, Robin Mansell, James Cornford and Malcolm Peltu, *The Information Superhighway: Britain's Response*, A Forum Discussion, ESRC Policy Research Paper No. 29, 1994.

George Gilder, *Life After Television*, Norton and Company, 1995.

Arthur Kroker and Michael A. Weinstein, *Data Trash: The Theory of the Virtual Class*, New World Perspectives, 1994.

K. Laudon, *Communication Technology and Democratic Participation*, Praeger Publishers, 1977.

Nicholas Negroponte, *Being Digital*, Hodder & Stoughton, 1995.

Howard Rheingold, *The Virtual Community: Finding Connection in a Computerized World*, Secker & Warburg, 1994.

Anthony Smith, *Books to Bytes: Knowledge and Information in the Postmodern Era*, British Film Institute, 1993.

——, *Software for the Self*, T. S. Eliot Memorial Lectures, Faber & Faber, 1996.

Alvin Toffler, *Future Shock*, Bantam Books, 1971.

Notes

1   Jon Katz, 'Guilty', *Wired*, September 1995, p. 100.
2   Marshall McLuhan quoted in Christopher Reed, 'Inter next world', *Guardian*, 20 March 1995, (Section 2), p. 15.
3   Stephen E. Arnold, *Internet 2000: The Path to the Total Network*, Infonortics in-depth Briefings, 1994, p. 9.
4   S. Flowers, 'Want it? Well Gopher it?', *Guardian*, 5 August 1993.
5   K. Laudon, *Communication Technology and Democratic Participation*, Praeger Publishers, 1977.
6   Ivan Horrocks and Lawrence Pratchett, 'Electronic Democracy: Central Themes and Issues', Joni Lovenduski and Jeffrey Stanyer (eds), *Democracy and New Technology*, Contemporary Political Studies, Volume 3, PSA, University of York, 18–20 April 1995, p. 1219.
7   Noam Chomsky, (interviews with David Barsamian), *Keeping the Rabble in Line*, AK Press, 1994, p. 148.
8   David Glencross, 'Convergence at Aspen', *Spectrum*, Autumn 1994, p. 3.
9   Graham Allen, 'Letter: net corner@guardian.co.uk.', *Guardian*, 16 September 1995, p. 26.
10   Chris Smith quoted from Patrick Wintour, 'Blair plans national information grid', *Guardian*, 28 November 1994.
11   William Dutton, Jay Blumler, Nicholas Garnham, Robin Mansell, James Cornford and Malcolm Peltu, *The Information Superhighway: Britain's Response*, A Forum Discussion, ESRC Policy Research Paper No. 29, 1994, p. 2.
12   Tony Blair, 'Help speed Britain down the superhighway', *Evening Standard*, 17 July 1995, p. 9.
13   John Heilemann, 'The Politics of Technology', *Wired*, December 1995, p. 104.
14   Ibid.
15   Ibid., pp. 103–4.
16   Rupert Murdoch in Trevor Hayward, *Information Rich and Information Poor: Access and Exchange in the Global Information Society*, Bowker-Saur, 1995, p. 193.
17   Alan Cane, 'An entertaining alliance: this week's multimedia tie-up between Rupert Murdoch and a US telecoms company', *Financial Times*, 12 May 1995, p. 15.
18   For further details, see Louise McElvogue, 'Fumbling in Silicon Alley', *Guardian*, OnLine Section, 8 February 1996, pp. 4–5.
19   James F. Moore in Howard Rheingold, *The Virtual Community: Finding Connection in a Computerized World*, Secker & Warburg, 1994, pp. 274–5.
20   Robert W. McChesney, 'Public Broadcasting in the Age of Communication Revolution', *Monthly Review*, vol. 47, no. 7, December 1995, p. 9.
21   Pat Coyne, 'Dielectrics: Tony Blair will find out that there is no such thing as a "free connection" ', *New Statesman & Society*, 13 October 1995, p. 25.
22   John Street, 'Remote Control: politics, technology and culture', in Iain Hampsher-Monk and Jeffrey Stanyer (eds), *Contemporary Political Studies 1996 (Volume 1)*, PSA, p. 505.
23   Howard Rheingold, *The Virtual Community*, p. 268.
24   Graham Murdock, 'Money Talks' in Stuart Hood (ed.), *Behind the Screens: The Structure of British Television in the Nineties*, Lawrence & Wishart, 1994, p. 158.
25   John Street, 'Remote Control', pp. 506–7.
26   Ibid., p. 507.
27   Tom Standage, 'Excalibur revealed', *Guardian*, On Line Section, 8 February 1996, pp. 2–3.

28 For further details see Andrew Adonis and Geoff Mulgan, 'Back to Greece: the scope for direct democracy', *Demos*, Issue 3, 1994, pp. 2–9.
29 Mike Holderness, 'Internet: A political climate change', *Guardian* (Section 2), 8 December 1994, p. 29.
30 Ibid.
31 J. Martin and R. D. Norman, *The Computerized Society*, Prentice Hall, 1970, pp. 298–9.
32 Howard Rheingold, *The Virtual Community*, p. 261.
33 Ibid., p. 33.
34 Joseph Gallivan, 'Internet: Battle brewing in cyberspace', *Guardian*, 1 June 1995, G2T, p. 24.
35 See Nicholas Negroponte, *Being Digital*, Hodder & Stoughton, 1995 and George Gilder, *Life after Television*, Norton and Company, 1995.
36 Nick Stevenson, *Understanding Media Cultures: Social Theory and Mass Communication*, Sage Publications, 1995, p. 119.
37 Marshall McLuhan quoted in Christopher Reed, 'Inter next world', *Guardian*, 20 March 1995, (Section 2), p. 15.
38 See Jon Katz, 'The Age of Paine', *Wired*, May 1995, pp. 154–214, or Jon Katz, 'Guilty', *Wired*, September 1995, pp. 50–100.
39 Thomas Paine quoted from Jon Katz, 'The Age of Paine', p. 156.
40 Ibid., p. 155.
41 Ibid., p. 210.
42 Mark Poster, 'The Net as a Public Sphere?', *Wired*, November 1995, pp. 42–3.
43 Ibid., p. 42.
44 Ibid.
45 Joseph Gallivan, 'Internet: Battle brewing in cyberspace', Guardian, 1 June 1995 G2T, p. 24.
46 Ibid., p. 43.
47 Mike Holderness, 'Internet: A political climate change', p. 29.
48 Louise Bernstein, 'Hate on the Internet', *Searchlight*, March 1996, pp. 12–15.
49 John Gray, 'The sad side of cyberspace', *Guardian*, 10 April 1995, p. 18.
50 Steven Barnett, 'Information superhighway or cul-de-sac?', *Media Moves*, Autumn 1995, p. 4.
51 Philip Dyer, 'Telecommunications: All wired up and nowhere to go', *Guardian*, 8 June 1995, G2T p. 25.
52 Ibid.
53 For further details see Mike Holderness, 'Falling through the net', *New Statesman and Society*, 13 October 1995, pp. 24–5.
54 Arthur Kroker and Michael A. Weinstein, *Data Trash: the theory of the virtual class*, New World Perspectives, 1994, pp. 6–7.
55 Howard Rheingold, *The Virtual Community*, p. 286.
56 John Gray, 'Virtual Democracy', *Guardian*, 15 September 1995, p. 17.
57 Howard Rheingold, *The Virtual Community*, p. 299.
58 D. Lyon, *The Information Society*, Polity Press, 1988, p. 93.
59 Jurek Martin, 'Internet smut law attacked', *Financial Times*, 23 June 1995, p. 6.
60 Ibid.

9
Conclusions: Citizenship, Politics and the Mass Media towards the Second Millennium

Introduction

The mass media should secure the citizen's civil, political and social rights. The print and the electronic medias' ability to disseminate critical information quickly and widely across society is crucial. The concept of freedom of information has underpinned the development of advanced media systems. Further, within traditional liberal thought, the media should act as a public watchdog or fourth estate to reveal state abuses.

Therefore, the mass media are key political actors, as individuals require universal access to knowledge to pursue their rights. They should facilitate citizenship through the provision of free and accurate information in three important ways. First, individuals must have access to knowledge and information that will allow them to pursue their rights. Second, they should be provided with the broadest range of information, interpretation and debate over public political choices. Thus, citizens can employ communications facilities to register criticism and propose alternative courses of action. Finally, they should recognize themselves in the range of representations on offer within the central communications sectors and be able to develop and extend their representation.

These rights indicate that the communications and information systems have two key features. At the production level, they should afford the maximum possible diversity of provision and the mechanisms for user feedback and participation. At the level of consumption, they should ensure universal access to services that càn guarantee the exercise of citizenship regardless of income or area of residence. To this end, the citizen's access to the market-place of ideas has been understood to be an obligation of national governments. Such rights have been established through a variety of laws, policies and regulations.

Alternatively, the media has been cast in a more invidious role as the means through which the values of the dominant ideology and governmental regimes are perpetuated. Further, the present technological advances (cable, satellite, telecommunications, the Internet) are bringing into question traditional concepts of public service in communications delivery and the very notion of mass media as many-to-many communication services are being advanced.

The Provision of Free Information

At the heart of this allocative system of information stands the free media market, which should act:

> like a political supermarket, in which customer-voters wander from counter to counter, assessing the relative attractions and prices of the policies on offer before taking their well-informed selection to the electoral checkout. The media play the part of consumer watch-dog, providing the means for the well-informed citizen to play his or her role to the full.[1]

The free market empowers people to register their preference as *consumers* of a product. The press's liberation is driven by the profit-motive. Consequently, to sell papers proprietors must ensure that a wide variety of opinions are expressed. Therefore, through their buying power, consumers act as the controllers of press output. This aids competition as papers, to be sold, must provide a wide variety of interpretations of the news. Thus, the consumer's choice of information will facilitate his or her own self-expression and will encourage political participation. The press promotes a free-thinking democracy in which no one should be subjugated to another's will but may freely express an opinion. In turn, this may promote public rationality and focus collective self-determination.

However, liberty not only emerges at the point of consumption but also within production. In theory, the market should allow for a diverse number of owners the freedom to publish through freedom of entry and competition. To protect freedom of ownership and to retain its independence from governments or regulators, the press should be lightly regulated, subject only to libel and obscenity laws and the tenets of taste and decency. Moreover, its political liberty is guaranteed as it has been independently funded through advertising revenues. Thus, only a privately-owned press, competing in a free market, can ensure complete independence from the government.

There are similarities and differences between the role of the press and broadcasting in liberal democracies. The broadcasters' political independence is closely tied to the freedom of the press. They remain neutral observers committed to the principles of accuracy, impartiality and objectivity. Yet society's response toward broadcasting has been different from its attitude to the print media. Whilst broadcasting organizations have been constitutionally independent, they have been regulated by and organized as public bodies.

Critiques

Despite constitutional and financial guarantees of independence, many criticisms have emerged over a media system which has been orchestrated by the market. Market allocation often unequally distributes the wealth, allowing for a concentration of ownership through closed entry. For true media diversity there should be public access to communication resources to advance a plurality of producers and opinions. A conflict exists between the rights of possession and expression.

For Marxists, media ownership is a key element in the mental domination of the bourgeoisie over the public. Some would suggest that mogulism produces a particular editorial outlook. However, political economists, such as Peter Golding and Graham Murdock, have shown how freedom is constrained by the interconnections between shareholders of different companies and by profit-making.[2] Golding and Murdock contend that greater concentrations of ownership, media diversification, conglomeration and imperialism have emerged. In effect, a new form of empire-building has evolved. We have seen how the global mass communications systems have become part of an increasingly conglomerate, multi-national order.

Thus, the history of the communications media is not only an economic history of their growing incorporation into a capitalist system, but also a political history of their centrality to the exercising of citizenship. The mass media are part of the information-cultural complex with close ties to the government. They are integrated into the political elite and remain generally supportive, although sometimes critical, of the dominant ideology.[3] This view is reflected in Jürgen Habermas's *The Structural Transformation of the Public Sphere*. He argued that the *public sphere* (the space between the state and civil society in which mass communications operate) eroded as *rational* public discourse was overridden by *power politics* when mass parties, monopoly capitalists and states dealt with one another. In the eighteenth century the press acted as a medium through which private opinions could be transformed into public convictions. The public arena framed the debates to influence public policy and criticize governments. Thus, the media expedited the political process by reorganizing private citizens into a collective body. However, as the press became dominated by corporatism, advertising and ownership, politics was defined as a predigested spectacle.

The Communications Revolution

These arguments have been located around the traditional print and electronic media. However, the technological revolution has meant that major transformations within the distribution of communications have become available for business and domestic use. These changes throw in relief some of the questions related to the exercising of citizenship through mass communications.

Technological reform

Effectively, several decades of new technology have been unleashed in the last fifteen years. The changes comprise: a computer revolution hastened by cryptography, the modem, domestic personal computers and more sophisticated software to be down-loaded; microwave technology, drawn from radar and rockets, for launching satellites; high-definition television reception; terrestrial broadcast reforms such as digital compression; the domestic videorecorder; and telecommunication advances including the long-running (now reaching fruition) introduction of narrow-band fibre-optic cable.

These advancements have complicated the communications industries' economic and social relations. Jill Hills has commented that these new hardware devices challenge the traditional monopolies which had dominated the communications industries.[4] The justification for a highly regulated broadcasting monopoly had been founded upon the scarcity of the air-wave spectrum. Yet 'the liberalisation of equipment (increased) the demand for the liberalisation of transmission which in turn (increased) the demand for the liberalisation of equipment.'[5] Rather than information being limited to terrestrial broadcast airwaves, it may be advanced on multi-channel systems through funding methods such as subscription.

So while the technological limitations had resulted in the previous compliance of these industries with the normative forms of control, the more recent technological developments have made these structures appear increasingly anachronistic, irrelevant, bureaucratic and inefficient. Moreover, the opening of the market-place to cable and satellite provided opportunities for the hardware manufacturers to invest in research and increase their profitability. Further, they mean that new or different media actors can provide broadcasting services. Consequently, the new communications are challenging the concept of public interest in press, television and communications industries. The advent of subscription-based services throws into relief some of very principles on which communications systems have been developed. With multiple, generic channels, the future more accurately may be seen as being representative of *'narrow'* rather than *'broad'* casting.

Globalization

The globalization of mass communications has emerged as worldwide satellite, telecommunication and broadcasting links have been established. Therefore, as information proliferates, the process of transmission cannot continue to be conceptualized by the boundaries of the nation state. These reforms have been accompanied by several different theories. For some, a global village will encourage universal citizenship and allow national cultures to interact. There are new opportunities for independent producers to create and distribute programmes. For others, media flows from the rich Northern states to the poorer Southern countries will exacerbate the gap between information rich and poor. Anthony Giddens has argued that 'time-space distanciation' establishes a complicated relationship between local involvements (circumstances of co-presence) and interaction across distance (connections of presence and absence).

Governmental Interventions and Responses

These changes demand new policy responses and reforms to existing laws and regulation. The problem remains how to effectively employ this new set of information highways for societal benefit. Technological changes carry with them the seeds either to promote or retard citizen empowerment. Invariably, in the wake of these technological reforms, national governments of all political hues have responded with policies located around privatization and deregulation.

The Thatcher government's response

In Britain, the importation of deregulation was particularly associated with the New Right.[6] Throughout the late 1980s, the Thatcher government ostensibly favoured a return to an eighteenth-century *libertarian* interpretation of communications. In particular, they advanced Adam Smith's market-liberal/utilitarian concept of society as a *competitive market*. In this construct no 'fixed' societal order exists. Instead society is composed of interactive and independent individuals. Following this, the individual is the principal source of economic activity through his or her enterprise. Individual economic liberalization equates with societal benefit. Social welfare is maximized by the individual's preferences which are supported by pro-competitive policies and minimal public regulation. By extension, state powers have to be limited so that individual enterprise may be fully realized.

Within this conception, social communication should satisfy individual preferences, rather than attempt to act as an unprovable public service good. As long as the public service tenets do not impinge upon the individual's right to choose, they remain acceptable. However, for libertarians, this has rarely been the case in broadcasting. Market-liberals have been unified in their unfavourable comparison between broadcasting and the press. Where the press has operated as a free market, it maintains that broadcasting has been duopolistic and subject to political pressure.

This critique provided the basis of the two main market-liberal approaches to broadcasting. First, that a form of *regulatory capture* has characterized relations in broadcasting. Second, that it is no longer acceptable to judge broadcasting as being good through the normal criterion of its ends (programmes); instead it is necessary to assess the *quality* of the system by the level of *access* it affords to the individual in order to determine what s/he wants to view or listen to. The process, rather than the product, was what mattered. Therefore, it was argued that the new technologies (cable, satellite) by removing the limited spectrum provided the means through which the viewer might fully participate in a form of *electronic publishing*.

Just as 'electronic publishing' would revolutionize the individual's access to programmes, it meant that the production and regulation of broadcasting would be transformed. The broadcasting system would no longer be vertically integrated, comprised of broadcasting organizations which produced and transmitted programmes. Instead, the new broadcasting market would enable the entrance of a greater number of independent production companies. These programme-makers could produce whatever they liked in exchange for the payment of a transmission fee. Like any product, the programme's success would ultimately be decided by its ability to attract subscribers. The regulators would become an irrelevance as the technological and industrial imperatives which had contributed to their existence had been overcome. This would be beneficial, as regulators had previously censored the individual's economic and societal rights. Consequently, government or legislative intervention could not be justified, except in applying the general print laws of blasphemy and libel.[7]

These ideological imperatives have led to governments pursuing some privatization and deregulatory policies to commercialize public terrestrial communications systems. However, governmental communication policies, most especially in broadcasting, have often produced compromised and confused legislation reflective of the practicalities of the policy-making process. These comprise political will, departmental jurisdiction, dissensions amongst the competing policy networks and negotiation with interested parties. The communications policy process often indicates a political fudge in which acquiescence to a number of competing interests overrides a coherent agenda for reform.

In British broadcasting, the government's political will was partly influenced by the efforts of the advertising lobby and their disdain towards the monopolism which pervaded the industry. However, in many respects, the principal motivation was political. After *Real Lives* the BBC had 'put its house in order' and made overt noises about becoming more efficient, whilst simultaneously seeking to limit the amount of political controversy. ITV, however, found itself at the centre of a high-level political storm after *Death on the Rock.* The IBA's reluctance to bow to political pressure clearly contributed to its own demise and channelled the government's desire to reform a monopolistic system. Further, British broadcasting policy stood on the cusp of the Thatcherite desire to deregulate the commercial sectors of the economy, whilst attempting greater state intervention in regard to individual rights and civil liberties. This dichotomy operated upon two levels; (1) a highly articulated concern over the potential programming output with the liberalization of the broadcasting market-place and (2) a more covert desire to retain, if not enhance, governmental controls over the flow of political communication. Consequently, the government was reluctant to remove the regulatory governors and paradoxically increased the number of agencies through the legislation. In this sense, what is often called deregulation is a misnomer, as there has been a shift in the rules rather than a removal of intervention.

Therefore the British government has altered communications systems due to the communications revolution and the ability to manufacture cheap domestic cable and satellite receivers. However, the government's approach was dictated by its relations with the established communications organizations. The policy did not indicate any overall coherent vision for communication. Instead, the process exhibited the government's preference for the expedience of commercialization over ideology. Commercialization became an end rather than a means to an end. This proved to be a politically convenient option as it satisfied the government ideologues by providing them with the political weaponry to reform, in the case of broadcasting, a perceived enemy. This usage of competitive practices also demonstrated the political nature of a government who saw the market as acting as the most efficient provider of resources rather than as a liberalizing force.

Throughout the 1980s and early 1990s, British media policy also exhibited a form of political clientelism in its dealings with Rupert Murdoch's News International group who held a considerable interest in satellite broadcasting. This close political alliance meant that there was no attempt to take Murdoch to the Monopolies and Mergers Commission, in spite of his significant (37 per cent) stake within the British Press. The government's inability and refusal to intervene served to lay the foundations for the monopolistic control which currently exists since the 'merger' between Sky and BSB. However, since the fall-out between Murdoch and the Major government, there have been pressures to regulate Murdoch's ownership power. The 1995 White Paper *Media Ownership* attempted to stem media monopolization by preventing groups from applying for a regional ITV licence if they have more than 20 per cent of the national newspaper market.

Yet government policy-making remains cursory as there was no attempt to deal with the media on a supranational level. National governmental legislation can do little to stem the international media conglomerates who have by-passed national ownership, regulatory and programming rulings by broadcasting on satellites technically outside of the jurisdiction of the state. This has been shown by the National Heritage Ministry's white paper attempting to stem cross-ownership. Its proposals may affect Rupert Murdoch's interests in Britain, but cannot reform the conglomerate nature of News Corporation in the global market.

Media Economics

Consequently, the new technologies, the government's laissez-faire responses and the globalization of mass communications have provided the framework to open up the new media markets to the international media conglomerates. The cumulative result of these shifts has been to strengthen and extend the power of the leading corporations. In Britain, the failure of British Satellite Broadcasting and the ascendancy of Rupert Murdoch's Sky Television, later BSkyB (which was a merger only at board level), has produced a situation in which a broadcasting monopoly dominates the satellite channels. This contrasts with market-liberal assertions that 'electronic publishing' could provide the foundation for a pluralistic pattern of independent productions in terms

Media conglomeration

The new media has allowed for the speculation of media conglomerates across Europe (Bertelsmann, Fininvest, Hachette, News International etc.). National governments have either loosened ownership restrictions or turned a blind eye to the expansion of these corporations. Market-liberal or deregulatory policies, designed to encourage the free flow of investment, have justified this state of affairs. Further, as media companies can aid politicians they have been perceived as valuable allies. Therefore, the new media's development may parallel the concentration of ownership within the newspaper and publishing industries, as the new outlets are controlled by fewer and fewer media moguls or conglomerates.

Public service broadcasters

As a consequence of technological and political imperatives which have opened up the system to conglomerate media competitors, public service broadcasting systems are being transformed from publicly regulated bodies into increasingly commercial organizations forced to incorporate public and private funding. This has taken several forms. In Italy, for instance, RAI has include spot ads between programming and after the recent referendum will be fully privatized.

In Britain, the broadcasting institutions continue to exist in a modified form and formally the system remains committed to the public service ideal, although this has been pitched as being predominantly the concern of the BBC and Channel Four. Through the franchise auction and the considerable sums of money that have left the companies to go directly to the Exchequer, the ITV sector is becoming increasingly commercial in terms of its organizational structure, constituent power blocs, labour practices and programme output.

Terrestrial broadcasting has evidenced gradual, but substantial, reforms in broadcasting organizational structures, ideology, ethos and outlook. The ITC is legally a regulatory body and is no longer required to preview programmes as a broadcaster. This has led to the ITV companies increasingly taking on the scheduling power through a new Network centre which has significantly different aims. As these companies are no longer legally bound by public service rules and, since the franchise auction, need to maximize their profits, populist programming has determined the schedule to secure high audiences in order to attract advertising. Company executives are keen to secure profits as they be-more commercial. As a result, the vertically integrated broadcasting producers are being replaced by broadcasting commissioners who transmit programmes from other regional franchisees or independents in order to save money and reduce staffing figures. Moreover, the legislation has allowed greater concentrations of ownership within ITV. For example, Carlton owns Central and has a major stake in ITN, Granada took over LWT and MAI merged with the newspaper group United Papers.

The changes within ITV have had an effect upon the broadcasting ecology. In response, the BBC has focused its attention on the continuing objective of receiving the licence fee, although it already predicts that it will have a substantially reduced audience by the end of the decade. Director-General John Birt has pitched the BBC's future upon; (1) an internal production market to promote transparent efficiency within the BBC entitled 'Producer Choice'; (2) a programming schedule pitched around a specialized form of 'public service' broadcasting which defines itself against the market in order to provide innovation which could not exist elsewhere; and (3) greater accountability to the licence fee payer.

Therefore, these developments indicate the increasing cross-media/industrial convergence and have started to question the relevance of national broadcasting systems. It may be suggested that we are entering into a world in which world-wide communication could be realized in which previously held public service assumptions, notions and structures are becoming more difficult to sustain. However, within this brave new world there is not so much a diversity of media sources, but an increasingly homogeneous international structure reflecting the media mogulism of Rupert Murdoch, Ted Turner, Time Warner and others. Public service broadcasters, faced with increasing programming costs, capped incomes and the commercial competitors are faced with commercialization of practices or marginalization.

Political Liberty in the New Media Order

Despite this concentration of ownership, the conglomerates maintain that the media has become too big for one person or elite control it. A free market encourages plurality of access and participation. The closed media systems will decline, as technology has provided a diversity of channels and outlets through which alternative views can be disseminated. Consequently, media moguls cannot shape the political discourse. Their influence is limited to the traditional role of 'public watchdog' and means that the media can now truly mirror the general consensus. Further, post-modern theory has conceived capitalist society in terms of the proliferation of images. The media syphons content, social reality, politics into a vortex of noise, meaninglessness and implosion. Within this new form of culture, reality is obliterated as the distinction between reality and irreality disappears. Proponents of hyper-reality claim that, as it is impossible to construct meaning, people use the media in a totally unstructured and irrational manner. It becomes futile to delineate between institutional structures, their historical trajectories or political effects. Therefore, as the owner's power is incomprehensible, it cannot be measured.

Conversely, media conglomerates have been subject to a number of major criticisms. Their unfettered growth means they can determine entry to the media market, thereby protecting their interests by excluding the opposition, cross-promoting their services or engaging in the takeovers of smaller competitors. Critics contend that global corporations either uncritically propagate political elites or have so many controls within the political mainstream that they are serving their own, rather than the public's, interest. Jürgen Habermas's argument, that the media have become the site for ideological manipulation, seems to be correct. Thus, due to globalization and conglomeration, the citizen's democratic rights are being undermined by the needs of the state and the media companies.

Reforming Models for Mass Communications

These problems have led to some commentators proposing alternate media models which, as they are independent from the state and the market, could put the citizen's needs first. Generally, they recognize that traditional public service homogeneity is undesirable within a cosmopolitan society. John B. Thompson has also argued that these pluralistic models will have to be regulated on both a national and international level due to the global nature of mass communications.[8]

To this end, John Keane has conceived of a mixed public service system comprising state-funded and -protected outlets, alongside a plurality of non-market, non-state communications institutions. These outlets will stem the political elite's power (undermining censorship) and, with constraints over private media markets, circulate ideas. Concurrently, James Curran advocated a core public service sector surrounded by different media outlets. As the core reaches a mass audience, it addresses general concerns, provides a forum for debate and encourages public discourse. However, as centrifugal forces may stem debate, four peripheral sectors comprising a civic media sector, a professional media sector, a limited private market and a publicly funded social market may provide checks and balances for pluralism.

The Multi-media Revolution

Alternatively, the multi-media technologies have been seen to challenge the problem of the media's political incorporation. This revolution is transforming business and domestic communications. Interactive fibre-optic cable systems are developing alongside the widespread use of the computer and videoconferencing. A new generation of networks promotes low-cost broad-band communication. These developments provide access to greater numbers of communications links, permit the distribution of commercial and entertainment material, and advance telephony along the same highways. New electronic services located around telecoms, computers and satellites have meant that a global electronic mail service has come on-line. There has also been the evolution of integrated computer networks, generically entitled the 'Internet'.

Computers increase data storage, retrieval and transmission. Mass participation technologies, such as broadcasting, which distribute information from a central source to millions are also enhanced. Further, interactive communications flows among individuals and organized groups may be established.[9] There are thousands of on-line Bulletin Board Systems (BBS) and news groups run by computer enthusiasts. Finally, they decentralize control over mass communication.

Futurists contend that a digital revolution may reform monolithic state edifices, corporations, political parties, schools, workplaces, orthodox economics and popular entertainment. The Internet will increase interactive citizen participation by circumventing the centralized, conglomerate and outmoded media structures. The Information Superhighway will provide the electronic landscape, or cyberspace, for a reinvented civil society so that citizens can engage in their civil, political and social rights.[10] Such interactivity can increase democratic participation through a constant series of referenda. Thus, the technological revolution will enhance freedom of belief, conscience, speech, movement, association and enfranchisement. Governments, regulators and owners will be impotent as millions adopt the interconnecting technology and engage in political discourse. In particular, the Internet offers instant global communication, in which all citizens can access the same informational and cultural resources. There will be a globalization of citizenship, the decline of nationalism and the reform of archaic political structures.

The information communication technologies and the public sphere

Currently, Internet newsgroups see themselves as nascent public spheres that will renew democracy.[11] However, these claims dismiss the profound differences between Internet 'cafés' and the *agoras* of the past. Traditionally, identity has been defined by physical contact. This enforces accountability and has enabled mutual trust to be developed. Disembodied video text cannot replace face-to-face interchange. Further, it creates shifting forms of identity which thwart political stability.[12] Whereas the public sphere enabled people to interact as equals, online *agoras* undermine equality by emphasizing irrational discourse.

The mass of undigested data misleads the public that they are accessing a great library. However, data is not information or knowledge. Human understanding, knowledge and wisdom lead to empowerment. The best ideas still go to the journals and important news stories are sold to media corporations. Therefore, access to limitless data does not enhance participation. Moreover, dissent on the net does not lead to consensus. A profusion of views exist without any public co-presence. Individual charisma has no force, and compromise, the hallmark of a democracy, evaporates. Since identities are fluid, dissent is encouraged and 'normal' status markers are absent. User groups tend to polarize political opinions.

Critiques of electronic democracy

Historically, technological reforms have not created new societies, solved intractable difficulties or redistributed wealth. Instead of encouraging greater access to different centres of power, they alter the terms for societal or political conflicts.[13] The public's consciousness is falsely distracted from state and capitalist power.

There are several critiques of electronic democracy. First, democratic decisions are not just based on citizen choice. They are often characterized by the electoral system as no natural majority exists and democracy is no more than a device for registering preferences. Second, information does not necessarily enhance a democracy as many decisions are matters of judgement. A distinction between information and knowledge has to be made. Cultural rights comprise four main entitlements: information, knowledge, representation, and communication. Information rights enable people to effectively determine personal and political judgements, and analyse the actions of public and private agencies with significant power over their lives. However, for information to be useful it has to be placed in context so that its implications are teased out.

As information is not an agency but conditional on those who govern it, our attention returns to a fundamental problem – that the electronic technologies promote the interests of the powerful. This belief partly draws on the gap between promise and practice in the operation of actual systems of electronic participation. It suggests that the problems of access that beset previous democratic forms will be reproduced as similar imbalances and inequality of resources may continue to distort participation. Electronic democracy may serve the ambitions of dominant groups, who depoliticize politics and may transform the citizen into the consumer.

Conclusion

The changes within mass communications and the burgeoning development of the multi-media are complex and still on-going. As a consequence, there will be a constant need for research to determine how these developments are being realized.

First, there should be a continuing analysis of media policy-making. The debates surrounding media ownership, commercialization within broadcasting and the relative decline of the public service remain controversial. Their relevance has been hastened by new technological developments, financial collapses, arguments over accountability and the implementation of legislation. There are problematic questions concerning the media's political liberty within a market-dominated environment. Such an assessment of industrial and organizational change must also consider the globalization of mass communications.

Second, a concern with content remains important. The cultural homogeneity in programming, advocated by public service broadcasters, has been challenged by the multiplication of channels and providers. This could provide greater access for women, ethnic or minority groups. Alternatively, with the dominance of the media conglomerates, a rather bland international cultural dominance may emerge as programming becomes dominated by imports and cheap productions. Such a study may question whether members of the media audience should be understood as a consumer of private goods or citizens enjoying their rights to a public good and freedom of information. This would also lead to questions concerning how the audience uses television in a multi-channel future and whether the traditional viewing patterns will remain stable or change. The new technology may also contribute to fragmentation of the audience.

The study of politics, citizenship and mass communications, therefore, remains vital. Throughout the preceding chapters, we have considered the political and philosophical implications of the changing communications landscape with the development of reformed policy agendas and as new technologies become domestically available and there is a greater globalization of the media economy. This book has been a modest contribution to widening understanding about these topics.

Notes

1 Peter Golding in Marjorie Ferguson (ed.), *Public Communication: The New Imperatives: Future Directions for Media Research*, Sage Publications, 1990, p. 84.

2 G. Murdock and P. Golding, 'Capitalism, Communication and Class Relations', in James Curran, Michael Gurevitch and Janet Woollacott (eds), *Mass Communication and Society*, Edward Arnold, 1977, pp. 12–43.

3 James Curran and Michael Gurevitch (eds), *Mass Media and Society*, pp. 87–8.

4 Jill Hills, *Deregulating Telecoms: Competition and Control in the United States, Japan and Britain*, Frances Pinter, 1986.

5 Ibid., p. 16.

6 Anthony Smith, *Books to Bytes: Knowledge and Information in the Postmodern Era*, British Film Institute Publishing, 1993, p. 145.

7 Peter Jay, *The Crisis for Western Political Economy and Other Essays*, André Deutsch, 1984 (9th edn), p. 225.

8 John B. Thompson, *Ideology and Modern Culture: Critical Social Theory in the Era of Mass Communications*, Polity Press, 1990, pp. 263–4.

9 K. Laudon, *Communication Technology and Democratic Participation*, Praeger Publishers, 1977.

10 Jon Katz, 'Guilty', *Wired*, September 1995, p. 100.

11 Mark Poster, 'The Net as a Public Sphere?', *Wired*, November 1995, pp. 42–3.

12 Ibid., p. 42.

13 John Gray, 'The sad side of cyberspace', *Guardian*, 10 April 1995, p. 18.

Select Bibliography

Official Reports and Legislation

Adam Smith Institute, *Omega Report: Communications*, Adam Smith Institute, 1984.

Annan Committee, *The Report of the Committee on the Future of Broadcasting (The Annan Report)*, HMSO, 1977.

British Broadcasting Corporation, *Extending Choice: The BBC's Role in the New Broadcasting Age*, BBC Publications, 1992.

Department of National Heritage, *The Future of the BBC: A Consultation Document*, HMSO, 1992.

Department of National Heritage, *The Future of the BBC: Serving the nation, Competing world-wide*, HMSO, 1994.

Department of National Heritage, *Privacy and Media Intrusion: The Government's Response*, HMSO, 1995.

Department of National Heritage, *Media Ownership: The Government's Proposals*, HMSO, May 1995.

Department of National Heritage, *Digital Terrestrial Broadcasting: The Government's Proposals*, HMSO, August 1995.

Department of National Heritage, *Broadcasting Bill (H.L.)*, HL Bill 19, 1995.

Home Office, *Broadcasting in the '90s: Competition, Choice and Quality*, White Paper HMSO, 1988.

Home Office, *Broadcasting Act 1990 (chapter 42)*, HMSO, 1990.

Independent Television Commission, *Invitation to Apply for Regional Channel 3 Licences*, ITC, 1991.

Peacock Committee, *The Report of the Committee on Financing the BBC (The Peacock Report)*, HMSO, 1986.

Books and Monographs

Arterton, F. Christopher, *Teledemocracy: Can Technology Protect Democracy?*, Sage Publications, 1987.

Aspinall, Arthur, *Politics and the Press, c. 1780–1850*, Harvester, 1973.

Barnett, Steven, *Games and Sets: The Changing Face of Sport on TV*, BFI Publishing, 1990.

—— (ed.), *Funding the BBC's Future*, The BBC Charter Review Series 2, BFI Publishing, 1993.

Barnett, Steven, and Andrew Curry, *The Battle for the BBC: A British Broadcasting Conspiracy*, Aurum Press, 1994.

Blanchard, Simon, and David Morely (eds), *What's This Channel Four?*, Comedia Publishing Group, 1982.

Blumler, Jay (ed.), *Television and the Public Interest: Vulnerable Values in West European Broadcasting*, Sage Publications, 1992.

Blumler Jay, and T. J. Nossiter (eds), *Broadcasting Finance in Transition*, Oxford University Press, 1991.

Bolton, Roger, *Death on the Rock and Other Stories*, W. H. Allen, 1990.

Bower, Tom, *Maxwell: The Outsider*, Mandarin, 1991 (2nd edn).

Boyce, George, James Curran and Pauline Wingate (eds), *Newspaper History: from the 17th Century to the Present Day*, Constable, 1976.

Briggs, Asa, *The History of Broadcasting in the United Kingdom: Volumes I–IV*, Oxford University Press, 1961, 1965, 1970 and 1979.

——, *Governing the BBC*, BBC, 1979.

——, *The BBC: The First Fifty Years*, Oxford University Press, 1985.

Briggs, Asa, and Joanne Spicer, *The Franchise Affair*, Century, 1986.

Broadcasting Research Group, *The Public Service Idea*, BRU, 1985.

Burns, Tom, *The BBC: Public Institution and Private World*, Macmillan, 1977.

Chippindale Peter, and Suzanne Franks, *Dished! The Rise and Fall of British Satellite Broadcasting*, Simon & Schuster, 1991.

Chippindale, Peter, and Chris Horrie, *Stick it up Your Punter: The Rise and Fall of the* Sun, Mandarin, 1989.

Chisholm, Anne, and Michael Davie, *Beaverbrook: A Life*, Pimlico, 1993.

Chomsky, Noam, (interviews with David Barsamian), *Keeping the Rabble in Line*, AK Press, 1994.

Coase, R. H., *British Broadcasting: A Study in Monopoly*, Longmans Green, 1950.

Collins, Richard, *Television: Policy and Culture*, Routledge, 1990.

Collins, Richard, James Curran, Nicholas Garnham, Paddy Scannell, Philip Schlesinger and Colin Sparks (eds), *Media, Culture and Society: A Critical Reader*, Sage Publications, 1986.

Collins, Richard, Nicholas Garnham and Gareth Locksley, *The Economics of Television; The UK Case*, Sage Publications, 1988.

Congdon, Tim, Brian Sturgess, National Economic Research Associates (N.E.R.A.), William B. Shew, Andrew Graham and Gavyn Davies, *Paying for Broadcasting: The Handbook*, Routledge, 1992.

Curran, James (ed.), *The British Press: A Manifesto*, Macmillan, 1978.

Curran, James, Michael Gurevitch and Janet Woollacott (eds), *Mass Communication and Society*, Edward Arnold, 1977.

Curran James, and Michael Gurevitch (eds), *Mass Media and Society*, Edward Arnold, 1991.

Curran, James, and Jean Seaton, *Power without Responsibility: The Press and Broadcasting in Britain*, Routledge, 1991 (4th edn).

Dahlgren, Peter, and Colin Sparks (eds), *Communication and Citizenship: Journalism and the Public Sphere*, Routledge, 1991.

Davidson, Andrew, *Under the Hammer: The ITV Franchise Battle*, Heinemann, 1992.

Docherty, David, David Morrison and Michael Tracey, *Keeping Faith?: Channel Four and its audience*, John Libbey, 1988.

Donald, James, *Sentimental Education: Schooling, Popular Culture and the Regulation of Liberty*, Verso, 1992.

Dowmunt, Tony (ed.), *Channels of Resistance: Global Television and Local Empowerment*, BFI, 1993.

Dutton, William, Jay Blumler, Nicholas Garnham, Robin Mansell, James Cornford and Malcolm Peltu, *The Information Superhighway: Britain's Response*, A Forum Discussion, ESRC Policy Research Paper No. 29, 1994.

Dyson, Kenneth, and Peter Humphreys, with Ralph Negrine and Jean Paul Simon, *Broadcasting and New Media Policies in Western Europe*, Routledge, 1988.

Dyson, Kenneth, and Peter Humphreys (eds), *The Political Economy of Communications: International and European Dimensions*, Routledge, 1990.

Evans, Harold, *Good Times, Bad Times*, Weidenfeld & Nicolson, 1983.

Ferguson, Marjorie, *New Communication Technologies and the Public Interest*, Sage Publications, 1986.

—— (ed.), *Public Communication: The New Imperatives: Future Directions for Media Research*, Sage Publications, 1990.

Franklin, Bob, *Packaging Politics: Political Communication in Britain's Media Democracy*, Edward Arnold, 1994.

Gamble, Andrew, *The Free Economy and the Strong State: The Politics of Thatcherism*, Macmillan, 1988.

Garnham, Nicholas, *Structures of Television*, BFI Monograph, 1980.

——, *Capitalism and Communication: Global Culture and the Economics of Information*, Sage Publications, 1990.

Giddens, Anthony, *The Consequences of Modernity*, Polity Press, 1990.

——, *Modernity and Self-Identity: Self and Society in the Late Modern Age*, Polity Press, 1991.

Gilder, George, *Life After Television*, Norton and Company, 1995.

Glasgow University Media Group, *Bad News*, Routledge, 1976.

Goldie, Grace Wyndham, *Facing the Nation: Television and Politics 1936–1976*, The Bodley Head, 1977.

Golding, Peter, Graham Murdock and Philip Schlesinger (eds), *Communicating Politics: Mass Communication and the Political Process*, Leicester University Press, 1986.

Goodwin, Andrew, and Garry Whannel, *Understanding Television*, Routledge, 1989.

Greenslade, Roy, *Maxwell's Fall: The Appalling Legacy of a Corrupt Man*, Simon & Schuster, 1992.

Hall, Stuart, Dorothy Hobson, Andrew Low and Paul Willis (eds), *Culture, Media, Language*, Hutchinson University Press, 1980.

Hayward, Trevor, *Information Rich and Information Poor: Access and Exchange in the Global Information Society*, Bowker-Saur, 1995.

Herman, Edward, and Noam Chomsky, *Manufacturing Consent: The Political Economy of the Mass Media*, Pantheon Books, 1988.

Hills, Jill, *Deregulating Telecoms: Competition and Control in the United States, Japan and Britain*, Frances Pinter, 1986.

Hirsch, Fred, and David Gordon, *Newspaper Money: Fleet Street and the Search for the Affluent Reader*, Hutchinson, 1975.

Hood, Stuart, *On Television*, Pluto Press, 1987.

—— (ed.), *Behind the Screens: The Structure of British Television in the Nineties*, Lawrence & Wishart, 1994.

Hood, Stuart, and Garret O'Leary, *Questions of Broadcasting*, Methuen, 1990.

Horrie, Chris, and Steve Clarke, *Fuzzy Monsters: Fear and Loathing at the BBC*, Heinemann, 1994.

Hughes, Gordan, and David Vines (eds), *Deregulation and the Future of Commercial Television*, The David Hume Institute, Hume Paper No. 12, Aberdeen University Press, 1989.

Isaacs, Jeremy, *Storm over Four: A Personal Account*, Weidenfeld & Nicolson, 1989.

Jay, Peter, *The Crisis for Western Political Economy and Other Essays*, André Deutsch, 1984 (9th edn).

Jenkins, Simon, *Newspapers: The Power and the Money, Faber & Faber, 1979.*

Keane, John, *The Media and Democracy*, Polity Press, 1991.

Kellner, Douglas, *Television and the Crisis of Democracy*, Interventions: Theory and Contemporary Politics, Westview Press, 1990.

Koss, Stephen, *The Rise and Fall of the Political Press in Britain*, Volumes 1 and 2, Hamish Hamilton, 1981 and 1984.

Kroker, Arthur, and Michael A. Weinstein, *Data Trash: The Theory of the Virtual Class*, New World Perspectives, 1994.

Kuhn, Raymond (ed.), *The Politics of Broadcasting*, Croom Helm, 1985.

——, *Politics and the Mass Media in Britain*, Harvester Wheatsheaf, 1996.

Lamb, Larry, *Sunrise: The Remarkable Rise and Rise of the Best-selling Soaraway Sun*, PaperMac, Macmillan, 1989.

Lambert, Stephen, *Channel Four: Television with a Difference?*, BFI Publishing, 1982.

Laudon, K., *Communication Technology and Democratic Participation*, Praeger Publishers, 1977.

Leapman, Michael, *The Last Days of the Beeb*, Allen & Unwin, 1986.

Lee, Alan J., *The Origins of the Popular Press 1855–1914*, Croom Helm, 1976.

Lichtenberg, Judith (ed.), *Democracy and the Mass Media*, Cambridge University Press, 1990.

MacCabe, Colin, and Olivia Stewart (eds), *The BBC and Public Service Broadcasting*, Manchester University Press, 1986.

McIntyre, Ian, *The Expense of Glory: A Life of John Reith*, HarperCollins, 1993.

McLuhan, Marshall, *Understanding the Media: The Extensions of Man*, Routledge, 1994 (repr.).

McQuail, Denis, *Mass Communication Theory: An Introduction*, Sage Publications, 1987, 1992.

——, *Media Performance: Mass Communication and the Public Interest*, Sage Publications, 1992.

McQuail, Denis, and Karen Siune (eds), *New Media Politics*, Sage Publications, 1986.

Madge, Tim, *Beyond the BBC; Broadcasters and the Public in the 1980s*, Macmillan, 1989.

Miller, Nod, and Rod Allen (eds), *And Now for the BBC*, University of Manchester Broadcasting Symposium, John Libbey, 1991.

——, *Broadcasting Enters the Marketplace*, University of Manchester Broadcasting Symposium, John Libbey, 1993.

Milne, Alasdair, *DG: The Memoirs of a British Broadcaster*, Hodder & Stoughton, 1988.

Morely, David, *Television, Audiences and Cultural Studies*, Routledge, 1992.

Mulgan, Geoff (ed.), *The Question of Quality*, The Broadcasting Debate 6, BFI, 1990.

Mulgan, Geoff, and Richard Patterson (eds), *Reinventing the Organization*, The BBC Charter Review Series, BFI, 1993.

Munster, George, *Rupert Murdoch: A Paper Prince*, Penguin, 1985.

Negrine, Ralph, *Politics and the Mass Media in Britain*, Routledge, 1994 (2nd edn).

Negroponte, Nicholas, *Being Digital*, Hodder & Stoughton, 1995.

O'Malley, Tom, *Closedown? The BBC and Government Broadcasting Policy, 1979–92*, Pluto Press, 1994.

Patterson, Richard (ed.), *Organizing for Change*, The Broadcasting Debate 1, BFI Publications, 1990.

Paulu, Burton, *British Broadcasting: Radio and Television in the United Kingdom*, Macmillan, 1981.

Perryman, Mark (ed.), *Altered States: Postmodernism, Politics and Culture*, Lawrence and Wishart, 1994.

Potter, Jeremy, *Independent Television in Britain, Volume 3: Politics and Control 1968–90*, Macmillan, 1989.

Raboy, Marc, and Bernard Dagenais (eds), *Media, Crisis and Democracy: Mass Communication and the Disruption of Social Order*, Sage Publications, 1992.

Rheingold, Howard, *The Virtual Community: Finding Connection in a Computerized World*, Secker & Warburg, 1994.

Said, Edward W., *Culture and Imperialism*, Vintage, 1994.

Scannell, Paddy, and David Cardiff, *Serving the Nation: Public Service Broadcasting before World War Two*, Open University Press, 1982.

Schlesinger, Philip, *Putting 'Reality' Together*, Routledge, 1987.

Seaton, Jean, and Ben Pimlott (eds), *The Media in British Politics*, Avebury, 1987.

Sendell, Bernard, *Independent Television in Britain, Volume 1: Origin and Foundation; Volume 2: Expansion and Change*, Macmillan, 1982 and 1983.

Seymour-Ure, Colin, *The Political Impact of the Mass Media*, Sage Publications, 1974.

——, *The British Press and Broadcasting since 1945*, Basil Blackwell, 1991.

Shaw, Colin (ed.), *Rethinking Governance and Accountability*, The BBC Charter Review Series, BFI, 1993.

Shawcross, William, *Rupert Murdoch: Ringmaster of the Information Circus*, Chatto & Windus, 1992.

Silj, Alessandro (ed.), *The New Television in Europe*, John Libbey, 1992.

Smith, Anthony, *The Age of Behemoths: The Globalization of Mass Media Firms*, Priority Press, 1991.

——, *Books to Bytes: Knowledge and Information in the Postmodern Era*, British Film Institute, 1993.

——, *Software for the Self*, T. S. Eliot Memorial Lectures, Faber & Faber, 1996.

—— (ed.), *Television and Political Life: Studies in Six European Countries*, Macmillan, 1979.

Snoddy, Raymond, *The Good, the Bad and the Unacceptable: The Hard News about the British Press*, Faber & Faber, 1992.

Stevenson, Nick, *Understanding Media Cultures: Social Theory and Mass Communication*, Sage Publications, 1995.

Stevenson, Wilf, *All Our Futures*, The BBC Charter Review Series 1, BFI Publishing, 1993.

——, *BFI/BAFTA Commission of Inquiry into the Future of the BBC*, The BBC Charter Review Series, BFI Publishing, 1993.

Storey, John, *An Introductory Guide to Cultural Theory and Popular Culture*, Harvester Wheatsheaf, 1993.

Thompson, John B., *Ideology and Modern Culture: Critical Social Theory in the Era of Mass Communications*, Polity Press, 1990.

Toffler, Alvin, *Future Shock*, Bantam Books, 1971.

Tomlinson, John, *Cultural Imperialism*, Pinter Publishers, 1991, (2nd edn).

Tracey, Michael, *The Production of Political Television*, Routledge, 1978.

Tunstall, Jeremy, *The Media in Britain*, Constable, 1983.

——, *Television Producers*, Routledge, 1993.

——, and Michael Palmer, *The Media Moguls*, Routledge, 1991.

Veljanovski, Cento (ed.), *Freedom in Broadcasting*, Institute of Economic Affairs, 1989.

Waters, Malcolm, *Globalization: Key Ideas*, Routledge, 1995.

Wedell, E. G., *Broadcasting and Public Policy*, Michael Joseph Books, 1968.

Whannel, Garry, *Fields in Vision: Television Sport and Cultural Transformation*, Routledge, 1992.

Williams, Raymond, *Television: Technology and Cultural Form*, Fontana, 1974.

Wilson, H. H., *Pressure Group: The Campaign for Commercial Television*, Secker & Warburg, 1961.

Index